THE MYSTERY OF THE HEART

THE MYSTERY
OF THE HEART

*The Sacramental Physiology of the Heart in
Aristotle, Thomas Aquinas, and Rudolf Steiner*

PETER SELG

2012

STEINERBOOKS

STEINERBOOKS
An imprint of Anthroposophic Press, Inc.
610 Main St., Great Barrington, MA 01230
www.steinerbooks.org

Originally published in German by Verlag am Goetheanum 2003 as
*Mysterium cordis: Von der Mysterienstätte des Menschenherzens
Studien zur sakramentalen Physiologie des Herzorgans.
Aristoteles, Thomas von Aquin, Rudolf Steiner.*
Second edition in German, Verlag am Goetheanum
2006, Dornach, Switzerland.

Translated by Dana L. Fleming;
verse on page 115 translated by Marsha Post

LIBRARY OF CONGRESS CATALOGING-IN-PUBLICATION DATA

Selg, Peter, 1963–
[Mysterium cordis. English]
The mystery of the heart : studies on the sacramental
physiology of the heart Aristotle, Thomas Aquinas, Rudolf
Steiner / Peter Selg.
    p. cm.
Includes bibliographical references.
ISBN 978-0-88010-751-8 (pbk.) — ISBN 978-1-62148-019-8
(ebook)
    1. Steiner, Rudolf, 1861–1925. 2. Anthroposophy.
3. Heart—Physiology. 4. Heart—Religious aspects.
5. Aristotle. 6. Thomas, Aquinas, Saint, 1225?–1274.
I. Title.
BP596.P47S45 2012
299'.935—dc23

                                                    2012019728

Contents

Foreword to the Second Edition

This book addresses the spiritual physiology of the heart in the works of Aristotle, Thomas Aquinas, and Rudolf Steiner. A second edition is possible only a few years after the first because of the high level of interest and demand. Numerous lectures, seminars, and opportunities for further study (in the field of esoteric medicine, as well) have arisen in the meantime. These allowed me to readdress the subject and reimmerse myself intensively in this work. Nevertheless, the manuscript appears here in its original, valid (or at least justified) form, corrected only for typographical errors. I saw no cause to make any changes either to the portrayal or to my chosen style of presentation, even in the face of criticism from prominent anthroposophical circles, claiming that the published "collection of essays" was too "lyrical, admiring, and judgmental"; too strongly obligated to the specific nature of the Christian Community and the sacramentalism of Catholicism; and rather deficient in its ability to show "spiritual connections."[1]

Despite having the text before them, my critics seem to have overlooked several important points. I was able to show a number of concrete "spiritual connections" for the first time in this text, and in significant detail. I had no intention of undertaking a conventional appraisal of the spiritual-intellectual-historical influences of "other authors" on Rudolf Steiner's understanding of the heart. Instead, I chose to present the evidence and allow the ideational and spiritual connections between the three streams of influences to become apparent. Every word was chosen with the utmost care. Individual contemplation and meditation on these ideas will bring even greater clarity on the subject. In my opinion, there is no need for any changes or corrections.[2] Together with Sergei O. Prokofiev,[3] I remain certain that Rudolf Steiner would have been pleased with this work in its present form.

My thanks to the Verlag am Goetheanum for making this second edition possible. Its external form fits nicely with that of my thematically related monographs, including *Vom Logos menschlicher Physis. Die Entfaltung einer anthroposophischen Humanphysiologie im Werk Rudolf Steiners* (The Logos of human physiology: the development of an anthroposohical human physiology in the world of Rudolf Steiner, Dornach 2006) and *Krankheit, Heilung und Schicksal des Menschen. Über Rudolf Steiners gesisteswissenschaftliches Pathologie- und Therapieverständnis* (Sickness, healing, and human fate: on Rudolf Steiner's concept of pathology and therapy in spiritual science. Dornach 2004). In addition, I would like to thank Dr. Walter Kugler of the Rudolf Steiner Archives in Dornach for permission to print a photocopy of the heart verse that Rudolf Steiner wrote for Johanna Mücke (see p. 113).

> *Peter Selg*
> *Director of the Ita Wegman Institute*
> *for Basic Research into Anthroposophy*

Introduction

"With matters as they are, one could state emphatically that we know 'heartily little' about what takes place inside the human being. Everything that we do not know or understand concerns the human heart. We still know only 'heartily little' about it. We know about what takes place in the physical world and what can be described using the laws of nature. We also know about the moral tasks that the human being performs, which can be described according to the laws of morality. However, every moral deed and every physical action in a human life are connected in the human heart. We will find the true fusion of these two parallel and independent phenomena, moral events, and physical events, only when we truly learn to understand the configuration of the human heart."[4]

During the 1920 celebration of Pentecost in Dornach, Rudolf Steiner held three important lectures concerning the philosophy of Thomas Aquinas on the subject of Thomistic philosophy and its importance in our time. Steiner portrayed the spiritual-historical path that led from St. Augustine to Thomas. Placing the greatest value on their learned stance on cognition, Steiner instructed us to develop these ideas even further. On Pentecost Monday, looking back at the end of his descriptions, both intensive and extensive, Steiner remarked:

I have shared these observations in order to demonstrate that a pinnacle of the intellectual development of the Western world was reached during the high period of Scholasticism in the thirteenth century. We in modern times have every cause to study the substance of this high point of European intellectual development with great attentiveness. An endless amount can be learned from this attentive examination, particularly with regard to our imperative need for a deepening of our conceptual ability, of our ability to develop our ideas. In this way we can rise above nominalism. Through the Christianizing of our ideas, we can once again find the Christianity that penetrates into our spiritual being.[5]

In the preceding days, Steiner had indeed shown that the task of Anthroposophy is to use spiritual science to bring the reasonable, down-to-earth elements of high Scholasticism into our age, the age of the natural sciences.[6] He had sketched the cognitive path that Goethe took in his work at the end of the eighteenth century and the beginning of the nineteenth. Working with the intentions of Thomas, Goethe chose an Aristotelian, realistic understanding of the world. He established a science of cognition based on ideas; such a science is able to demonstrate the concrete nature of objects. In contrast to Thomas, Goethe took it upon himself to make decisive advances in the natural sciences by studying the human organism.[7] According to Steiner, twentieth-century spiritual science was the logical consequence of continued work with Goethe's ideas:

> In this Goethean view of the world lies the impetus for a nascent intellectual movement. It is the logical result of earlier work with Thomistic thought, adjusted to reflect the new emphasis on the natural sciences in modern scientific research. The soul-spiritual element has a powerful effect on every single activity and function of the human organs. Thomas Aquinas could express this only in an abstract manner, stating that everything which lives and works in the human body,

right up to the most vegetative of functions, is directed by soul forces; and it must be recognized and identified by its soul forces. Goethe marks the beginning of this change in direction in his "Theory of Colors," which has been completely misunderstood on this point. Goethe [too] marks this new beginning with his "Morphology," his work on plants and animals [*On the Metamorphosis of Plants*]. We will be able to bring this Goethean work to completion only when we have a spiritual science that can clarify these observations from the natural sciences.[8]

On Pentecost Sunday, Steiner continued to clarify this with a very consciously chosen example, referring to the recent series of lectures he had held for physicians during the Easter season:

Several weeks ago in this same location, I attempted to demonstrate how spiritual science could play a corrective role vis-a-vis the natural sciences. Let's use the study of the human heart as an example. Those favoring a mechanical and materialistic viewpoint have made the heart into a pump that pushes the blood through the human body. However, the heart is quite the opposite. The circulation of blood is a living thing, as the study of embryology would show us quite precisely if embryologists chose to do such study. The heart is set into action by the blood, as the blood is set in motion internally. The activity of the blood takes place within the heart. In the heart, the activity of the blood is taken up into the entire human individuality. The action of the heart is a consequence of the action of the blood, not vice-versa. Indeed, we can understand the material characteristics of the human being only when we can understand the human as a spiritual being. I have shown this in great detail during this lecture series for physicians, with reference to each individual organ of the body.

In a certain sense, we can express concretely what Thomism could grasp and express only abstractly—specifically, that the spiritual-soul element permeates every aspect of the physical. This has now become a very real, concrete insight. Thus we see how the ideas of Thomist philosophy, kindled anew by the study of Goethe's work, have progressed from their original, abstract form in the thirteenth century to become the spiritual science of our own age.[9]

"At Pentecost, when thought finally comes down the cleared path, it will acquire an empire of riches."[10] Rudolf Steiner's continuation of the spiritual-scientific work of Thomism marked a turning point in the evolution of human consciousness. It defined the epoch without attracting the attention of the general public. This was the work of a single individual; but Thomas, too, and Aristotle before him, had followed their sovereign paths. Each was led by his individual "I," though each found himself spiritually connected to the intellectual steps of his predecessor. Thomas Aquinas began his university studies in Naples in 1239, at the age of fourteen. He occupied himself intensively with the work of the great Greek philosopher and natural science researcher throughout his life. This began with the first lectures on Aristotle he ever attended, given by the Irish professor, Peter of Hibernia. Six years later, in Paris, Thomas is said to have had his first encounter with Albertus Magnus, who became first his teacher, and later his friend. Albertus Magnus was offering lectures on Nicomachean ethics at the Dominican abbey there. Soon after, Thomas began to compose commentaries on Aristotle's works, explicating the texts in a new, truly congenial style entirely unfamiliar to readers of his time. He took the greatest pains to stay true to the original texts, although he did not (in the strictest sense) adhere to the ancient Greek writer's exact words, as Thomas himself reported. Instead, he strove to honor the *intentio Aristotelis* (intention of Aristotle), as perceived by Thomas himself. He consistently referred to his own work as "what Aristotle actually intended to say."[11] According to Thomas's own very clear statements in one of

his commentaries, he was not interested primarily in "what others have thought," but rather in "the truth of matters as they actually stand."[12] He strove to find his own layer of meaning, directly associated with Aristotle's own. According to Josef Pieper, who first referred to the "deeply established connection between the two thinkers," Thomas recognized "his own thoughts" in the works of Aristotle.[13] The same is true of Steiner's later continuation of the work on the *intentio Aristotelis* and the spriritual work of Aquinas, undertaken in the twentieth century.

Thomas Aquinas belonged to the Dominican order, which he joined at the age of nineteen, despite the significant resistance by everyone who knew him. He was ordained in Cologne in 1250 or 1251. As a member of that order, he belonged to a group of priests who had decided to devote their lives to the Gospel in every sense. The Dominicans were simultaneously occupied with challenging the scientific status quo of the time. In stark contrast to the order of mendicant friars established by Francis of Assisi at nearly the same time, the Dominicans turned their attention to the universities from the start. They swelled their ranks with students and professors who sought acceptance into this spiritual community. In the course of Thomas's short life span, he became the greatest teacher of his order, without exception. His excellence was the result of his impassioned oral presentations, his spiritual conversations, and the *disputatio,* or highly formalized academic debates. Even the argumentative confrontations he faced served as an indication and consequence of his controversial devotion both to Aristotle *and* to Christianity.

In contrast to the prevalent views of the leading clerical and academic circles of the time, Thomas did not limit himself to the concrete, earthly, representational connection to the natural world proposed by Aristotle of Stagira (the Greek philosopher and scientist). Thus, Thomas distanced himself completely from the "symbolic unreal-making of the world of the senses" passed down to us by succeeding generations of theologians (Pieper).[14] He also championed the spiritual truths of Christianity and the spiritual individuality of each human being with equal fervor.

During Thomas's lifetime, the university in Toulouse had actually advertised for students by offering lecture courses on Aristotle, although this topic of study had been forbidden by the Church. "Lectures on the [Aristotelian] books about nature, *libros naturales,* are forbidden in Paris. Here they are available to anyone with a desire to penetrate more deeply the innermost aspects of nature."[15] Thomas paved the way for a concrete understanding of the "I" in a preliminary sense—that is, for an understanding of the being and existence of each person, at once both eternal and individual, choosing to incarnate on Earth, and realizing one's biological potential with the help of one's body.

Writings on these physiological issues make up only a relatively minor portion of Thomas's work. Nevertheless, Rudolf Steiner believed that Thomas's attempts to describe his insights were of great importance. Thomas had made these matters accessible for continued and intensified exploration, particularly the *intentio* that came to light in this work.

> In a certain sense we can express concretely what Thomism could grasp and express only abstractly; namely, that the spiritual-soul element permeates every aspect of the physical. This has now become a very real, concrete insight. Thus we see how the ideas of Thomist philosophy, kindled anew by the study of Goethe's work, have progressed from their original, abstract form in the thirteenth century to become the spiritual science of our own age. (see note 5)

This "symbolic unreal-making of the sensory world" (as described by Josef Pieper) was perpetrated by theologists and the church establishment. Increasingly, it left the field free for the type of natural scientific research motivated purely by materialistic goals. This surrender to materialism constituted a shot straight to the heart (literally) of the study of the human being. Though it was more often hinted at than explicitly stated, the human heart had played a central role in the events described in the Gospels. Even in the centuries and millennia before Christ, the heart had played a central role in much questioning and research in mystery centers and philosophical academies; in the thinking of philosophers and physicians; and (to name but one further example) in the lives, words, and, deeds of the ancient Jewish prophets. Aristotle occupied himself with the same topic. Several essential questions about the heart's importance to human existence in both the physiological and spiritual senses were of great concern to Thomas as well; and we should remember that Thomas lived a life filled not only with thinking, but also with sacramental activity. While carrying out the tasks of the Christian religion and its mantra-like use of the spoken word, the "word of the heart" (*verbum cordis*) played a role of primary importance. Nevertheless, during Aquinas's lifetime, and to an even greater extent in the centuries that followed, much of the spiritual knowledge about the heart organ was lost. Often it was set aside by the majority of theologians and scientists without being understood. The heart remained a pale metaphor in mainstream Christianity. Although ever-present in religious and literary texts and seldom missing from emotional sermons, the heart was lacking in the ever-more extensive study of spiritual-physiological reality. Meanwhile, the natural sciences were busily conquering the territory that had been left to them. With forced expansiveness they pushed their idea of the "mechanizing of the heart." A detailed description of this mechanization appeared in a scientific work at the end of the twentieth century.[16] Rudolf Steiner reintroduced this physiological "site" in his research, study, and publications on spiritual science at the beginning of the twentieth century. He brought it to our attention again very deliberately at Pentecost in 1920.[17]

The present study sheds light on some aspects of these questions. It is the revised manuscript of a lecture series that I held this year (2003) in February at the Hamburg Seminary of the Christian Community. Rudolf Steiner composed many texts for the newly formed "Movement for Religious Renewal" based on the intrinsic mystery of the human heart. The liturgy of the Act of Consecration of Man (the communion service of the Christian Community) begins with, "My heart be filled with your pure life, O Christ." These texts take the spiritual physiology of the heart into account as they establish a unique continuation of the intentio of the holy Thomas. Our culture as a whole has not even begun to recognize the possibilities inherent in the *intentio* of this Dominican, who died in the Cistercian cloister of Fossanuova in 1274.[18]

The lectures I gave in Hamburg were intended to clarify these connections, both within and outside of the Christian Community. My wish was also to shelter and protect the words spoken about the heart in these religious gatherings by explicating their intellectual context and spiritual background. The "symbolic unreal-making of the sensory world" is a phenomenon by no means seen only inside clerical circles and outside anthroposophical circles. Within this religious-cultural sphere of influence, we must exert ourselves. We must remain aware of the spiritual-physiological aspects of meaning when speaking these meditation-based words. It goes without saying that the spiritual science of Anthroposophy and its detailed body of knowledge take on a central, even decisive, role. This is especially true in light of the connections that Rudolf Steiner established in the paradigmatic statements of his Pentecost presentations on Thomas Aquinas and the tasks of Anthroposophy in the twentieth century. Here, in Steiner's words, we find the first building blocks leading us toward a sacramental physiology of the heart. These words must be understood, penetrated, and internalized in freedom. "At Pentecost, when thought finally comes down the cleared path, it will acquire an empire of riches."

Consciously intended as a simple study aid, this work has something to offer every reader. It is based on a thorough study of the source texts. Deliberately eschewing bibliographic completeness in the field of scientific history, it avoids perfectionism and the temptation to offer elaborate academic digressions. Although these would certainly have been appropriate in light of the truly extensive thematic scope of the book, they are not absolutely necessary. The text is accompanied by numerous helpful endnotes, which may lead to further reflection.[19] For the first time, this small book places Rudolf Steiner's teachings on the heart squarely back in the spiritual realm, from which they arose. In this sense, this work is also an indirect contribution to the documentation of Rudolf Steiner's spiritual development.

I wish to thank Dr. Gunther Dellbrugger, who invited me to speak in Hamburg, and my indefatigable publisher, Joseph Morel. My thanks also to Peter Schnell. His foundation, which helps so many, helped to support my own fundamental research on the medical and scientific works of Rudolf Steiner. Further, I would like to thank the Medical Section of the Goetheanum (Free University for Spiritual Science, Dornach, Switzerland); the Ita Wegman Clinic; and the Ita Wegman Archives (Arlesheim, Switzerland), with whom I work.

This book is dedicated to the seminaries of the Christian Community in Hamburg and Stuttgart and to all of those who teach and learn there. In his day, Thomas Aquinas ascribed significant importance to the spiritual study and scientific teaching of the Dominicans. He set these tasks above even the care of the soul and the religious-cultural work of the priests. Perhaps it would be appropriate to renew this historical priority in our own age. Perhaps it will be possible for the Christian Community seminaries to increase their contributions to this endeavor. Aided by academic, scientific, and practical pastoral efforts, Rudolf Steiner's twentieth century Christological spiritual science might make its way into wider circles of our culture.[20]

> *Arlesheim and Dornach,*
> *Pentecost, 2003*
> *Peter Selg*

I.

The Anthropology of the Heart in the Gospels

"Where your treasure lies, there, too, lies your heart."
(Luke 12:32–4)

> *"Why are you still worried*
> *because you have no bread*
> *Have your thinking and your understanding*
> *still not been awakened?*
> *Is your heart still hardened?"* (Mark 8:17)

The heart plays a significant, if not central, role in all four Gospels, especially Luke. The anthropological points of view or, more precisely, anthropological assumptions of the relevant passages of the Gospels are complex and markedly differentiated. It will be worthwhile for us to examine the Gospels as a whole, and also to note each individual passage where the heart is mentioned. This enterprise will reveal many astonishing and important new perspectives.[21]

According to all four Gospels, the heart is an organ of sympathy. It signifies the soul's participation in the events of the world, and its emotional consternation in the face of those events. Jesus Christ's "heart was touched" by the Widow of Nain, whose only son apparently had died. "As the Lord saw her, her sadness touched his heart, and he said to her, Don't cry! [*Quam cum vidisset Dominus, misericordia motus super ea dixit illi: Noli flere!*]" (Luke 7:13).[22] In contrast, it was grief that filled the hearts of the disciples as they tried to imagine the approaching death of Christ (John 16:6).

Christ's parting words indicated that this heartfelt grief should give way to great inner joy (in this same organ, the heart) following his resurrection and reappearance. "But I want to see you again, and your heart will rejoice, and no one will be able to rob you of your joy [*Iterum autem videbo vos, et gaudebit cor vestrum, et gaudium vestrum nemo tollit a vobis*]" (John 16:22).[23]

In several passages a "hardening of the heart," or a "hardness of the heart" (*duritia cordis*), is mentioned. Jesus Christ points out the lack of empathy and the absence of sympathy for those who suffer, and for those who are pushed aside. The sick man with the withered hand is one example. Those present in the synagogue watch with suspicion and inner apathy as Christ begins his healing work with the man. "And he said to the man who had the withered hand, Rise and stand forth in the middle. And he arose and stood forth. Then said Jesus unto them, I will ask you one thing: Is it lawful on the Sabbath days to do good, or to do evil? To save life, or to destroy it? They said nothing. Then he looked at the angry men around him, full of sadness at the hardening of their hearts" (Mark 2:4–6 in Ogilvie translation). The same lack of empathy is seen in the passage about the wives who are left behind, abandoned, and otherwise discarded by their husbands.[24]

As we are examining the anthropology of the heart we should take note that this organ as portrayed in the Gospels is seldom or never the instrument or expression of human feelings alone. The heart is also deeply connected to the individual thinking and cognitive capacity of the human being. The previous references demonstrate not only the human capacity for empathy, but also the level of general readiness and willingness to enter fully into the situation at hand and grasp its meaning. Each person present is at a certain stage of situational cognition, or (at the very least) situational acknowledgement. The overwhelming majority of the additional Gospel references show, with great clarity, the inner connection of our heart activities to our higher intellectual capacities. This is often shown by negative example as failure, holding back, or refusal. In just this manner, the hearts of the disciples were lastingly blinded, or hardened (*cor obcaecatus*). Despite having seen the miracle of the loaves and fishes, they were unable to arrive at a true understanding of the working of the Christ being. The disciples were fearful during the storm, and were beside themselves when Christ intervened (*non enim intellexerant de panibus, sed erat cor illorum obcaecatum.* [Mark 6:52]). According to Mark, Christ repeats this striking expression shortly thereafter, as the disciples once again become anxious about being fed:

They were worrying together about having no loaves of bread. Jesus noticed this and said to them, Why are you worried about having no loaves? Do you not yet perceive, nor understand? Have you hardened your heart entirely? [*Et disputabant ad invicem, quia panes non haberent. Quo cognito ait illis: Quid disputatis, quia panes non habetis? Nondum cognoscitis, nec intellegitis? Caecatum habetis cor vestrum?*] (Mark 8:16–17)

Even if the heart is not portrayed in the Gospels as the actual, or only, organ of thinking, the spiritual and physiological processes that take place in the heart are clearly the decisive premise for the recognition, acceptance, and comprehension of each event. These processes of the heart allow us to connect our individual selves with our experiences.

Some of the disciples did not live in conscious awareness of the actual events of Golgotha, despite the Easter reports of Mary Magdalene and the experiences in Emmaus. Mark and Luke both report that the risen Christ reproved these disciples. "And he upbraided them for the weakness of their belief and the hardness of their heart" (Mark 16:14). The heart processes of the disciples worked "too slowly" (*cor tardus*) and remained unmoved even while these events were unfolding before them—even in the midst of events foretold centuries before by the prophets concerning Christ. "O you ignorant ones, so slow of heart, unable to believe all that the prophets have spoken!" (Luke 24:25). Matthew and John, in turn, make a direct reference to the prophet Isaiah, who had spoken thus after an explicit reference to the weak and untrained, if not actually defective, processes of the heart:

You will listen with your ears, but not hear. You will see with your eyes but not perceive. The heart of this group is obstinate [*incrassatum est enim cor populi huius*], their ears have become deaf, and they have closed their eyes, so that they cannot see with their eyes nor hear with their ears, nor understand with their hearts and turn to me [*et corde intellegant et convertantur*] so that I could heal them. (Isaiah 6:9–10; compare to Matt. 13:14–15 and John 12:40)

In this sense, every instance of doubt among the disciples has to do with the heart organ. "For assuredly, I say to you, whoever says to this mountain, 'Get up and jump into the sea!' and does not doubt in his heart [*et non haesitaverit in corde suo*], but believes that those things he says will happen, he will have whatever he says" (Mark 11:23). As the risen Christ meets the disciples in the circle where they had gathered, shortly after the events in Emmaus, Luke reports that Christ speaks to them thus: "Why are you so confused, and why do such doubts rise up in your hearts? [*Quid turbati estis, et quare cogitationes ascendunt in corda vestra?*]" (Luke 24:38).

In the Gospel, the heart is connected not only with the dependable, determined trust in the truth of what we recognize or experience intellectually, but also, significantly, it is connected with the intentionality of our thinking, with its origin, with its deliberately moral core, and with the deepest concerns of the human being. In the contorted form of the failure—or, to put it another way, in a mode of deficient soul-spiritual attitude and activity—this heart activity becomes clear in the words of Christ, spoken during a debate about the purity laws for meals and eating:

> Do you lack insight here, as well? Can you not comprehend that no external substances taken into the human body make it impure? These things are not taken into the heart [*non introit in cor eius*] but into the stomach. They then leave the body. For that reason, all the food which we eat is pure.... That which goes out from us can desecrate the body, because evil thoughts have their origin inside the human heart [*ab intus enim de corde hominum cogitationes malae procedunt*]:

obscenity, theft, murder, adultery, greed, anger, guile, lack of
self-restraint, envy, blasphemy, pride, and rashness. All this
evil comes from within and makes the human being impure.
(Mark 7:18-23)

Just as God knows the hearts of human beings, as we read in
Luke [*Deus autem novit corda vestra*] (Luke 16:15), likewise (as
we read in the story of the apostles), God's son is clearly capable
of perceiving human thoughts as they spring from the heart,
before they have found a form of expression.[25] This happened
repeatedly while Christ was together with his disciples, who
often absented themselves from their assigned tasks, caught up
in their preconceived notions and idiosyncrasies. "They often
pondered together over the question of who was the greatest
among them. Jesus knew about the thoughts in their hearts
[*Iesus sciens cogitationem cordis illorum*], took a child, placed
it next to them, and said to them: If one of you cares for this
child in my name, you care for me; and if you care for me, you
are caring for the one who sent me. Whoever is the least among
you, he is great" (Luke 9:46–48). In the meetings between Christ
and the Pharisees and learned men as well, who were offended
by the spiritual healing ("forgiving of sins") of the paralyzed
man of Capernaum, Christ knew their thoughts:

> Some of the learned men sat there, thinking in their hearts
> [*cogitantes in cordibus suis*]: How can he talk like that? He
> is blaspheming! Who can forgive sins besides God himself?
> At once Jesus perceived their unspoken thoughts in his spirit,
> and he spoke to them: Why are you thinking such thoughts in
> your hearts? [*Quid ista cogitatis in cordibus vestris?*] (Mark
> 2:6–8; also Matthew 9:3–4 and Luke 5:21–22)

By contrast, thirty years before, the aged Simeon had held
the child Jesus (whom he had long awaited as the bearer of the

Christ being) in his hands and blessed the parents. On that occasion, Simeon had spoken the following foreshadowing words to Mary: "Observe, he is sent so that many in Israel will fall and rise up again, and he is sent as a sign which will be contradicted. A sword will pierce through your soul, as well. The thoughts of many hearts shall be revealed [*Ut revelentur ex multis cordibus cogitationes*]" (Luke 2:34–35).

*

Language and words hold a particular meaning for what springs from the human heart, according to the Gospel. The movements of the heart gain their first perceptible shape in human language, even if Christ was already able to perceive them before they took this form. The formed word and the thought it carries constantly refer to their origin in the heart; and also refer to the quality of this origin, to its inner composition. In Matthew and Luke, Jesus Christ expresses himself on the subject with great clarity. In both of these accounts, we find the significant term *treasure chest,* or *coffer* (thesaurus) of the heart. Here Matthew tells of Christ's speech to the Pharisees:

> Either you plant a good tree, and there is good fruit, or you plant a rotten tree, and there is rotten fruit; by the fruit one knows the tree. How could you, offspring of snakes, speak of good when you are evil? Because the mouth speaks that which overflows out of a full heart [*Ex abundantia enim cordis os loquitur*]. A good person brings forth good things out of his good treasure chest, and a bad person brings forth evil out of his evil treasure chest. I tell you, though: on the Day of Judgment, people will have to answer for every unnecessary, inappropriate word they speak; what emerges from your words will acquit you; and what emerges from your words will condemn you. (Matt. 12:33–37)

The corresponding passage in Luke states:

> A good person brings forth good things out of the good trea-
> sure chest of the heart, and a bad person brings forth evil out
> of his evil treasure chest. The mouth speaks of whatever over-
> flows out of the heart [*Bonus homo de bono thesauro cordis
> profert bonum, et malus homo de malo profert malum: ex
> abundantia enim cordis os eius loquitur*]. (Luke 6:45)

If one examines the other closely related Gospel passages, col-
lectively, it becomes very clear that the "treasure chest" of the
heart organ does not refer to an unchanging being or existence;
but rather to nothing less than the spiritual-physiological site at
which the moral-spiritual becoming or development of the individual can take place, by means of inner training and meditative practice. Ultimately, the heart can become "abundantly rich"
and "overflow," if this hidden process is carried out with much
inner work, in the best sense. Luke refers to this when speaking
of Mary, as she was telling the shepherds of the field about the
angelic annunciation: "But Mary guarded and pondered all of
these words in her heart [*Maria autem conservabat omnia verba
haec conferens in corde suo*]" (Luke 2:19).

"She kept all these words [of the twelve-year-old Jesus] in her
heart," as well, after Jesus' visit to the temple (Luke 2:51). When
considering the birth and later spiritual work of John, observers
took those events into their hearts in an initiative-taking, active
way (as Mary had very possibly also done), questioning the meaning of what they were seeing, and their hearts were moved (Luke
1:66 and 3:15). To the same realm of meaning belongs the idea
(found in both Luke and Matthew) that the words of Christ were
"sown" in the hearts of humanity, like a spiritual seed. Inside the
heart, these words can ripen and take effect in individual freedom
(Matthew 13:18–23 and Luke 8:12–15). Precisely the opposite was

achieved when satanic power seized the heart of Judas Iscariot, manipulating his deeds and his fate with its influence: "During the evening meal the devil had put the idea of betraying Christ into the heart of Judas, son of Simon Iscariot [*Et in cena, cum Diabolus iam misisset in corde, ut traderet eum Iudas Simonis Iscariotis*]" (John 13:2).[26]

From this we learn that the process of overcoming evil, baseness, misrepresentation, or distortion takes place in the heart, by means of inner soul-spiritual activity. The heart is the central organ of human morality. It is the site of the innermost directing of one's individual existence.[27] "Let not your heart be troubled; neither let it be fearful [*Non turbetur cor vestrum neque formidet*]" (John 14:27). Each instance of actual "forgiveness" also takes place in the heart (Matthew 19:35).

Now we have gained an overview of the statements made about the heart in the Gospels. The precise order in which we follow these references is essential. We can begin to see the outlines of the form and nature of an organ that enables us to connect our souls to the reality of the outside world. We must also acknowledge the central role of the heart for each individual, in the processing of knowledge and intention. The heart is entirely responsible for our spiritual existence in the world. Spiritual activities take place in the heart, which determine the moral path of the individual. They regulate what we "take to heart," and how intensively (Luke 21:14). They define what sense and meaning we carry in our hearts (Luke 1:51). They also determine how our intentions will influence all of our thinking and actions. The result of these spiritual activities has consequences on both the soul-spiritual and physical levels.[28] The outcome determines the development and evolution of the world; the biographical form a human life will take; and the person's future fate—the developmental path of one's individuality. At different points in the Gospels we read of someone attaining a "treasure in the heavens" by virtue of his thoughts and deeds on Earth (Matthew 19:22; Mark 10:21; Luke 18:22). It is Luke who adds validity to the idea that this spiritual "treasure" is intimately connected with the heart organ:

> Do not be afraid, little flock! For your father intends to give you his kingdom. Sell what you own, and give it to the needy. Acquire the sort of treasures that do not age, an inexhaustible treasure in the heavens, which no thief can reach and no moth can destroy. For where your treasure lies, there too lies your heart [*Ubi enim thesaurus vester est, ibi et cor vestrum erit*]. (Luke 12:32–34)[29]

2.

De Essentia et Motu Cordis

ARISTOTLE AND THOMAS AQUINAS

"Because in the heart the life source of the entire creation is found, the heart comes into being first of all."

—ARISTOTLE

"The motion of the heart in the sensory being corresponds...to the motion of the heavens in the world."

—THOMAS AQUINAS

"I want to put a new heart and a new spirit in you; and I want to take the stony heart out of your body and give you a living heart."

(Ezekiel 11:19)

The events that took place in Palestine in the first decades after the "turning point in time" (after the coming of Christ) signified a new beginning in the spiritual history of humanity. These events were given linguistic and conceptual shape by the accounts of Christ's life and deeds written later by four of his students, Matthew, Mark, Luke, and John. This heralded an entirely unexpected and intensive revision of all previous notions about the human being in the world, including physical, social, and spiritual existence. This concept of "intensive revision" includes the idea of progressing beyond what was previously thought; beyond what happened previously; and beyond the historical past, by taking up the older ideas about the human being in a qualitatively different and newly sophisticated way. If we wish to try to judge what is truly new and different in a period of radical historical change, it is essential for us to make an intensive and significant effort to understand the time before that change, as well as more recent events.[30] This is just as important as our attempts to determine what became of these new beginnings; how the understanding and existence of the human being changed; and what hindered and what helped this process.

Against the background of the centuries just before and just after the life of Christ, we now bring forth the question of the anthropological meaning of the heart organ; or at least each successive historical perception of the significance of the heart. Nearly overwhelming obstacles stand in the way of such an undertaking. The scientific, academic, and historical documents exist in great number, but are obtained only by means of a tedious process. There are no easy means of gaining an overview of what is available, and what might be pertinent. The greatest difficulties, however, lie not so much in the challenge of obtaining the necessary documents, as in the documents themselves. The texts, which were written down, collected, and preserved for centuries and millennia, do not accurately represent the thoughts and research of those earlier times. It is difficult to determine what Ezekiel, Plato, Aristotle, or Thomas Aquinas (for example) actually thought about the heart. We know little about which spiritual experiences and physiological discoveries were within their conceptual reach as they explored themselves and their world. We must speculate as to what they held to be possible or probable. They did not entrust these essential matters to the manuscripts to which we now have access. Even the words and concepts they used often bore entirely different meanings in their time, and we can gain only a sketchy idea of their true intentions. Human intellectual and spiritual history is much richer, more subtle, and more differentiated than accessible documents would indicate.

Looking back at the centuries before Christ, we must note that the vital progress and development in the spiritual knowledge about humanity took place in the seclusion of the mystery schools.[31] Even in Plato's Academy, in the fourth century before Christ, everything that was essential, valuable, and original was considered and taught only orally.[32] Their methods of research, and the concrete results of these intensive efforts, have been entirely forgotten. Their attempts to understand the human being in the cosmos, and the physiology and pathology of the human, exist only in the collective world memory.

It does not contradict the statements above in any sense, to note that in isolated instances, views and ideas arising from these entirely different realms of understanding did eventually leave the seclusion of the mystery centers and find their way into mainstream thought. At some point, these ideas reached even the developing systems of philosophical thought and the collective culture. The attempt to establish an accurate picture of the progress made in cognition at that time, and the attempt to interpret this progress appropriately, leads us onto decidedly divergent and misleading paths. This phenomenon is exaggerated even further if we begin this work with the hubris of modern humanity and its immoderate overvaluing of the contemporary ways of seeing and current thought paradigms. Take a good look at contemporary historical portrayals of the development of views on the heart during the past 2,500 years. You will see that they begin, almost without exception, with a short report about what was apparently (but not actually) thought and taught by Empedocles, Hippocrates, Plato, and others on the physiological and anatomical aspects of the heart. In this way, every author on the subject contributes, willingly or unwillingly, to the further characterization of this very different research and thought.[33] In the meantime, we have come to lack nearly every requirement for gaining a true understanding of this work of the past.

These are fundamental difficulties we find with any historical research based exclusively on written documents. Despite these challenges, reflecting on the phenomenon of heart research and teachings from the centuries immediately before Christ will prove valuable. Of particular interest are the events of the "turning point of time," especially the mystery of Golgotha and the surrounding events as depicted in the Gospels. Some passages we discover in these old texts have a premonitory effect; that of a probing, questioning effort to describe the heart, and with it the mysteries of blood and breathing. In the six centuries before Christ the many views and questions on the human body took on a more concrete and thus more physiological form. These investigations had taken place for eons in all highly developed cultures. In China, India, Babylon, Egypt, and Palestine, such work on the heart had been pronouncedly complex and profound for millennia.[34] Those cultures investigated the human body as the active, effective organ of cosmic and earthly forces, and increasingly also as the site and instrument for the soul-spiritual and existential development of an individual—a particular, unique, individual human being. The concept of the "I" was still strange and foreign to all cultures before the coming of Christ. Particularly in the Greek cultural realm, though, steps were being taken that would lead to the concept of the individuality of each human being. The entire course of events of this history of consciousness, which can be followed indirectly in literary and philosophical documents, appears to us today to have been a process of the incarnation of the human spirit, in which substantial importance was ascribed to the heart organ.[35] The heart was essential not only for the active completion of this process, but also for the analysis of the scientific and cognizant consciousness. These events, while taking place, made themselves into the questions to be answered. They chose themselves, as it were, as the central theme of inquiry.

*

If one studies the available documents from this point of view, it is remarkable to see how the Greeks referred to the elements of air and fire as they thought and wrote in their philosophy on the phenomenon of the living, feeling, and spirit-endowed organism. These ideas were being set before the general public for the first time, beginning with the Ionic philosophy of nature, and continuing into their contemporary medical practices. Very different approaches were formulated, at great variance to one another. The pneúma, changing itself in the blood, is described as a carrier of feelings and consciousness, in close connection with human breathing. In addition, an ever greater emphasis is laid upon its "native warmth" (*émphython thermón*), in combination with the blood, designated as the physiological source of the life of the organism and the movement of the self. This is shown in contrast to the sun, which works macrocosmically. The upper breath (*pneuma*) and the lower blood (warmth) processes culminate in the heart. This fact focused interest on the heart organ as the apparent center of life and consciousness. Historical documents credit the Sicilian philosopher Empedocles (ca. 483–423 BCE) with being the first to draw attention explicitly to the physiological importance of the heart organ in human intellectual development, with an emphasis on the processes of the blood: "The heart is nourished in the corridors of the blood, as the blood pulses against the spot where thinking takes place in the human being. The blood that streams around the human heart is human thought. Human insight grows as this process takes place."[36]

Plato and his Academy's important student, Aristotle of Stagira, who broke new ground with his work in the sciences, did their work during the fourth century before Christ, in the decades following Empedocles' lifetime.

Plato and Aristotle, both still intensively ensconced in the world of the mysteries, did more than introduce the principle of initiation to the general civilization.[37] More important, this was the start of a firmly grounded, extensive, and highly systematic anthropology. The interrelationships of the body, soul, and spirit, the *conditio humana,* were successively elucidated in this anthropology. The heart organ itself played a rather subordinate role in the dialogues of Plato, to which we now have access. However, there was an extensive reference to the heart in *Timaeus,* which explored the receptive and regulatory powers of the heart for the soul and body forces of the lower organism, and for the processes of the blood with which they work in close connection.[38] On the other hand, we can assume that the heart and all heart-related events stood in the background, or even the center, of some investigations and Academy courses. Scientists and high-ranking lecturers from other cities, including doctors, mathematicians, and astronomers, were invited to take part in them. There was an extensive and differentiated study of motion in the work of Plato, for example—with its additional questions about the causes of planetary motion. In this work a transition was described from the idea of a body to the idea of a body being moved by outward forces, with the help of the soul. The soul is able to move of its own accord and moves between idea and manifestation.[39] It seems reasonable to analyze an organ whose clearly defined and elementary dynamic of movement and definition of movement for the entire organism was already recognized in those times. For Plato, who had extensive contact with the Sicilian medical school of the great Philistion, the soul was unquestionably the force behind both the formation of the body and its function. The collective view of the body depended on this spiritual-ideational organization—in sickness and in health—and on the existence of one of its central active organs, the heart.

ARISTOTLE'S STUDY OF THE HEART

"The heart lies at the front, in the center; and according to our theory, life depends upon it, and all movement and perception, as well."[40]

Aristotle's father served as the royal physician in the Macedonian court. From the age of seventeen (367 BCE), Aristotle studied with Plato in Athens, where he remained for two full decades.[41] Starting at the beginning of the sixth decade of the fourth century, with close attention he followed the radical change in scientific methodology.[42] Very soon, in fact, his own lectures helped to shape that change. We have proof that he possessed a library, perhaps the first on European soil. He personally took the historical step from being a "listener" to being a "reader."[43] In the fifty years of his active intellectual life, he worked his way through the entire collective knowledge of the age, examining and testing everything he read.[44] How he managed this task is incomprehensible, even today. He developed comprehensive epistemological points of view.

Active and productive in every branch of science known in his time, Aristotle played a fundamental, innovative, and pioneering role. Only in the field of medicine did he deny himself the opportunity to put forth his own independent theory or philosophy. He did have intensive contact with anatomical, physiological, and pathological–therapeutic research, nevertheless; and he formulated numerous points of view that pointed the way toward a new theory of health and sickness.[45] Aristotle continued working on Plato's intentions, while making necessary corrections to Plato's statements: "I love Plato, but I love the truth even more."[46] In particular, he centered his attention even more lastingly and empirically on the living developmental process of creatures and on the substantial effect of forming, shaping forces.[47] Throughout his life, he occupied himself extensively and intensively with biological investigations, with a constant emphasis on processes directed toward the progressive realization of a higher unity.[48] In the field of anthropology he gave priority to assessing how the nature of the human body leads to the development of intellectual-spiritual cognitive processes, moral actions, and individual responsibility. Aristotle devoted himself to a phenomenological investigation of the differing conditions of body and soul in animals and humans; and he worked to clarify how these conditions led to their species-specific ways of experiencing events.

Plato had begun this work, but Aristotle's work was both more extensive and more specific. His research shifted the heart organ to the very center of the physiological process. Aristotle's work stepped away from the seclusion of the old mystery schools and their ways of seeing; and he achieved a fundamentally new, forward-looking perspective consisting of clearly formed concepts.[49] The real history of empirical natural science began here. The sense-perceptible world received its first great recognition, comprehension, and appreciation, not as a mere reflection of reality, and not as an absolute, final, fully independent object, but as the fulfillment of the encounter between earthly and cosmic forces, influenced by the body and the soul, by both perceptible and suprasensory processes. Aristotle performed a systematic investigation of meteorology and cosmology, as well as hibernation and autumnal bird migration, without the desire or the technical means to change or manipulate the results. *"Pantes anthropoi tou eidenai oregontai physei"*—all people are naturally driven to seek knowledge.[50] Aristotle took a close look at every known aspect of the cosmos, learning from fishermen, shepherds, hunters, beekeepers, pig breeders, veterinarians, and others. He wrote precise descriptions of hundreds of hitherto unknown animals, inspecting every aspect of their existence, even to the hidden eyes of the blind mole, which he had unambiguously identified during a dissection.

> There are miracles in every natural object. Some strangers wanted to visit Heraclitus, then stood stock still upon entering, after seeing him warm himself by the oven. "You should come in," he called out to them; "there are gods here!" And in accordance with these words, one should approach the observation of any animal, every animal, without making a face, and tell oneself that in every single one there is a bit of nature and perfection.[51]

In his work with anthropology, Aristotle completed a first and momentous attempt to describe the mystery of incarnation as the deepest connection of soul-spiritual and physical events. In his work with cosmology, he worked out the familial relationship between every part of the creation, a connection that Aristotle validated with emphasis on the *logos,* a term introduced by Heraclitus.

Aristotle took charge of the Platonic Academy, in which the individual students were expected to work toward intellectual and moral maturity, educating themselves to assume responsible state tasks and positions. Aristotle transformed the previous organizational structure of the Academy and allocated research projects with a firm hand. His student Theophrast, for example, was assigned the composition of an independent botanical study. This was all part of an ambitious cognitive project that included very different sorts of people, teachers and students alike, in the newly expanded scientific organization of the Lyceum.

The nineteen documents published by Aristotle during his lifetime are considered to be lost without a trace. We still have the manuscripts of the lectures of this great teacher, which are known up to the present day as his writings. He himself continually reflected upon these texts, making notes in the margins and adding comments. These were first published in Rome many centuries after his death.

*

As mentioned in the introductory remarks, Aristotle focused his attention less on the unchanging nature of existence and more on the world as it is constantly coming into being and fading away, the world of movement and processes. He was one of the first to follow, intensively and systematically, the question of how a being appears on Earth with a form or shape, and becomes reality. The nature of physiology (*physis*) was for him the world in the process of becoming, revealing itself in its manifestations, and at the same time making these manifestations possible. "Nature in the sense of becoming is defined by its transition into its own being and essence."[52] This process of becoming is completed, said Aristotle, in confrontation with the sphere of earthly materiality, but also in confrontation with the dynamic forces of destruction, breakdown, and disintegration, standing in opposition to the formative forces. This leads to the concrete forms and organs that serve the being. From this standpoint, Aristotle observed the formation of the individual organs (and the nature of the being as an entirety, as well) primarily from the point of view of the function they serve. "For that reason the body exists for the sake of the soul, and the limbs exist for the sake of the activities that nature has assigned to them."[53] Aristotle vehemently protested every materialistic interpretation that attempted to invert the relationship between physicality and soul-spiritual development. "Anaxagoras said that possessing hands made humans into the most intelligent living beings. It would be more sensible to say that humans possess hands because they are the most intelligent living beings."[54]

According to Aristotle, the nature of all creatures contains both a formative force, a shaping capacity, and the eidos (image, form, shape), which enables the learning processes and contains within itself the goal to be reached (*en telei*), allowing fulfillment. The concept of *entelecheia,* developed by Aristotle, describes the goal-directed form of this developmental process, as well as the inherent foreknowledge of where each process leads. For the living beings (the plant, the animal, and the person), Aristotle used the broad term *soul* (*psychê*), which encompasses narrower or broader abilities, depending upon the being's relative level of importance in the creation. These abilities lead to the functions of nurturing (in the plant), to sensory perception and movement (in the animal), and to the development of thinking (in the human). The *psychê,* in this sense, is constantly shaping the form of our physicality, and it is the "physio-logical" principle that determines that form, and thus constitutes the primary reason for its effectiveness. "The soul must necessarily exist in the form of a natural body, because doing so enables it to live. The being, though, is the fulfillment, *Entelechie.* And the soul is thus the fulfillment and completion of such a body."[55]

> If we were to name something that every soul has in common, we would say that the soul is the element that completes and perfects each natural, organic body. For that reason we should no more ask if the body and soul are one than we should ask if the [sculptor's] wax and the figure are one; and definitely not ask if matter, and what constitutes matter, are one. "Unity" and "being" have many possible interpretations, but the most proper and fundamental sense of both is the relation of an entity to that of which it is composed.[56]

On the other hand, Aristotle pointed out that the body loses its life, its function, and gradually its form after the departure of the soul. "When the soul leaves, the body flees from itself and decomposes."[57]

In light of the historical and intellectual background of this cognitive attitude, it should not surprise us to learn that Aristotle was one of the first natural scientists to take up the study of human embryological formation.[58] He followed the early appearance of the heart organ and the centralized blood–heart system (the first functional and conjoined organ system) with great attentiveness.[59] "It is so!" he called out in his writings on the origin of the living being (*Peri zôôn geneseôs*).[60] In the developing heart organism, Aristotle recognized not only the first sign of life and the "organological" beginning of the body; but also, in a certain sense specific to human beings, the beginning of the earthly process of becoming a person. He also saw the effective principle on which all further development is based, which he called the "source of life" in the sense of a "creative power" that invokes (and thus initiates) all further development.[61] Aristotle discussed this in more detail in *Peri zôôn geneseôs*, one of his later works:

> The beginning of the development of plants is already found in the seeds, at first only as an inherent structure. When this potential is realized, the stem and the root start growing out from this point, enabling the plant to draw in nourishment and continue growing. The same thing takes place in the embryo [of the animal life forms], which contains all the parts of the structure. In this case, the first step of the developmental process is marked out especially clearly. The heart develops first, and one can actually observe this—it is so!— and also list the reasons for it. When the embryo has freed itself from the material contributed by both parents, it must construct itself, like a child who has moved out of the home of its parents. There must be a source, therefore, which is responsible for all further development of the body from that point on. If this power comes from outside, and first enters

the body at a later point, we would naturally wish to determine the point in time when it appears. Whatever is needed for the first steps of development, and initiates that development, must already be present at the time when the limbs are being formed and begin to move.

He who teaches, like Demokritos, that the outer form of a being arises first, and only later the inner organs, is incorrect. This would be the case only with animals made out of wood or stone. These have no life source, but living beings do; and this life source is found inside of them. For that reason, the heart blossoms forth first in all blood animals, because this is the source of all of the evenly divided and unevenly divided limbs and organs. We are justified in seeing the heart as the source of the being's life, shape, and organization.[62]

At another point, coming back to his previous remarks, Aristotle continued these observations with a glance at the end of the organism's life, and wrote:

> The life source (the heart for animals with blood, and the corresponding substitute, for others) first takes the form I have described so often. The fact that the heart is formed first is something we learn, not only from our own observation. It can also be proven by examining the end of the life of the animal, because the very last signs of life are seen here also, in the heart.
>
> What developed last is always the first thing to disappear, and what developed first is the last thing to disappear, as if nature were running a race around a track and always returned to the starting point again at the end. Birth is the step from not-being to being, and death is the step from being back into non-being.[63]

*

Aristotle noticed and described not only the early presence of the heart organ in the embryonic state, but also the early movement of the heart, the activity that is specific to the heart, and appropriate for it, "as if it were itself an independent being." In his text *On the Limbs of Beings* (*Peri zôôn moriôn*), he added, "In the unborn child, the heart can be observed moving as if it had an independent existence, because it is the origin of life for this being, and indeed for all blood creatures."[64]

According to Aristotle, the heart is formed by the blood and for the blood. The individual, moving form of the heart originates there, in the living, moving blood. Only in the heart do we find the blood directly in the organism without the blood vessels that usually surround and shield it. The heart organ is both the creator and the point of origin of the blood vessels and the blood itself. "Blood and blood vessels necessarily have the same origin. Blood vessels exist as containers for the blood. The same is true of blood for all creatures; blood vessels originate in the heart."[65] The organological independence of the being develops itself first in the living, moving blood. "The other viscera constitute a sort of deposit as the blood flows through the veins, just as mud separates itself from flowing water. The heart naturally consists of that from which it receives nourishment. The heart is the origin of all blood vessels, holding the origin of all the blood-forming forces within itself."[66]

According to Aristotle, the heart is the "origin and source of the blood and its carrying vessels" in the embryological and genetic sense and in terms of function.[67] The blood flows out from the heart, where its formation takes place, and into the vessels of the body. To this extent, it is also possible to say that the blood and its blood vessels are the "original source of life."[68]

In connection with this, we must consider just how far-reaching and profound Aristotle's concepts are—those concerning the "blood-forming forces," the substance of the newly formed blood,[69] and the nurturing process.[70] He knew about the blood-rich nature of marrow and made special note of this in his *Natural History of Living Beings (Peri tôn zôôn historiai)*. Nor did the strong relationship between the liver and the blood escape his attention.[71] Most important, he gave validity to the idea that we must see the heart as the source of the blood and the place of its definitive formation. There, in the heart, the blood "brings itself forth from certain prepared fluids," and there the actual "blood-forming forces" do their work.[72] Certain preparatory stages of this process may have taken place elsewhere, and those other locations may have thus helped to enable the process in a preliminary sense. Significantly, the formation of the substance is completed in the heart. "We must look to the heart to discover where the blood is created. From there, it spreads itself through the entire body."[73]

First, Aristotle tells us, the heart organ must absorb and transform the "prepared fluids." Only with this can we speak of this substance as blood. Various processes specific to human beings can then commence. Aristotle repeatedly pointed out that the characteristics of the blood differ significantly within the human organism as a whole, particularly between the upper and lower organism.[74] There are also pronounced differences between the blood of human beings and the blood of other creatures.[75] Human blood has certain special, unique qualities that are essential for the realization of our constitutional and soul-spiritual potential.[76] The actual nourishment process of each living thing is involved intrinsically with the entire process of forming the blood. The formation of the blood constitutes "the final step" of internalizing and transforming nourishment.[77] Aristotle wrote that this step is "completed" in the heart,[78] the "origin" and "final source" of this nourishment process, the physiological site in which "the center of the soul function lies, which regulates growth and nourishment."[79]

Aristotle elucidated this further in his article "On Youth and Age, Life, and Death," in which he wrote, "The other parts of the body carry out their nourishment-related functions so that the heart can carry out its nourishment-related functions."[80]

*

Warmth is fundamental, decisively important, for the entire process of the transformation of substances, and thus also for the final steps in blood formation and the subsequent development of the body.[81] In fact, warmth enables digestion, as Aristotle repeatedly explained. Thus warmth also brings about the "overcoming," surmounting, and internalization of outside, "foreign" qualities. At the same time, warmth finds its own center, origin, and source in the heart. In the article just named, Aristotle wrote:

> Each animal possesses inherent natural warmth in its body as a whole, and in every part of its body. That is why animals are warm while they are alive and cold when they die, when the life goes out of them. The origin of this warmth for blood-filled animals lies in the heart. For bloodless animals, the source of this warmth lies in the body part that corresponds most closely to the heart. All parts of the body and, most important, the central organ [the heart] process and digest nourishment by means of this natural warmth. Life continues, even if the other parts of the body cool down, as long as the heart remains warm. However, the entire body perishes if the warmth leaves the heart. All other parts of the body depend on the heart and have their source, or origin, in the heart.[82]

Compared to all other living beings on Earth, the warmth of the human heart is "the most purely formed and developed," according to Aristotle's statements in his work *On the Creation of Beings*.[83] This makes two things possible: both the specific formation of the general life processes and the further development of the soul-spiritual. At one point, Aristotle said that the particular prerequisites for human thought activity are grounded in the polar opposite and painstakingly balanced processes of warmth and cold in the human heart and brain.[84]

Aristotle knew a great deal about the human brain and the entire central nervous system, though certain details of its inner structure were far beyond the level of empirical understanding during his time. He nevertheless saw the essential importance of the brain and the nervous system and described their early formation in the embryonic development process, as well as the impressive, predominant role they play at that stage. In many respects, they serve as the functional counterpart of the heart. Taking up the case of the heart as the center of life and the source of warmth for the entire organism, in *On the Creation of Beings* Aristotle wrote, "Because the source of life in the entire being is in the heart, it develops first. Because of the heart's warmth, nature chose to place the brain above, where the blood vessels end, to serve as a cool counterbalance. From the very beginning, the brain is large and moist. For this reason, the head and the surrounding area develop immediately after the heart. The size of the head differentiates it from the other limbs."[85]

Aristotle's views on this matter differ sharply from those of various contemporaries and from those of the nature philosophers who came before him (Alcmaeon of Croton, for example, but also the Pythagoreans, Democritus, Diogenes of Apollonia, and Plato). In contrast to those philosophers, Aristotle repeatedly emphasized the essentially participatory and ultimately metaphorical role played by the brain in various physiological processes, including the organ processes upon which human intellectual accomplishments are based.[86] He warned against overestimating the role of the central nervous system and against the idea of identifying the higher mental and spiritual functions with the mechanical processes of the brain, even with regard to our sensory perception and ability to move.[87] Aristotle stressed the essential participation of the brain in certain heart-centered activities, which served unquestionably as the focal point of his work on physiology. He described the inclusion and preparatory role of the brain in the processes of nourishment and substance transformation, which are completed in the heart, characterizing the heart and the brain in their corresponding, if opposite, roles as the "most important tools of life."[88] "The largest and strongest membranes surround the heart and brain, with good reason, because they are most in need of protection, the sort of protection most suited to the most important parts [of the body]."[89]

Aristotle's work on the senses is extensive and was formulated in several of his written works, in particular in *On the Soul* (*Peri psychês*), but also in smaller, condensed lecture transcriptions: "On Sensing and What is Being Sensed," "On Memory and Reminiscence," "On Sleep and Waking," and "On Dreams," as well as in the treatise "On the Interpretation of Dreams."

We wish to discuss and clarify certain physiological questions about the heart. In this context, let us confine ourselves for a moment to discussing the vital role played by the heart as it aids the other organs in the process of perception. Of primary importance, according to Aristotle, is the fact that all isolated sensory impressions of the individual senses are coordinated to a certain extent in the heart. They must be brought into connection and synthesis with one another. This process serves as the basis for every unified assessment of the form and quality of what has been perceived. To this extent, the heart is the "center of the perception process of the soul"[90] for the sensory environment of the human being, because the human capacity for "community spirit" (*koine aisthesis*) is physiologically based.[91] Aristotle described this phenomenon together with the absolute necessity of its presence:

> Each of our senses has an individually appropriate function, but also a more far-reaching, comprehensive ability. Seeing is appropriate for our sense of sight; hearing is appropriate for our sense of hearing; and so forth with each of the senses. There is also a more general ability befitting all of the senses, by means of which we are aware that we are seeing and hearing; we see that we are seeing, not by means of our sense of sight. Indeed we differentiate, and are able to differentiate, that there is a difference between sweet and white, not by means of our sense of sight or taste, nor by means of a combination of the two. Instead, there is an organ bridging all of the sense organs. There is, in fact, a unified sense organ that governs and dominates.[92]

It becomes clear from the various accounts of these events that Aristotle found the heart fundamentally capable of carrying out this higher function of sensory perception, because in every act of perception of the individual sense organs there are processes of movement taking place.[93] This is true in the case of pathophysiology, as well. These processes imprint themselves upon the blood and are conveyed by the blood to the centralizing heart. In the heart, these impressions are perceived, detected, bound together, and thus first truly felt and understood. For this reason, the heart organ, according to Aristotle, should be called the "starting point for all sensory impressions."[94] In particular, his detailed writings on the physiological aspects of dream figures show that he worked under the assumption of movement phenomena in the arena of the sense organs. In a certain sense, these movements remain continually available to the organs whenever they are in a waking state. "Even when the external object [being perceived] is no longer present, the product of the act of perception remains in a condition of perceptibility."[95] At the same time, the sense organs, in a certain respect and to a certain extent, are able to communicate this to the heart. This last action can take place at night in an accelerated or exaggerated sense (that is, without hindering influences) or in pathological states of mind (such as the delirium of fever). This can lead to dream phenomena that are completely organologically based and, causally speaking, constructed out of real sensory impressions. Aristotle had this to say on the subject in *On Dreams:*

> These movements are called forth by the results of the perception of external objects. From the earlier material, it has become clear that these movements take place not only in the waking state, but also under the condition we call sleep—and far more so during sleep. During the day, when the senses and power of reason are active, these movements are crowded out and extinguished, like a small fire next to a large one; and minor feelings of pain and desire next to overwhelming feelings. When these stronger sensory impressions cease, the tiny ones rise quickly to the surface and make themselves felt. At night, the individual senses are inactive and are incapable of carrying out their functions, and the heat from outside flows inward. As a result, when peaceful quiet sets in, these movements affect the center of perception [the heart] and make themselves distinctly noticeable.[96]

Aristotle continued, explaining his previous statements and giving us more concrete examples:

> You must make it clear to yourself that every movement continues in much the same way as small whirlpools in rivers. They repeat their motions once again as they did the first time, then lose their original form when they encounter an obstacle, taking on a new form. For this reason, there are no dreams for very young people (namely children); and no dreams if one falls asleep right after a meal. In such cases,

the inner movement arising from the heat (as a result of the recent meal) is simply too great. It is the same as it is with water; if you stir it up too intensely, you cannot see a picture reflected upon its surface, or only a distorted picture that shows the object in a completely changed form. Once the water is still again, pure, clear pictures appear. While we are sleeping, our imagined pictures and other ongoing movements disappear completely under the powerful influence of the movement named. Only indistinct, peculiar pictures appear. Our dreams are disjointed as they are with melancholics, those sick with fever, or those who are intoxicated. All of these conditions are associated with air, and all of them cause a great commotion and churning. However, when the blood quiets itself and the substances it contains separate out, then the movement arising from each individual sense organ brings forth logically connected dreams. Something appears before us then, and we believe that we are seeing and hearing it on the basis of what is still flowing within us from our sense of sight or sense of hearing, and it is the same with the other sense organs.... When we are asleep, most of the blood floods to the heart, and these movements flow along, partly provisional and partly actually present.[97]

*

The various explications from Aristotle on the genesis and physiological basis of sensory perception, sensory impressions, and the consequent formation of mental images do not permit a definitive judgment on the concrete meaning of the sense organs themselves or on their cooperative work with the heart organ as part of the "common sensory center." Aristotle seems to have considered this center to be the "controlling authority" for the accuracy and appropriateness of individual perceptions.[98]

Nevertheless, in all of his descriptions, he amply clarified the central importance of the heart in this regard. Aristotle pointed out unambiguously in *On Memory and Remembering* that the mental image (*phantasma*) sparked by a sensory impression owes its existence to a creative power of imagination (*phantasia*), whose active presence he also located in the central organ of perception—that is, in the heart. In the same context, he explained that this central sense organ is also responsible for the preservation of mental images and, as a result, also responsible for the work of the human memory and the subsequent work of recollecting.[99] After a long and highly differentiated series of observations, he stated this very succinctly: "The memory arises in the central organ of perception, which is also responsible for our sense of time."[100]

Aristotle connected the entire exchange between our waking and sleeping constitution with the activity of the heart. He took into account the changes in the warming processes between the heart and the brain for the transfer to the physiological level.[101] Aristotle emphasized the essential role of sleep for our vitality and regeneration; sleep exists for the purpose of "supporting and maintaining us as living beings."[102] He also described sleep as the immobilization and temporary cessation of certain heart functions. "If sleeping and waking are the two functional states of this organ, then it is clear which organ brings about the sleeping and waking states."[103] In a highly complex sense, we now note clearly the close connection Aristotle saw between the human heart and the life of the senses, the imagination, and human consciousness. Physiologically, the heart is the center of human "everyday consciousness." Sensory impressions and mental images, formed creatively, then constitute the central core of our conscious life. They are led together and stored, while a connection with the full completion of the biography is maintained.

The heart organ, said Aristotle, is "responsible for our sense of time"; it enables our achievements in memory and recollection and enables the transition between the day and night sides of human existence. This is the transition from consciousness into an unconscious, regenerative state, from conscious experience (*Erleben*) into a reduced state (*Leben*), still very much alive but exhibiting physiological phenomena that only vaguely resemble the actions of our bodies in a waking state. The heart thus stands in the center of our daily, contemporary existence, constantly renewed by additional sensory impressions, while simultaneously building a bridge to the past, the world of our previous experiences, both passive and active, and into the world of sleep, in which we merely exist.

*

The heart is connected primarily to the present. In light of this, Aristotle also saw the possibility of direct soul reactivity: "Apparently all stirring of joy, pain, and indeed all sensations arise there, go forth from there, and return there; this is entirely sensible."[104]

The heart is not just the physiological "source" of life, warmth, nourishment, and growth, but also the center of sensory perception and closely connected with conscious life. It is also the "source of sensations."[105] The special nature and constitution of the heart organ enables, shapes, and manifests the actual soul life in the present moment, while the corresponding processes of sensation and feeling are accompanied by warmth processes.[106] "The reason is as follows: warmth offers the greatest assistance for the bodily work done to activate the soul."[107] Thus, "angering oneself" or "making oneself fearful," as we read in *De Anima,* can be described on the psychological level as, in a certain sense, "the heart feeling moved."[108] In the same text, Aristotle asserted that we are dealing with changing, reactive warmth processes, focusing on the blood as it moves in and around the heart. These warmth processes correspond to the soul's affect on the material level, as well as psychologically enabling this affect to occur.[109]

*

As Aristotle reiterated in his work *On Memory and Remembering,* the human soul life extends into the past with help from the memory and recollection work done by the heart. At the same time, the human soul life lives in the present as it works with our current sensory impressions, the associated powers of thinking and imagination, and our processes of sensing, feeling, and sentiment. The blood assists with all of these functions.[110] Like the activity of our memory, they are all centered on the heart. In one of his lectures, Aristotle also made an explicit connection between the human heartbeat (or, rather, the psychologically intensified "pounding of the heart") and the general tendency to focus on the future in human soul life. He even found that our entire human existence tends to remain directed toward and focused on the future. He formulated this as follows: "This process [the pounding of the heart] is confined to human beings, because only human beings live in the hope and expectation of things to come."[111]

From this, it may be possible to conclude that the psychological responsibility of the heart for our human "sense of time" (as asserted by Aristotle) leads us not only to the remembered past or the present moment, but even into the future. Particularly in light of Aristotle's persistent interest in the question of the heart's movement, we should see the heart as the origin and source of the human capacity for movement. This movement constitutes a temporality that reaches out ahead of itself, leading us out of the past and into a future time. He dedicated two individual texts to the movement of living beings and to questions associated with that movement: *On the Movement of Living Beings* and *On the Forward Movement of Living Beings.* In those texts, he attempted to explain his own theory of movement more precisely, focusing on its physiological aspects.[112] He had already discussed a nascent

form of the theory in several other texts. Here, Aristotle differentiated carefully among localized movements: quantitative changes
(in the form of increases and decreases); qualitative changes (under
the influence of the processes of sickness and health); and substantial "life movements" (such as the genesis and exodus of living
beings). Also in his text *On Breathing,* Aristotle pursued with
great subtlety the question of the heart's movements and their
importance for the entire organism.

If we gather and examine these complex explications, it
becomes clear that Aristotle considered the activity of the heart
to be the first, original movement of the organism, making all
other movement possible. He saw the heart's movement as the
beginning and end, as the source and goal, not only for all psychological-soul sensations, but also for all underlying, basic forms
of movement necessarily connected with psychological-soul phenomena. "Every stirring of joy, pain, and other sensation originates and ends there. This is entirely sensible." Aristotle summa-
rized briefly in *On the Limbs/Parts of Beings,* "According to our
theory, life itself, every movement and every perception, depends
on the heart."[113] Aristotle asserted that the soul has the ability to
influence and even direct the "hinges" of the heart organ. Its influence is particularly strong at the decisive point in the "swinging
of the door" when minor modifications in the heart's movements
have enormous consequences for movements of the entire being:

> When changes take place in the body, some are more mean-
> ingful and some are minor. Nothing, though, can conceal the
> fact that a small change, made at the starting point, causes
> multiple, significant modifications later, even far away. If the
> steering wheel changes its orientation just a bit, for example,
> the movement of the boat's bow undergoes significant change.
> When a change takes place in and around the heart because
> of warmth or cold (or any similar affect), it has a considerable

consequence on the human body. This is true even when the change takes place in a spot so tiny that it seems to vanish into the vastness of the heart as a whole. We can observe the change as a blushing or blanching, or as shuddering, shivering, or their opposites.[114]

Aristotle also developed his complicated theory of the "congenital pneuma" in this context, which he also considered to be of an etheric-warmth nature.[115] With help from this pneuma, the soul attempts to turn its movement intentions for the central heart organ into real actions. "This principle is found in the heart, and nature designed it to set the soul's intentions in motion and endow them with strength."[116]

At the same time, in connection with the above, the heart organ finds itself in constant motion from the very first stages of embryonic development. In *On Breathing*, Aristotle attempted to shed more light on the way this complex, individual movement is performed: "Three phenomena are found at the heart: the pounding of the heart, the movement of the pulse, and the breathing."[117] They appear to have the same character, but actually do not. Aristotle called the physiological contraction and dilation movements of the heart the "pulse movement" (*sphagmos*), bringing them into a causal relationship with the movement of the blood. He contrasted these with the illness- or fear-related "pounding of the heart" (*I edois*), an intensified beating caused by a change in the warmth organization of the heart. According to Aristotle, these continual blood-building processes, with their increasing levels of warmth and the resultant changes they cause, are responsible for the onset of the beating of the embryonic heart. They also account for the lifelong continuation of these specific forms of movement, carried forth by the blood as it follows its pattern of circulation. In *On Breathing*, Aristotle stated:

Moisture is obtained continually from the sources of nourishment and led into the blood. The increased volume of moisture brought about by the warmth of the blood in the heart causes the heart to beat by pressing upward against the external cloak around the heart. This continues without interruption. The substance called blood arises from the moisture that flows uninterruptedly to the heart. First and foremost, the moisture is transformed there. This is also clear from the first steps of development. It is obvious that the heart contains blood even before the veins are completely developed. Because of this, the pulse beats faster in younger people than it does in older people. In younger people, the vaporization is stronger. The blood vessels pulse together, with the same timing, because they lead out of the heart. This process causes the movement to continue without interruption, so that the blood vessels move together with the same timing each time the heart initiates this movement.[118]

We can ascribe the constant moderating of the warmth processes in the heart region to the "cooling" influence of breathing (whose movements are primarily driven by impulses from the heart).[119] This contributes decisively to each respective contraction of the heart organ. The cooling effect of breathing constitutes a functional counterbalance to the blood-bound powers of warmth in the lower body, with their tendency to work expansively and effectively. This makes it possible to achieve a balance between the warming and cooling processes.

In addition, Aristotle described the movement of the heart in *On the Movement of Beings* (*Peri zôôn kinêseôs*) in a general sense as "involuntary" and differentiated it from the "voluntary," or intentional, movement decisions carried out on the basis of rational decisions or those based on desire. He also differentiated heart movement from movements classified as "non-voluntary," which he grouped with processes such as breathing and sleep, which are conditioned purely physiologically and are characterized by a high degree of inner autonomy. The movement of the heart, on the other hand, as explicated by Aristotle, is influenced by internal and external impressions, as well as by as thoughts, emotions, and strivings, and lying mostly beneath the level of consciousness and intentional decision.[120] In this way the movement of the heart (and thus the entire heart organ) is permanently exposed and endangered, in a certain sense. In and of itself, Aristotle tells us, the heart exhibits no signs of sickness. Through its interaction with other organs and negative internal and external influences, however, there can be serious pathological consequences. In his manuscript *On the Limbs/Parts of Beings,* Aristotle spoke briefly of this danger: "Alone among the organs and all parts of the body, the heart cannot tolerate poor treatment. We can easily understand this. If the source [the heart] is corrupted, there is no other way to bring help to the dependent organs."[121]

*

The heart organ stands in the the absolute center of the physiological theory of Aristotle of Stagira, a student of Plato and the most effective natural scientist and humanities scholar of pre-Christian antiquity. The heart is in the "center" of the body, as Aristotle frequently reiterated. "Wherever it is possible, the point of origin should be unified, and the most appropriate sphere is the center."[122] The heart is in every sense the primary and leading organ in the service of existential reality. For human beings, this reality includes advanced soul-spiritual development. Only in human beings does the heart develop itself further (in its interaction with the circulation of the blood) into the actual "time-sensing organ." Only in humans, Aristotle wrote, does the heart become a tool serving higher mental and spiritual activity. For the movement, sensory perception, and feeling nature of all animals the heart is simultaneously both "origin and end" of both their active and sympathetic-empathetic connections with the world.

Aristotle could not yet present us with a concept of the human being that included a place for an individual sense of self or an individual biographical path. His concept of the spirit, much discussed in later centuries, contained neither the notion of the spiritual individuality of the human being nor a concrete dimension of fate in human development. Aristotle tended to be a bit vague regarding human physiology, as well.[123] The exceptional form, content, and phrasing of his works nevertheless set the stage for a new scientific study of anthropology that would know how to differentiate between the soul-spiritual powers and organological tools of the human being and would wrestle with the first objective, practical expression of these concepts. In addition, his ethical and anthropological presentations of the fourth century BCE were able to demonstrate the extent to which the moral autonomy of the individual personality actually exists or, at least, whether the possibility of such autonomy lies within the realm of human powers and within our capacity for development. Aristotle intended to demonstrate the extent to which we can realize and individualize the spiritual ideals described by Plato, taking individual responsibility and setting our own pace on this path of spiritual development.

Aristotle's concept of what it means to be human and his descriptions of how the earthly bodies of humans are organized were broadly conceived and spiritually based. He quite deliberately distanced himself from Plato's characteristically creative-imaginative style of expression, adopting instead a technical, conceptual style of description. Nevertheless, everything he wrote still corresponded to the view of cosmic events appropriate to his era, which accounts for many of his observations. We must always regard Aristotle's physiological studies through the filter of this imposing backdrop.[124] Though some of his concrete, individual remarks on the heart were markedly restrained in some of his cosmological lectures, he still regarded the sun as the unmistakable macrocosmic equivalent of the human heart organ, speaking of the sun as the "creator of all life."[125]

*

Aristotle was a pioneer and prophet whose work prepared the world for a new epoch to come. In contrast to Plato, he found few like-minded students and successors. As a result, with severe and devastating rapidity, his work nearly sank into oblivion following his death. After leading so many scientific debates so energetically, this deeply religious man died in almost complete isolation at the age of sixty-three in his mother's house in October 322 BCE in Chalkis, on the island of Euboia.[126] The first complete edition of his remaining works appeared more than 350 years later in Rome, at almost exactly the same time as momentous events were taking place in Palestine that would change and shape the world to come.[127]

Aristotle: On the Athenian State. *Manuscript*

THOMAS AQUINAS

"God's love is poured into our hearts [in cordibus nostris diffunditur] *by the Holy Spirit, who is given to us as a gift."* (St. Paul, as quoted by Thomas Aquinas)[128]

Thomas Aquinas[129] was fourteen when he took up the study of Aristotle's lectures at the University of Naples, 1,561 years after the death of the Greek philosopher. A completely different era had begun. For many centuries, an almost exclusively Arabic view of Aristotle's work had dominated.[130] Now, in the very heart of Europe, a new exploration of this enormous intellectual and spiritual inheritance was beginning. This study began in the monasteries and was increasingly taken up in the newly founded universities, as well. Texts from antiquity were considered in light of Christianity and the Christ event itself. Ancient source texts were rediscovered and reexamined in the context of newer, Christian texts: the reports in the Gospels, the letters of the Apostles, and the interpretations and descriptions written by the Church fathers. In particular, there were attempts to unify the ideas of the ancient texts with the widely read texts of St. Augustine. An unparalleled learning process took place in the effort to unite pre-Christian thought with "Christian philosophy."[131] The "reader" and teacher Thomas Aquinas was destined to become the leading figure, rising above all others in this unique, almost volcanic event in the history of consciousness and the humanities. Thomas's capabilities and knowledge allowed him to absorb and comprehend the larger implications of these developments, even to anticipate what would come of them, setting him far above his contemporaries. It was this superior grasp of developments that had characterized

Aristotle so precisely, as well. Despite everything that took place in the intervening millennium and a half, this vision bound the two of them together, as we saw when examining Aristotle's own highly unusual curriculum vitae. Between the two of them, to be sure, stood the events of the new millennium, particularly the incarnation of Christ. Everything that Thomas experienced, thought, taught, and worked to accomplish was based on and centered on that seminal event.[132]

The lifespan of Thomas Aquinas was shorter and more troubled than that of Aristotle.[133] Thomas lived to be just forty-nine years of age. Following his early entrance into the Dominican order, his years were spent in a great spiritual community, although never in peace or in seclusion from current events. Even his attempt to gain permission to join the order constituted an affront to his extended family; members of the order chose quite deliberately to live in radical, evangelical poverty. Everything else also served as an indicator of the battles being fought—the spiritual conflict and his unconditional, passionate commitment to spreading the message of the true faith, the *propositum nostrae intentionis,* the issue of greatest importance to him. His biography was characterized by numerous changes of residence and spiritual duties, which placed him at the front lines of the academic conflicts at the University of Paris, the most important academic institution of the time. These conflicts also led him to Naples, Rome, and elsewhere to establish institutes of higher learning for his order. He wrote the important work *Summa contra gentiles* while traveling between cities, for the most part using tiny scraps of paper when he ran out of proper sheets. He would later die on one of those journeys.

The Dominicans sought scientific work, debate, and discussion from the start. Immediately after receiving official recognition for the order, St. Dominic sent members of the order to the university cities. There, they placed themselves quite deliberately amid the controversies of the time, which centered on Christian philosophy and thus around the most essential anthropological and epistemological questions. In September 1217, just a year after their order was founded, the Dominicans reached Paris. Eleven months later, in August 1218, they had succeeded in opening their own monastery there. In the time that followed, Thomas would use this as his base of operations for his academic duties. Not until 1256 did he finally receive a *licentia docendi* (license to teach) for the University of Paris, after prolonged and vehement opposition from within the university. A year later, he was officially accepted as a member of the faculty.

Thomas Aquinas became the master teacher of his order, even of the entire epoch. His lectures, instructional talks, and answers to questions carried a sense of self-evident truth, their content serving as a sign of his *propositum nostrae intentionis,* with a style characteristic of the specific inner tasks he had set for himself. For Thomas Aquinas, teaching constituted a singular unifying and connecting point between the spiritual and meditative sphere and the exterior sphere of active social work. It created a bridge between the two sides of life, combining aspects of the *vita contemplativa* with the vita active. "*Docere est opus activae vitae* [To teach is the work of an active life]."[134] Thomas was a highly schooled thinker, with great powers of meditation and concentration. He carried the results of his research into the social realm through his teaching.[135] He possessed quite extraordinary pedagogical skills and was able to adjust his teaching to suit his audience, even to think as they were thinking if it served a need. Following the same pedagogical rules, his written formulations also changed according to the needs of the readers. Even the largest and most extensive of his writings, *Summa theologica,* was determinedly written "for the instruction of beginners" (*ad eruditionem incipientium*). In this sense, his recorded works, like those of Aristotle, consist almost exclusively of "instructional works" and revised "lecture texts." Nevertheless, Thomas was always aware that the truly uplifting and life-changing "instruction" from his works and words would take its effect indirectly:

> When teaching, one exercises an exterior effectiveness like that of the physician when healing [*sicut medicus sanans*]; but just as the inward biological self is the principle reason for the healing work [*natura interior est principalis causa sanationis*], so, too, is the inward light of cognition [*interius lumen intellectus*] the principle reason for knowledge and wisdom. Both come from God.[136]

*

Thomas began to refer to the work of the "heathen" Aristotle in his earliest writings and lectures. His first publication, *De ente et essentia,* which appeared in 1254, when Thomas was twenty-nine years old, opened with a citation from the person Thomas called "the philosopher" (with great simplicity and consistency). He continued to use this expression until his death. Thomas Aquinas placed himself in a lifelong dialogue and debate with the instructional writings of his ancient predecessor, despite all of the resultant hostility he faced from the traditional church and clerical factions.[137] Thomas also openly and vehemently opposed contemporary interpretations of Aristotle proposed by the circle of philosophers at the Paris University led by Siger von Brabant.[138] "For truth and falsehood never reveal themselves more clearly and obviously than when they stand in opposition to contradiction, as in the saying 'iron is sharpened by rubbing it against iron'" (Prov. 27:17).[139] Thomas opposed these Brabantian interpretations, because he saw them as a belated distortion of the most important spiritual-intellectual messages of Aristotle and the goals set by

the philosopher as contradictions of the *intentio Aristoteles*.[140]
Thomas's own teacher, the great Albertus Magnus, was the first
Dominican to take up the study of Aristotle's complete oeuvre with
resolve and determination. Albertus Magnus developed a plan
(which he was unable to complete) to translate single-handedly all
of the writings of the Greek philosopher into Latin. He wanted to
make these works accessible to those in his own cultural sphere;
"Nostra intentio est, omnes dictas partes facere Latinis intelligibiles
[Our intention is to make Latin intelligible to everyone]."[141]
Albertus did, however, succeed in writing commentaries for all
of Aristotle's works. Thomas's own examination of Aristotle's
writings was significantly more intensive, more authentic, and
more intimate than that of his monumental, argumentative
teacher. Thomas understood Aristotle more deeply, listened with
greater stillness, and penetrated the works more thoroughly.
Thomas read Aristotle, quill in hand, against the backdrop of
the events (and subsequent changes) of the new millennium. He
read with an eye for the actual intentionality of the work, with
an awareness of both the historical setting and the stage in the
history of consciousness that had been reached by that time. Both
are implicit in every word of the texts, and both help explain why
Aristotle appeared at that precise moment in history. Thomas read
with immense, selfless (and thus truly objective) calm, peace, and
devotion. At the same time, he read Aristotle with the intention of
expanding upon his work:

> To understand Aristotle, we must take the trouble to under-
> stand the dynamics that form the basis of his thinking as
> a whole. We must determine the truths that emerged in the
> course of his investigations, despite his somewhat clumsy abil-
> ity to articulate them. Precisely for these reasons, Thomas felt
> himself justified in placing himself in this position in order to
> expand his own thinking and to be exposed to things that he

would not have thought of on his own. A historically correct reconstruction of Aristotelian thinking for its own sake did not interest him in the slightest.... He preferred to determine Aristotle's plan and to complete the work that Aristotle considered to be of greatest importance. The completion of this work would not have been possible without the light of revelation. (Jean-Pierre Torrell)[142]

Thomas Aquinas thought something had been brought to light in the fourth century before Christ through the work of Aristotle (*sicut patet per Philosophum:* "as it has been made clear by Aristotle," not "as Aristotle said"). This meant, first and foremost, the order of the natural universe, the orderliness of created reality, and the natural fit of all things. This also comprised a true understanding of the role of humanity in the cosmos and thus also an understanding of anthropology. Aristotle's intellect and spirit were demonstrated by the spiritual order (*ordo*) of the graduated steps occupied by all forms of life, from the minerals up to the plants, then the animals, and then to human beings (and from here up to the upper hierarchies and godly beings).[143]

This natural order was clearly delineated, accessible, and comprehensible to all. In contrast to the many clerical and theological tendencies of his time, Thomas argued emphatically for Aristotle's approach. For the first time, Aristotle had conceptually defined the cognitive tasks and practical, scientific experience of the world's physical reality, placing a high value on each.[144] This was very different from the popular approach to the Gospels, Plato, and Augustine at that time, which renounced the body and the physical world. Instead, Thomas saw in the physical world the effectiveness of spiritual, intellectual, and creative powers, in all that they had brought forth. In addressing a grave misunderstanding on the part of these theological circles, Thomas once wrote:

There are those who state that it is important only to have the correct view of God himself. With regard to the truth of religious beliefs, they consider it to be a matter of complete indifference how one views God's creation [*de creaturis*]. This opinion is clearly false. A mistaken understanding of the creation results in a false understanding of God [*nam error circa creaturas redundat in falsam de Deo scientiam*].[145]

Following the patterns of Aristotle's thoughts, and taking them further, Thomas said that all created beings are formed by godly and spiritual powers, and thus bear an eternal connection to those powers. "If we look at things thus, we see that God touches everything directly, because of his unlimited power. He causes all things to come into being and remain in existence. It follows that God is in all things, in the most direct sense, through his being, presence, and might [*per essentiam, praesentiam et potentiam*]."[146] Against this background, Thomas Aquinas even understood the theological concepts of sin and grace not as counter to nature, but having, instead, the most intimate connection to the lawful and orderly world of the natural. "Grace" was not a contradiction of nature in his eyes, but rather its intensification and highest state. "Grace does not destroy nature. Instead, grace presupposes nature, and makes it complete."[147] In much the same way, however, Thomas did not, in traditional theological fashion, define the occurrence of sin as a lapse into the "lower sensory nature." Instead, he considered it to be quite the opposite: "Sin is counter to our natural inclination [*peccatum est contra naturalem inclinationem*]."[148]

*

With regard to Thomas Aquinas's great love for the creation and constant reference to Aristotle, we should never forget to take into account this important fact: Thomas's orientation toward the world of the natural (the earthly world) was primarily Christologically based. In Thomas's eyes, Christ, the Logos, was not connected primarily with the creation of the world.[149] Rather, Christ had connected himself with the earthly and human substantiality (materiality) in the process of his incarnation and the sacrifice of his earthly being (*mysterium incarnationis et passionis Christi*). In the process, he transformed all that is earthly, uniting it once again with its original, cosmic, and godly source:

> In a certain sense, the entirety and unity of God's work are made complete when we humans, the last creatures to be created, return to our origins. We do this as if it were part of a cyclic process. We become one again with the original, fundamental source of all things as we work to become truly human [*ipsi rerum principio per opus incarnationis unitus*].[150]

This fundamental understanding of world-historical development, emphatically transformed since (and because of) the millennial events surrounding the earthly life of Christ, led Thomas Aquinas far beyond the conclusions of Aristotle. This is reflected in the basic structure of the *Summa theologica:* "In the first segment we deal with God directly. In the second, we speak of the movement of the spiritual beings toward God. In the third, we speak of Christ, who in his humanity becomes the path we can take to reach God."[151] These events enabled a Christological reconnection of the creation with the origin of its being. For Thomas, this reconnection necessitated a definitive emphasis on the basic anthropological and anthropocentric insights first revealed by Aristotle. In the incarnation situation of the highly effective Logos of Christ, Thomas Aquinas saw the intensified connection of a higher spirit–soul with a living earthly body actually taking place. "Because of that, the oneness Christ achieved by becoming man is deeper and more profound than the unity of soul and body that we ourselves can achieve."[152] This connection had stood in the center of Aristotle's "physio-logical" intentions, and was now continually taken up by Thomas, ever-more intensively.

*

"*Manifestum est, quod homo non est anima tantum, sed aliquid compositum ex anima ex corpore* [Apparently the human is not merely a soul, but the unity of soul and body]."[153] Building on the work of Aristotle, Thomas held and justified the idea that the soul is the principle of existence[154] for the body; its primary reason for living (*primum principium vitae*);[155] its shaping form and reality;[156] its occupation;[157] and its completion.[158] At the same time, more distinctly, clearly, and decisively than Aristotle, he emphasized that the human being should be seen as a real unity of body and soul. The body (contrary to conventional theological thinking) undoubt-edly belongs to the essential nature of the human being.

Plato, among others, asserted that the soul simply serves the body, existing separately from human physicality, wholly or com-pletely, and serving as the actual essence of the human being.[159] According to Thomas, this is simply not the case. Instead, the soul has a real, concrete, and direct relationship to the body, which takes on material substance. "The nobler the form, the more eas-ily it masters the substance of the body."[160] Together they form an incarnating connection, which is the first definitive characteristic of the human being: "To the extent that the soul is the existential form [of being] of the body, it does not have an existence that is separate from the existence of the body. Instead, the soul is directly connected to the body by virtue of this existence-being [*sed per suum esse corpori unitur immediate*]."[161]

An inclination "to be unified with the body" is part of the innermost nature of the soul.[162] This implies that the soul is striving for a particularly human form of existence:

> The most important task of the soul is to unite itself with the body, just as it is the task of the light object to float [while the heavy object sinks]. A light object stays light when moved away from its usual place, but keeps its inclination toward, and sense of belonging to, its own place. So too does the human soul keep its sense of being, when it is separated from the body, and it keeps its inclination toward, and sense of belonging to, a state of union with the body [*aptitudinem et inclinationem naturalem ad corporis unionem*].[163]

Because the soul itself is only one part of the human being, it possesses the "totality of its nature" only when united with the body.[164] The opposite is also true. The earthly substance shows a tendency to be part of a comprehensive human spirit–soul. In that union, we become truly human. "The soul is given to the human, rather than to any other life form, because the human being is the whole of existence, in a certain sense."[165] In *Summa contra gentiles,* Thomas formulated it in this way: "At the highest level of the entire creation is the human soul, and matter strives to reach this stage, as if stepping into its predetermined external form.... The human being is, namely, the goal of the entire creation [*Ultimus igitur generationis totius gradus est anima humana, et in hanc tendit materia sicut in ultimam formam.... Homo enim est finis totius generationis*]."[166]

*

In connection with these foundational explications on anthropology, and thus on human body-soul reality, Thomas emphasized (at several points) that he considered the actual incarnation to be an unmistakable sign of discernible soul activities and their physiological organizational structures. In other words, he considered the spirit not to be simply meta-physical (*substantia separata*), but rather to be a portion of the soul, and to that extent to be a part of the previously explored relationship to physicality (even if in a specifically differentiated sense).[167] Not the capacity for thought itself but rather the capacity for imagining earthly objects shows Thomas that there is a physiological basis for his theory. "The body is necessary for the activities of reasoning and understanding, not as the organ that carries out those tasks, but rather with respect to the object."[168] Thomas made the sensory activity of the body and the connected, resultant imaginative activity [the activity of picturing something] identifiable as the explicit starting point for our higher cognitive capacity. He characterized the sphere of the senses as the essential "source of our ability to know and understand [*primum principium nostrae cognitionis*]."[169] In this context, Thomas made a decisive choice not to speak of different "levels," "layers," or "parts," of the soul as existing next to one another, varying in proximity to the body. Instead, he consistently and rigorously supported the idea that the spirit–soul (or the soul that has been granted a spirit, *anima rationalis*) is the single substantial form of the soul appropriate for the human body. He considered it to be effective in each part of the body.[170] It portrays the higher principle of the body, which determines everything else that is specific to human beings.[171] The spirit–soul forms the body and shapes it for functionality, including the activities and functions of nourishing and growing, perceiving and moving.[172] To support this view, Thomas wrote these indicative words on the organization of the human senses in the *Summa theologica:*

> What brings a being to completion also constitutes its greatness and dignity. In the case of animals, the sense life is the

highest and final step that this portion of the creation, the animals, can achieve. In the case of human beings, the life of the senses is not the highest level to which we aspire. It becomes nobler, nevertheless, when united with the higher, ennobling life of the spirit.[173]

If this spirit–soul, as the highest form of being, constitutes the dominant reality of the human body, and its single determining and completing principle, then (according to Thomas) we must take certain things into consideration.[174] The cognitive activities are related only indirectly to the substance and functionality of the body, as Aristotle had already attempted to describe.[175] Although the sensory processes are actually dependent on the physical organization and inner state (condition) of the senses in a very direct way, in which the outer world is "objectively" present, to a certain extent, the same is not at all the case for the actual intellectual activities.[176] In the *Summa theologica,* Thomas wrote:

> In one sense, [the relationship of] sensory perception to the visible manifestation is similar to [the relationship of] the understanding to the understandable. This is true to the extent that the first term in each of these exists as a possibility and the second as a concrete object. In another sense, though, they do not behave in the same manner. This happens when the visible manifestation (affected by a change of the body) harms the sensory perception. The inappropriate intensity of the manifestation destroys the sense of perception. This does not occur with the intellect. The mind, which recognizes the highest [things] in the realm of the comprehensible, is afterward even more capable of recognizing the lowest things. If the body tires while it is thinking, however, all necessary imaginative images are prepared for it by the imagination on the sidelines (to the extent that the work of the mind requires the activity of the sensory-imaginative powers).[177]

Thomas stated that the activities of the mind develop themselves by means of sensory impressions and imaginative pictures. We obtain these with the help of the body. Concepts are acquired from these through processes of abstraction. These concepts form the instrument used for the higher cognitive activities actively performed by the spirit–soul. Thomas repeatedly turned his attention to this stage of cognitive activity, because he believed that the active development of self-knowledge takes place in this realm: "Our spirit uses the senses to abstract concepts from sensory impressions. The spirit recognizes itself and knows itself to the extent that it becomes real and active by using these concepts.... Our spirit comes to know itself not by its nature, but rather by the force of active work."[178]

In the same textual context of the *Summa theologica,* Thomas also remarked briefly, "Socrates or Plato was able to perceive that he has a spirit–soul by observing that he is thinking [is capable of thinking]."[179] In the process of this thinking experience, each of us becomes aware that spiritual material is present in us, in an individualized form. It is we ourselves who are thinking responsibly and actively. Thomas understood and described this process as a "return" of the human spirit to its own essential state.[180] This process takes place when we turn ourselves toward the earthly, sensory environment. We lean toward the other, the stranger, the one standing opposite, with a primarily sense-related orientation. We are meant to recognize this "other," and in the end, we do come to recognize him. The "return" of the human spirit to its own essence, experienced by the self as a result of its activity, takes place in the world. Here the human being takes part and has a share as a sensory being, although without the capacity for self-reflection in this aspect of our lives.[181] We human beings come to ourselves by means of the impressions, experiences, and insights gained in this manner.

No one retains the fact that he has perceived something, except by means of perceiving that fact; because perceiving something happens before the realization of perceiving. Moreover, this is how the soul first explicitly perceives its own existence—through the things it observes and perceives. Our spirit is unable to become self-aware in this way, by becoming aware of itself directly; rather, it becomes able to perceive its own existence by recognizing other things.[182]

The process of conceptualization brings about a subsequent, resultant aptitude for higher perception. This process is present not only in the deeply spiritual process that helps determine the future of the spirit–soul, but also, Thomas tells us, forms the basis of the capacity for freedom that we experience as earthly, incarnated spiritual beings. Thomas argued that the concepts we acquire through this process have importance for the existence of the human soul after death.[183] Godly spiritual powers play a significant role in these higher processes, as well.[184] The actual development of the human intellect takes place at this time.[185]

Thomas repeatedly pointed out that the "root of all freedom" lies in the ability of the human being to perceive (*"unde totius libertatis radix est in ratione constituta"*).[186] Freedom is experienced in the active use of this perceptive ability. Perception constitutes the preliminary requirement for the ability of the individual to act responsibly and to take responsibility for one's actions. "Wherever there is intellectual perception, there is also free will."[187]

Thomas sharply differentiated himself from the interpretative work on Aristotle done by the Latin Averroist movement, which argued for a negation of every notion of the individual possessing an intellect.[188] Latin Averroism also denied the capacity for freedom and responsibility of the individual human being. "If, according to this, the intellect were not something that belonged to each individual person, something that is truly part of us...then the will would not be part of the individual human but part of a spirit that existed quite separate from the body. As a result, such persons would not be the master of their own actions, and none of their actions could be praised or criticized. To accept this would be to destroy the basis of all moral philosophy."[189] Thomas staunchly represented the viewpoint that the "'I'-centered," perceiving human beings are, in fact, free to take action and are responsible for themselves (independently responsible). Consequently, we shape and take responsibility for our own development as truly incarnated spirit beings, grappling with earthly conditions and circumstances. Here on Earth, in the midst of the sensory world, Thomas tells us, the perceptive, active person completes the developmental steps that are indispensable for one's own individual future. He stated this simply and succinctly (but built it on a deep Christological foundation) in *Summa contra gentiles:* "The soul needs the body to achieve its goals to the extent that it attains its completeness, in both knowledge and strength, by means of the body [*Anima enim indiget corpore ad consecutionem sui finis inquantum per corpus perfectionem acquirit, et in scientia et in virtute*]."[190] Thomas believed that the human heart plays a significant, even central, role in carrying out these developmental activities.

*

"Now it is a matter for religious scholars to contemplate the nature of the human being from the perspective of the human soul (*ex parte animae*); but to study the nature of the body only in terms of its relationship to the soul [*secundem habitudinem quam habet corpus ad animam*]."[191] In contrast to Aristotle, Thomas Aquinas did no independent research in the natural sciences. He spent little time considering more recent work in the natural sciences. At the same time, he spent a great deal of time in deep and concentrated thought about the human heart. Thomas knew all of Aristotle's key biological expositions and the countless statements about the heart in the New Testament. He could draw upon an abundance of cultural, sacramental, and contemplative inner experiences. These permitted him, as no one else, to place his investigations of the heart in a larger Christological context for the first time. In addition, Thomas was an exceptional authority on the subtle phenomenology of human soul life. He moved about in this realm with an unprejudiced objectivity. This was of great help in his efforts to penetrate the full context and connections of "the nature of the human being."

Thomas was building upon, enhancing, and augmenting the *intentio Aristoteles,* taking those ideas much further. For these reasons, Thomas expressed himself on the human heart in his written works, again and again. In the last years of his life, probably at the request of a professor of medicine of his acquaintance, Thomas composed *De motu cordis.* This sensitive, important treatise discusses the forces we possess as a result of the movements of our hearts. Well known and widely read in Thomas's lifetime, the volume was gradually forgotten after his death.[192]

Together with Aristotle, Thomas understood the heart to be the central principle of the life of the body, and of the human being as a whole (*"principium vitae in homine"*).[193] The heart is the first organ system to appear and begin functioning in both humans and animals (*"in generatio animalis primo generatur cor"*).[194] The heart in motion maintains the life[195] and the life forces of the organism (*"cor est principium virium vitalium in toto corpore"*).[196] In the manner identified by Aristotle, the heart also enables and facilitates the comprehensive capacity for motion in the body (*"est principium omnium corporalium motum"*).[197] This ability arises from the first movement of the heart (*"Primus autem motus animalis est motus cordis"*).[198] To a certain extent, we can view this movement as being equivalent to life itself.[199] Thomas reached these conclusions as he did his own work, by building upon the work of Aristotle. In his exegesis on the prologue to the Gospel of John, Thomas wrote about the particular quality of life and movement in the human being:

> What moves itself in some manner is often called "alive." Moreover, things that can move themselves fully and completely are thus fully, completely alive. Among all the creatures of the lower order of created beings, only the human being can move in this full and actual manner. Even if other beings are able to be moved by an inner impulse [*ex seipsis ab aliquo principio intrinseco moveantur*], that impulse is based not upon contrasting possibilities, thus they move out of necessity and not out of freedom. The human being, on the other hand, moves freely in a chosen direction [*homo vero, cum sit dominus sui actus, libere se movet ad omnia quae vult*].[200]

The movement of the heart is the original source of all movement for the entire organism. When the heart stops moving, the living existence of the body ceases. In *De motu cordis*, Thomas wrote, "Nothing is more characteristic of the sensory beings than the movement of the heart. When that ceases, life also ceases. [*Nihil autem proprium magis est animalibus quam motus cordis; quo cessante, perit eorumvita*]."[201]

What is the source of the movement of the heart, though? Thomas Aquinas, it seems, was not fully convinced by Aristotle's reasoning in *De respiratione*. To be sure, Thomas was also of the opinion that the exceptional "pounding" of the heart, and the accompanying change in the intensity and rhythm of the heartbeat, takes place in a soul-situational context. The heart, he felt, is generally characterized by involuntary forms of movement. Aristotle had ascribed the contraction and dilation of the heart and the resultant movement of the pulse to warmth processes. These could also be described as the ascending of life fluids, resulting in the blood's formation and the "cooling" influences of the lungs working in opposition. Thomas clearly rejected these as being (respectively) the last and first reasons for the movements of the heart. He explained this in *De motu cordis* as follows:

> The reason for the heart movements must be what happens within us before all else. In a sensory being, however, the movement of the heart seems to take place first, coinciding with the onset of life to a greater extent than every possible change based on warmth. It follows that no change brought about by warmth can be the reason for the movement of the heart. It would be more accurate to say that the movement of the heart instigates the changes brought about by warmth.[202]

In the *Summa theologica,* Thomas had already asserted that the actual movements of the heart were neither determined by outside stimuli nor subject to the will; and he discussed the fact that the movement of the heart was "in accordance with nature [*motus cordis secundum naturam est*]." Additionally, "As if by chance or accident, the movement of the heart follows the onset of life, which comes about as a union of the soul and the body."[203]

In *De motu cordis,* as well, Thomas argued that the specific type of movement made by the heart is intrinsic to this organ and that it correlates to the force shaping the human soul, which becomes effective in the heart and even has its center there. This shaping force, Thomas tells us, originally induces the movement of the heart. This shaping force also establishes a constellation of forces whose natural expression is the movement of the heart: "Accordingly, the movement of the heart is natural, as it arises out of the soul, because the soul corresponds to the form of the body and above all, is of the heart [*inquantum est forma talis corporis, et principaliter cordis*]." [204]

Accordingly, the heart does not react primarily heteronomously to environmental conditions, whether of an elemental, cosmic sort or of an inner, physiological sort. Instead, the heart performs mainly an idiosyncratic type of movement that is related intimately to the formational relationship between the body and the soul (also known as the "union of the soul and body"). Thomas emphasized repeatedly in his treatise that the soul does not initiate and carry out the regular movement of the heart by itself, as it would in the case of an intentional action. Instead, this is done by the spiritual and physiological structure of the organism, composed jointly of the body and soul. This structure can become functional and effective without further soul activity, in the narrower sense. [205]

It was not by chance that Thomas viewed the eventual entirety of the heart's "pulling and pushing" (*pulsu et tractu*) movement as approximating a circle. For the circle is the consummate cosmic and spiritual archetype of all movement, constantly cycling back upon itself. "The movement of the heart in a sensory being corresponds to the movement of the heavens in the world [*Sic enim est motus cordis in animali, sicut motus caeli in mundo*]." [206]

This correspondence exists because the soul, uniting itself with the body and thereby shaping the heart, "bears a similarity to the cause of the movement of the heavens." [207] In other words, the soul stands in connection with the godly and spiritual forces that are the root cause of the (hierarchically led) planetary principle of operation. The movement of the heavens is the "cause of all movement in the world," as Thomas said in *De motu cordis* (and in *Summa theologica* [208]: "*motus caeli...est principium omnium motuum mundi*"). [209] The movement of the heart, which precedes all movements in sensory beings, stands in a subordinated position with relation to the cosmic pattern of movement. However, the heart movements, working imitatively, cannot reach the perfection of their uninterruptedly active model. "The movement of the heart, however, must lag behind the movement of the heavens, as the effect always follows the cause."[210] Between the two movement gestures of the heart ("pushing" and "pulling"), there must come a short pause for rest (*morula media*). Nevertheless, even here in the area around the heart, a movement takes place that comes very close to being circular and approaches perfection. As Thomas pointed out, Aristotle had already made accurate suggestions in this direction. All of the movements of the soul return, in the end, to the source of the body's movements, Thomas taught, building on work done by Aristotle. The movements of the soul contribute to the unsettling of the stable rhythm of the heart's activities, intensifying their estrangement from the archetypal cosmic model: "Because of this, the movement of the heavens remains uniform. The movement of the heart, however, changes in accordance with the different moods and perceptions of the soul. The moods of the soul are not caused by changes of heart. Instead, they bring about the changes of heart."[211]

In regard to this last hierarchy of effect (the primacy of the soul's perceptions in relation to the physiological organ of expression), Thomas added the following explanatory remarks in *De motu cordis*:

> Thus, there is a formal aspect that, arising from the mood, lies in the state of the soul. Anger, for example, consists of the desire for revenge. The material aspect arising from mood, on the other hand, is related to the movement of the heart—for example, as an inflammation of the blood in the area surrounding the heart. Nevertheless, as in all matters of nature, form does not exist because of matter. The opposite is true, which is clear from Aristotle's second book, *Physics*. Matter

does carry within it a predisposition for form. It follows that someone does not long for revenge because the blood around the heart is inflamed, but rather because one is predisposed to anger.[212]

In *De motu cordis,* Thomas gave no further explanation of his remark that the soul is above all else the form of the heart (*"et principaliter cordis"*).[213] Despite this, his remarks on the spiritual and cosmic "dignity" of the movement of the heart indicate that the heart is the anthropological center of the process of human incarnation. All indications point in this direction. Thomas glimpsed the innermost origin of the process of becoming fully human when he contemplated the human heart.[214] He described this often with great subtlety in all of his texts. Thomas gave a precise interpretation of this bodily heart mystery in *De motu cordis,* but did so with notable caution, perhaps with an eye to his audience and the academic and journalistic character of his treatise.

Like Aristotle, Thomas saw the heart in the processes of sensory perception. The heart, wrote Thomas, is the "principle of the senses"[215] and activates the senses through warming influences.[216] He also considered the heart to be involved in the enabling of actions guided by our power of imagination. This he saw as an emotional resonance brought about by warmth as the soul is moved, or touched, by the imaginative content that determines our actions.[217] According to Thomas, the heart is constantly affected as it carries out its life-giving motions at the center of human existence and responds accordingly. First and foremost, it responds from the very center of the soul, for the heart is the organ of our perceptions and various states in the life of the soul.[218] These "soul states" (*passiones*) are usually translated as "passions"[219] and intervene in the physiological functionality of the heart. Sometimes they use the heart as their own organ of effectiveness and expression. Thomas illustrates this in the foregoing passage from *De motu cordis* and discusses it extensively in *Summa theologica*, as well:

> Every state of the soul causes there to be either more or less natural movement in the heart, provided that the heart works more strongly or more weakly while contracting and expanding (*inquantum cor intensius vel remissius movetur, secundum systolen aut diastolen*). To this extent, the movement of the heart has a characteristic of the state of the soul (*et secundum hoc habet passionis rationem*).[220]

> *Cor... est instrumentum passionum animae* ("The heart... is the instrument of the soul's passions").[221]

This is how Thomas describes the physiological changes that take place in the region of the heart in states of anger,[222] fear,[223] or shame,[224] but also joy[225] or love.[226] He pays particular attention to the modification of the blood processes centered in the heart.[227] These subtle processes always have far-reaching and wide-ranging consequences for the organism as a whole. The consequences are visible even out at the periphery of the circulatory system (when we grow pale or blush, for example), even causing changes in the speech or the coordination of the limbs. Thomas wrote the following on the subject of the soul states and the consequences of anger in the *Summa theologica* (and elsewhere):

> The confusion of the heart [*perturbatio cordis*] can sometimes get so far out of control that the movements of the extremities are hampered by the disorganized agitation of the heart [*quod per inordinatum motum cordis impediatur motus exteriorum membrorum*]. Even death sometimes follows the occurrence of this silence and immobility. However, if the confusion is not so extreme, a torrent of words can

result from the superabundance of rage in the heart [*si autem non fuerit tanta perturbatio, tunc ex abundantia perturbationis cordis, sequitur oris locutio*].[228]

*

Reasonably enough, the heart stands in the emotional-spiritual and feeling-oriented center of the human being. It has effective inner connections to sensory perception and the willful development of actions. However, this is still not an exhaustive list of the anthropologically significant traits of the human heart. Thomas tells us that the heart organ carries out predominantly "hidden effects [*sed cor habet quamdam influentiam occultam*]."[229] To a certain extent, these are part of an "occult physiology" and move in the spiritual sphere of the human spirit–soul and in the realm of all of the cosmic and Christological connections to the spirit–soul. Nevertheless, these events take place in the closest possible connection to the bodily functionality we have read about thus far, not "off somewhere."[230]

Thomas repeatedly pointed out that the heart is related to the higher cognitive activities, which take place after sensory perception and the development of imaginative images. He spoke of the "word of the heart" (*verbum cordis*), by no means only in a metaphorical sense. This "word" is the end result of the other activities. In the *Summa theological*, Thomas wrote:

> The external sound [*vox exterior*] is called...the word [*verbum*], because it signifies the inner concept of the mind [*significat interiorem mentis conceptum*]. Thus the inner concept of the mind [*interior mentis conceptum*] is called *word*, first and foremost, and only on secondary consideration do we use the term for the external sound, used to signify the inner concept.[231]

Something takes place in people whenever they perform an act of perception. This is the act of receiving and conceiving the perceived object (*conceptio rei intellectae*). It results from cognizance of the object. This concept designates the sound, and the concept itself is called a word of the heart (*verbum cordis*).[232]

According to Thomas (quoting John of Damascus in this matter), the word that results from this conceptual work of perception is "uttered inventively in the heart" (*in corde pronuntiatur*).[233] This concept, necessarily general, serves as the final segment in the process of sensory perception. For Thomas, it was merely the beginning (*principium*) and the tool for the spiritual and intellectual activity of thought. This thought process takes place in the individual penetration and unification of the act of perceiving with what is being perceived. This leads, in the end, to the formation of the word. This is a spiritual conception process in which the spiritual and intellectual forces of thinking and willing in the human being are united in the very center of our being. Thomas described this high and essential quality of human intellectual and spiritual activity as *mens* (*interior mentis conceptum*) or as *cor* (*conceptus cordis*), but not as ratio, despite all of its receptive and creative qualities. As human beings, we unite ourselves with the content of the world by means of sensory perception. Our receptive and creative qualities enable us to perceive the world's content after the fact. "The word inherently has more in common with the reality it expresses than with the individual who speaks it, even if it lives within the speaker, dependent upon the speaker's support."[234] These receptive and creative qualities also enable us to assimilate the world in an individualized form, in the form of (externalized) speech (*verbum vocis*) or in the form of individual conduct, led and shaped by our perceptions. Before the spiritual word again externalizes itself in this way (before it returns to the material world as a completed reflection of the process of creation), it lives entirely within the human being. It is formed within us, internally quickened and examined by the spirit–soul in the meditative space of the heart, in which the individual's knowledge of the active spirit also takes place, as described above.

Understood in this way, the spiritual knowledge of the heart gains its form in the *verbum cordis*. In the mind of Thomas Aquinas, this spiritual knowledge is closely connected with the human capacity for love and the effectiveness of the Holy Spirit (*Spiritus sanctus*). Thomas considered the actual perception to be a real internalization of the quality of what is perceived. By the same token (though with a subtle differentiation),[235] he pointed out that "the beloved lingers in the receptive perception [*in appre-hensione*] of the lover." In so doing, Thomas quoted Paul's letter to the Philippians (1:7), "because I have you in my heart [*quod habeam in corde vos*]."[236] In this same passage, he also wrote:

> We say that the lover lingers in the beloved through per-ception, as long as the lover is not satisfied with a super-ficial familiarity with the beloved. Instead, the lover must be determined to search through every detail, scrutinizing the beloved's innermost soul, and even entering it [*et sic ad interiora ejus ingreditur*]. We say of the Holy Spirit, who is God's love, that he searches "even the deep things of God." (I Cor. 2:10)[237]

To this extent, the human heart is essentially an organ of knowledge and love, mediating between Heaven and Earth, thinking and willing, human and environment. This organ shares, spiritually, in the "endless love, which is the Holy Spirit [*infinitae caritatis, quae est Spiritus sanctus*],"[238] since the time of Christ's activity on Earth. Thomas placed a renewed emphasis on this with a word-for-word reference to Paul (Rom. 5:5): "It is...God's love that is poured into our hearts [*in cordibus nostris diffunditure*] by the Holy Spirit, which is given to us as a gift."[239]

This quality of the *"Spiritus sanctus"* has been working with and through the human heart organ since that essential turning point in time when Christ came to Earth. It moves the heart in a spiritual sense. It belongs to the very substance of the processes of cognition and the forming of words. At the same time, it stands in a significant relationship to the elemental, physiological quality of warmth that Thomas (building on the work of Aristotle) characterized as *"spiritus vitalis."* He described it with reference to its meaning for the performance of actions mediated by the heart and carried out by the will.[240] The warmth quality, too, for its part, may have experienced an elevation and reforming in the direction of the *Spiritus sanctus* as a result of the earthly activities and effectiveness of Christ. In any event, Thomas wrote the following in *Summa contra gentiles:*

> When we recite the Creed, we say that we believe in the Holy Spirit, "the one who brings us to life [*in Spiritum Sanctum vivificantem credere profitemur*]." That is also true for the name "breath of the spirit [*quod etiam et nomini spiritus consonat*]." The bodily life of the sense beings exists because of the living breath [*per spiritum vitalem*] that streams through the limbs from the foundation of life [that is, from the heart].[241]

The heart is moved—spiritually—by the Holy Spirit. According to Thomas Aquinas, this spiritual orientation of the center of our human selves[242] also enables the conscious, willful connection of the human being to the godly spiritual world, "to the extent that the heart of this person is moved by the Holy Spirit to believe, and to love God [*alicujus cor per Spiritum Sanctum movetur ad credendum et diligendum Deum]*"[243] and enables the *credulitas cordis* (faith[244] of the heart). Here, in the heart region (*locus circa cor* or *praecordia*), Thomas tells us, is where cognitive exercises, meditation, and prayer experiences take place, initiated by the individually active will. "Now prayer has its place mainly in the heart [*Sed oratio praecipue in corde consistit*]."[245] The actual developmental actions of the human being also take place here, right up to their final intensification: "Clarity of the eye makes us capable of clear sight; so, too, is it promised to those who are pure of heart that they shall look upon God [*unde mundis corde divina visio repromittitur*]."[246]

The corresponding processes of the heart are all included, from the cognitive activities up to and including religious experiences and spiritual intentions, from the *cogitatio cordis* to the *voluntas cordis*. Moreover, all of these are perceptible to the godly spiritual world, as Thomas taught, as he explicated the applicable passages in the Holy Scriptures. "Only God recognizes the thoughts of the heart [*cogitationes cordium*] through himself."[247] He "probes" into our hearts (*quid corda scrutatur*) and their secrets (*occulta cordorum*).[248]

*

Christ, as well, the Godly word, the Logos, (Thomas tells us) was himself brought forth in the "heart of the father," in order to be realized in the world, and given a bodily shape. This is the macrocosmic form of the process, which can now take place perpetually in each individual person, by means of the *verbum cordis*. As he developed these thoughts, Thomas wrote the following in the Summa contra gentiles:

A word that has been taken into the spirit by us is invisible [*sicut verbum nostrum in mente conceptum invisibile est*];

but after it has been projected outward, and made audible by the voice, it becomes perceptible to the senses. So it is with the word of God. It has an invisible existence, appropriate to its eternal creation in the heart of the Father. Through the incarnation of Christ, however, it becomes visible to us. For this reason, the incarnation of the Word is like the vocalization of our word [*unde Verbe Dei incarnatio est sicut vocalis verbi nostri expressio*]. The vocalization of our word takes place by means of a breath of air, which lends form as our word is voiced. It is justifiable to say, therefore, that the body of the Son of God was formed by the breath of the Holy Spirit.[249]

The Logos of God's Son stands closely conjoined with the entire creation. In addition, Christ united himself with human beings in a "higher and inexpressible manner."[250] In his earthly incarnated form, and in his spiritual form of existence following the resurrection, Christ clearly became the necessary precondition for changes in the area surrounding the human heart. This includes the *Spiritus sanctus* in its present empowered state, working together with the being of Christ:

> Since the uncreated Trinity is differentiated within itself in keeping with the emergence of the word out of speaking and love out of both words and speaking, one could say that even in creatures blessed with reason [that is, in humans], there is a picture, an allegorical likeness, of the uncreated Trinity. The emergence of the word takes place following cognition [*processio verbi secundum intellectum*], and the emergence of love takes place following the will [*processio amoris secundum voluntatum*]. In the other creatures, however, there is no source of the word, no word, and no love [*non invenitur principium verbi et verbum et amor*].[251]

Making a renewed reference to Paul, who wrote in his Letter to the Galatians (4:6) that God the Father had sent the spirit of his Son into the hearts of the disciples, Thomas Aquinas spoke of the everlasting spiritual "birth of Christ," precisely in this center of being within each person.[252] This spiritual birth completes the deeper mysteries of the *"verbum cordis"* and the "meditations," primarily in the ritual, sacramental event,[253] which touches the human within the transformed heart. The "secret of the incarnation and passion of Christ" (*mysterium incarnationis et passionis Christi*), and indeed the entire sacrifice of Christ in his oneness with humanity on Earth, was present and active for Thomas in the sacraments and, in particular, in the celebration of Communion. He considered this to be the highest point of spiritual life and the goal of all the sacraments.[254] "In the other sacraments, Christ himself is not existentially present as he is in this sacrament."[255] Thomas began his workday with two holy Masses (one he celebrated, and one he heard),[256] and he repeatedly referred to the meaning of the ritually spoken word.[257] "The form-giving words gain their holy power and effectiveness not by being heard but by being spoken."[258] He understood the sacramental baptism (the "gate to the sacraments") as a preparation (*praeparatio*) of the heart for "taking in" spiritual truths[259] wrought directly by Christ. "A person who baptizes carries out an external act. It is Christ who baptizes us inwardly."[260] Thomas placed great emphasis on the singular relationship of the heart to the Eucharist.[261] According to the teachings of Aristotle, it is here in the heart that the substance of Earth reaches its highest stage on the path to the spirit—and becomes blood. Christ's central sacramental power also takes place in this sphere, as do the reception of his existence and the transformation into him in closest connection with him. It follows, Thomas tells us, that it is Christ himself who speaks the holy words of this highest of all sacraments through a consecrated priest. It is Christ who completes this spiritual process:[262]

The form-giving words are spoken by the person who is administering the sacrament [except in the case of the Eucharist]. The form-giving words of this sacrament [the Eucharist], however, are spoken by the person of Christ himself, who speaks. Through this we are given to understand that the celebrant of this sacrament does nothing other than to speak the words of Christ.[263]

Christ the Logos, conceived in the "heart of the Father" long ago, worked and continues to work into the center of the human being, into the sphere of the heart, from which the human being forms a path for life. Christ, perceiving, suffering, and acting, unites himself with the world in its development and obligates himself to the future.[264] The whole of humanity finds its point of departure here in the heart, which Thomas tells us is capable of pure completeness (*munditia cordis*). There exists a "new law," the law of love, the law of the "spiritual grace that has sunk into the heart [*lex nova consistit in ipsa spirituali gratia indita cordibus*]," which refers to the free and responsible "I" of the human being—not to the Old Testament "law of fear."[265] Christ and the work of the Holy Spirit, for which he prepared the way, can be very effective in hearts prepared in this way. They can enable the spiritual development and the independent moral responsibility of the individual, which imprint themselves upon the individual hearts. In his exegesis, written late in his life, on the Last Judgment and the setting of the Resurrection, Thomas reminds us of the words of Richard of St. Victoire, who once said that the hearts of human beings would one day become "like law books," recording the conscience, containing records of all completed deeds, and deciding our individual future.[266]

*

After returning from Holy Mass on the morning of December 6, 1273, Thomas abruptly stopped his work on the *Summa theologica*. At the time, he was right in the middle of his explanations of the sacraments in part three, intended to be the concluding portion of the work. Thomas was deeply changed, and silent. Despite receiving every sort of encouragement from Reginald of Pipernos, his secretary (*socius continuus*), he chose not to continue writing his Christological anthropology in the winter of 1273 to 1274. Thomas's silence continued, and he was deep in thought. Reginald's repeated queries received only this answer: "Everything that I have written up to this point appears to me to be nothing but chaff compared to what I have now seen and what has been revealed to me."[267] Three months later, the forty-nine-year-old Thomas Aquinas prepared himself for death, moving into a Cistercian cloister nearby. His last instructive words, spoken to the Cistercians from his sickbed, made a lasting impression upon them, as did his departure from Earth, which followed soon afterward. The burial of his body was not celebrated with the usual Mass for the Dead, but rather with the Mass *os justi*. This unusual choice was made quite spontaneously, as noted in the proceedings of the canonization. It begins with the following chanted words: "The mouth of the righteous man senses wisdom, and his tongue speaks righteousness, and the law of God is in his heart."[268]

Fifty years after his death, Thomas Aquinas became the first teacher to be sainted in the West[269] (despite the fact, as Josef Pieper notes, that Thomas did not find any true students in his lifetime).[270] He spent his life seeking both Eastern and Western knowledge through deep meditation and rigorous scientific work. In the words of the *Summa theologica:*

> As the morning is the beginning of the day, the evening is the
> end. Knowledge of the absolute beginning of the existence of

things is called morning knowledge [*cognitio matutina*], but this refers to the existence of things in the Word [*in Verbo*]. Knowledge of the existence of the things that were created, to the extent that they exist on their own, however, is known as evening knowledge [*cognitio vespertina*]. The existence of things streams forth from the Word as at their absolute, primordial beginning [*primordiali principio*], and this streaming finds its goal in the existence of things, which possess it in their very nature.[271]

Thomas sought this "morning knowledge" in his own heart forces. This is the first, original organ of development, which stands in the closest connection with the word. Out of the loving powers of his own highly developed spirit–soul, Thomas took his own path to perception and knowledge, which stood as a sign for Christianizing human thought and human heart forces:

A brighter light blots out the lesser light of another glowing body, but it does not extinguish the light of the illuminated body. Instead, it becomes complete. When the sun comes, the light of the stars is dimmed, but the glowing of the air is complete. It is permeated with light. The cognitive power or spirit of the human being is like a light that is illuminated by the light of the Godly word. The spirit of the human being is not extinguished by the presence of the word. Instead, it becomes complete. It is permeated with light.[272]

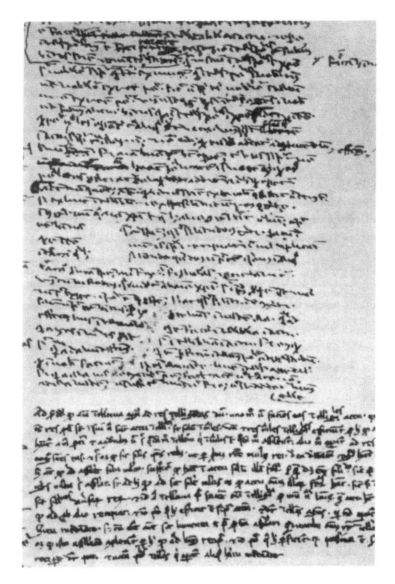

A page from Thomas' manuscript Quatuor libros super Sententiis,
*continued (at the bottom) with dictation taken by Reginald of
Piperno. The handwriting at the top of the page is Thomas's.*

3.

The Heart and the Fate of Humanity

Teachings on the Heart
in Rudolf Steiner's Spiritual Science

"When you look into your heart, you are able to perceive rather well what you will undertake in your next life. You can see only traces, of course—not a fully executed likeness. One can thus say, and not only in general, in abstracto: what will take place karmically in the next life is prepared in this life. One can practically point out the volume [in the Book of Life] in which the karma is worked out for the times to come."

—RUDOLF STEINER

"Spiritual science takes a different view of the heart and its relation to the so-called circulation of the blood. Contemporary physiology believes this relationship to be entirely dependent on mechanistic and materialistic ideas. This mechanistic and materialistic theory of life sees the heart as a sort of pumping apparatus that drives the blood through the body in a persistent, regulated way. From this point of view, the heart is the cause of the blood's movement. Spiritual-scientific perception shows something entirely different. Spiritual Science sees the pulsing of the blood and all of its inner movement as an expression and effect of soul processes. The soul is the reason the blood behaves as it does. Becoming pale because of feelings of anxiety or blushing under the influence of sensations affecting the soul are unrefined results of soul activity in the blood. However, everything that takes place in the blood is simply an expression of what takes place in the life of the soul. The connection between the pulsing of the blood and the impulses of the soul is deeply secret. The movements of the heart do not cause the blood to pulse, but are rather the results of that pulsing." (Cosmic Memory)[273]

As Rudolf Steiner wrote these sentences during the first decade of the twentieth century, he was writing in much the same spirit as Thomas Aquinas and Aristotle did. Like them, he stood largely alone, albeit in a completely different era. The "mechanizing of the heart" and the accompanying interpretation of the human organism as a soulless machine, in the spirit of a technically aimed manipulation, had found and held its position in civilization. Since the second half of the nineteenth century, this view has determined nearly all scientific thinking and action. The last traces of Aristotelian natural philosophy now belong to the past,[274] as does the spiritual mysticism of the heart, spread chiefly by Dominican orders, which characterized the religious life of central Europe for several centuries after the death of Thomas Aquinas.[275]

As an understanding of the body-soul relationship, and indeed the entire study of medicine, Descartes' mechanical interpretation of blood circulation was revolutionary and set the tone for further investigations.[276] Descartes' work was a powerful reinterpretation of the findings of William Harvey, an Aristotelian.[277] These new interpretations emphasized the automaton-like nature of a soulless human body, functioning exclusively according to physical laws. This includes, of course, the mechanical beating action of the heart. The new concept understood the blood circulation to be bound to the nervous system in a regulated cycle, and the substance of the blood itself to be "nothing other...than a collection of small nutritive components."[278] For Descartes, for the school of thought associated with him, and for the powers behind this movement, all Aristotelian and Thomistic concepts of warmth and motion were obsolete and nullified, including the entire incarnative connection between the soul and the body. "The heart became a mechanical apparatus, which it has remained until the present day, basically, for most of the so-called physiologists and physicians."[279]

Steiner quickly completed the university education in the natural sciences that was available in the 1880s, earning a doctoral degree in philosophy. By the age of twenty-three, he was already editing Goethe's works on the natural sciences. Steiner outlined fundamental areas where he felt the stress should be different, emphasizing in particular the original Aristotelian nature of research and cognitive theory, which Goethe (against all dominant trends of his time) had continually emphasized ever more extensively in his work from the end of the eighteenth

century into the nineteenth century. Like Aristotle and Thomas
Aquinas before him, Rudolf Steiner recapitulated the knowledge
of his age and the directions, trends, and forces that were part of
the development of the natural sciences in bygone eras. He did
this extensive work in the finest detail.[280] Even in this first publication (*Goethe's Theory of Knowledge*), Steiner formulated the
necessity for a methodically extended and broadened study of
nature and spiritual science.[281] He devoted the rest of his life to
the further development and teaching of these ideas, publishing
more than twenty books on the subject, and giving thousands
of lectures. Aristotle founded his academic Lykeion in Athens,
and Thomas Aquinas helped to found and then briefly lead a
number of colleges for his order, in addition to his long ten-
ure at the university in Paris. In much the same spirit, Rudolf
Steiner founded a "School of Spiritual Science," in which this
work could be continued in marked contrast to contemporary
scientific thought, particularly in the case of empirical research
done in the individual scientific fields.

Six months before the opening of the Goetheanum in Dornach,
Steiner spoke these words (already cited in the introduction to
this work):

> In this Goethean view of the world lies the impetus for a
> nascent intellectual movement. It is the logical result of ear-
> lier work with Thomistic thought, adjusted to reflect the
> new emphasis on the natural sciences in modern scientific
> research. The soul-spiritual element has a powerful effect
> on every single activity and function of the human organs.
> Thomas Aquinas could express this only in an abstract man-
> ner, stating that everything that lives and works in the human
> body, right up to the most vegetative of functions, is directed
> by soul forces and must be recognized and identified by its
> soul forces. Goethe marks the beginning of this change of

direction in his "Theory of Color," which has been completely misunderstood on this point. Goethe [also] marks this new beginning with his "Morphology," his work on plants and animals [*The Metamorphosis of Plants*]. We will be able to bring this Goethean work to completion only when we have a spiritual science that can clarify these observations from the natural sciences.[282]

*

"Thomas was able to state his conviction only in the abstract, that the soul-spiritual forces play an active role in every last aspect of the workings of the organs in the human body." *Theosophy* was Rudolf Steiner's first work of the new century that was no longer focused primarily on scientific methodology or the history of philosophy. In this work, written in 1904, Steiner described the parts of a human being and the steps of its incarnation very precisely. In both private and public lectures during the following years, he demonstrated the extent to which the human being forms various organizational structures and takes functional advantage of them in the process of incarnating, as well as in carrying out biographical development. Expanding on the work of Aristotle and Thomas Aquinas, Rudolf Steiner spoke not only of the individual elements of the soul or of a general spirit–soul (*anima rationalis*) of the human being, but also of an individual "I," or Ego. (This "I" is united with its own sphere of the soul, which is just as deeply linked to the fate of the individual.) The "I" incarnates into a living body and thus takes part in various relationships between the organs. It should not be forgotten that the "I" had a role in shaping these organs during the period of development after death and before a new birth. To this extent, Steiner's descriptions always focused on the development of the human being in the individual sense, as well as in the macrocosmic, cosmogenetic sense. The formation of the heart was of primary importance during this process, together with initiation of the blood circulation. Steiner refers to the heart as the "noblest" human organ.[283]

The heart is the central instrument of the process that makes us human. It is not only the first functioning organ to appear in the development of the embryo, but is also of central importance from a broader evolutionary point of view, as well.[284] First appearing in an extrasensory form, the heart was formed in the earliest stages of the planetary evolution of the Earth. Shaped by the dynamic movements of warmth, led by the hierarchies, coming to a state of rest,[285] it then transformed itself further at each stage of cosmic evolution.[286] In the end, it became an integral part of our physicality in connection with the development of the human "I" and the final formation of the Earth. In this process, the blood played a decisive role. According to Steiner, "the principle of the development of the 'I'" is found in the blood.[287] With the help of the blood and the processes of warmth, human individuality has long been able to incarnate, and continues to incarnate, into an earthly body.[288] A certain arrangement or organization of the blood circulation[289] is needed, including the further development of the body and its organological and functional structures, so that the human being becomes an "I" organism, centered on the blood and the heart.[290]

This evolutionary process of development of the human heart and our physicality as a whole is not ended or finished but open to the future. The actual process of becoming human is just that: a work in progress. This is true in the sense of the incarnative relationship being developed between the spirit–soul and the living body, as well. In various lectures just after the turn of the century, Steiner pointed out that the higher spiritual development and "I" development of the human being are contingent upon extensive changes that the heart itself will undergo.[291]

The heart's relationship to the body will also change over time. Moreover, these changes will affect the future bodily substance of the organism,[292] as well as the involuntary and thus deeply unfree quality of the heart's movements frequently discussed by Aristotle and Thomas Aquinas.[293] According to Steiner, the coming metamorphoses of the heart will be able to provide the necessary requirements for the development of a new physicality, directed by the central warming forces of the heart.[294] These changes will bring about a changed relationship between the body and the soul in the sense of an even more extensive individualization and spiritualization of the human being and his or her physiology. Referring to the future movements of the heart, Steiner wrote:

> The heart will not always remain as it is now. In the future, it will have an entirely different form and different task. The heart is moving toward becoming a voluntary [rather than involuntary] muscle. In the future, it will carry out movements that will be the workings of inner soul impulses of the human being.... In the future, the heart will be the result of what is woven in the human soul, carried into the outer world by voluntary movements.[295]

*

According to Rudolf Steiner's descriptions, the heart belongs to the collective physiology of the body. One part of it belongs to the "rhythmic system," a balanced central system that maintains equilibrium between the divergent forces of the upper nerve–sense organization and the lower metabolic sphere connected with the dynamic system of the limbs. All of the nerve processes, Steiner tells us, function in the service of the perception and imagination. However, development of the human will serves subtle processes of the metabolic system. The rhythmic system is between the two and balances them. It also serves as the organ of expression and attainment, or realization, of the human feeling life:

> The connection between the feeling life (no matter how odd that sounds to us today) and every rhythmic occurrence in our bodies is just as direct as the connection between the imaginative life and the nerve–sense system [and the will life with the metabolic system]. These rhythmic activities are dependent upon and held in check by the rhythm of our breathing and, by extension, the rhythm of the blood. I refer not merely to the simple rhythm of breathing and the circulation of the blood, but also to the finer branches of the rhythmic system. We must think about the true nature of rhythm and rhythmic movement if we wish to seek the physical, bodily basis for our feeling life.[296]

Steiner contends that the direct, physiological expression of the feeling and sensory life of the soul is not the action of the heart in its narrow sense. Nor is it primarily the warmth processes of the blood near the heart (despite the fact that Aristotle and Thomas Aquinas hinted that it was so, in their descriptions).[297] Instead, Steiner tells us, it is the rhythmic movement processes connected with (and culminating in) the activity of the blood and the heart.[298] These rhythmic processes in turn stand in a particular relationship to our breathing, the most important life rhythm of the organism. The "world rhythm"[299] lives in our breathing and in the cosmic "world events."[300] "We become part of our cosmic environment precisely through this breathing system, and we do not observe our participation because we exercise this rhythmic 'organizing' as an unconscious activity, taken largely for granted."[301] Breathing, says Steiner, constitutes the stable center of the autonomous rhythmic system. Our breathing exercises a balancing and correcting function for the other rhythms of the body, each of which is unstable and susceptible to disruption from other influences. Thus breathing also strongly influences the blood circulation, which is always subject to the metabolic events taking place. "There must be a progressive healing of the blood circulation through the breathing."[302]

As an instrument of the feeling life, the human rhythmic system mediates between events of sensory perception and the imagination, as well as between the development of the will and movement. This connection to the past and future with respect to the unfolding of a human life through time was made known by Aristotle and Thomas Aquinas. Steiner expanded considerably upon these anthropological points of view in his physiological study of the human being. According to his descriptions, the corresponding forms of soul activity are not linked solely to the past and the future. They are also the concrete expression of our individual origin and our own future (with respect to the bodily, physiological organs, which take what is potential and make it real). The human nervous system is cosmically oriented and works actively in processes of decay, or deterioration. Steiner contends that the human nervous system is the concrete result of the last earthly existence and will serve as a further development of this existence in the time after death, as the human being, still in the realm of the earthly metabolic system and movement, prepares and builds up forces for the future, which will form and shape the body.[303]

Against this backdrop, the nerve–sense system and the metabolic–limb system, which are polar opposites, so to speak, try to achieve a balance in the realm of the rhythmic center. The consequent opposition between the nerves and the blood[304] should be seen as a physiological confrontation of the human being with the developing self.[305]

Steiner repeatedly portrayed this in a "downright drastic" manner:

If the decomposition process of the nerve–sense system works its way into the metabolic–limb system by means of rhythm, then something is present that works against the metabolic–limb system; this is in fact poisonous to the metabolic–limb system. Moreover, the opposite is also true. If something present in the synthesizing [digestive] system works its way into the head [system], it is poisonous to the head [system]. And because the systems...are spread out through the rest of the entire organism, there is a perpetual system of poisoning and detoxification taking place, which is brought into equilibrium by the rhythmic process.[306]

Within every connected system of the body, a meeting of the past, already experienced, with the future is being prepared. This pronounced instance of opposition is potentially pathogenic, or even destructive. Even the central feeling life of the human being exists within this ongoing polarity. As Rudolf Steiner explained more extensively in various lectures in 1917, human feelings and mood at a specific moment of one's biography can never be understood completely on the basis of the experiences of the immediate present or the recent past. It is more accurate to say:

If we feel something in this moment, the person within us who is feeling is the one who is just beginning to live—who will live on tomorrow and the next day, and next year, until our death. In that moment, when we feel something, the subject (the otherwise unknown subject) is our life, which is within us between the moments when we feel and our death. What we perceive is the life that we have experienced from birth up to the moment when we are having this particular experience.[307]

Everything we feel at one particular point is the effect of our own future on our own past.[308]

In this sense, the rhythmic system, and the underlying events experienced by each part of the being, respectively,[309] enable the physiological equilibrium of the self-reincarnating human being, binding itself repeatedly with earthly connections. In this way the rhythmic system configures a center between the cosmos and the Earth.[310] Within this highly dynamic event, the actual confrontation and balance achieved between the "head" and the "limbs," the upper and lower functional poles of the human being do not take place within the central breathing system but in the heart. This is because, Steiner tells us, breathing, which carries healing rhythmical forces within itself and makes itself available to the entire body, is itself part of this controversy. The breathing stands in the upper, cosmically oriented pole of the rhythmic system, inwardly related to the sensory functions and serving as a bridge to them. In much the same way, the activities of the blood circulation (circulatory activities) border the sphere of the actual metabolic activities. "In the circulatory system, equilibrium is reached between the metabolic system and the rhythmic system. In the breathing system, equilibrium is reached between the rhythmic system and the nerve–sense system."[311] In the heart organ, however, these opposites "crash together," as Steiner describes it. They must find an active balance. Centered here in the heart, the central organ of human development, are the upper and lower organic processes;[312] the nerves, blood, breathing, and circulation; the cosmic world order and the transformative earthly power of the organism; participatory cooperation and active internalization; the external being and the internal being; but also "lightness" and "heaviness," form and dissolution. "One can say that the entire organic process shifts toward the heart, both the process in the upper human being and the process in the lower human being. They shift from the very bottom through the lower limbs and upward. The entire formative process of the human being crowds into the heart (the actual collecting organ) from both sides."[313]

In the heart, says Steiner, the opposing aspects of our physiology are perceived and overcome. These opposing forces are deeply bound up with the conditions of our existence. The heart thus serves as the central physiological organ and as the organ of balance for the nerve–sense and metabolic–limb systems. It also brings together the individual past and future of the human being. In the middle of childhood, around the ninth year of life, "I"-consciousness is established organologically, bringing about a rhythmic equilibrium between the breathing and blood circulation,[314] which develops of its own accord. This is the actual "earth consciousness"[315] of the experienced present (time).

*

According to Steiner, the "observable heart movements" are the "expression of the balance between the upper [self] and the lower [self]."[316] All activities of perception and mediation centered in the heart take place directly by means of the blood processes[317] that come together in the heart. "The heart is nothing less than the organ that balances both circulatory systems of the blood— namely, that of the upper self, the 'head being,' and that of the lower self, the 'limb being.'"[318]

Rudolf Steiner continued to speak about the relationships between the blood and heart processes following his first lectures on spiritual science. Before various audiences, he referred frequently to the developmental processes of the heart and circulatory systems of the human embryo. He emphasized that the blood is basically lively and moved, and that the circulation of the blood is "the original" and first,[319] the Aristotelian *arché:* "One must see the heart, to a certain extent, as a creation of the movement of the blood. One must place the heart, to a certain extent, into the living movement of the blood."[320]

There are forces at work in this "primary" movement of the blood—cosmic forces[321] and the development of power within the higher elements of the human being that are connected with the cosmic world order:

> The blood is moved through the organism, through the spiritual existence of the human being. In the will [system] and in the feeling impulses, the spiritual existence reaches directly into the metabolism and the breathing (that is, into the rhythmic system). The entire inner movement, this entire inner rhythmic activity comes directly out of the spiritual human being. The heart (the activity of the heart) is not the cause, but rather the result of the circulation of the blood, the circulation of the fluids. Only in its own movements does the heart express how it is inwardly aroused and moved *by the movement that actually arises from the spiritual human being.*[322]

> As I consciously perceive the outer world through my eyes, I make it my own in my imagination. I also unconsciously perceive what I develop unconsciously in my blood as a pulse sensation, using my spiritual and soul forces through this inner sense organ of the heart. The heart is not a pump; the heart is the inner organ of perception. Through it, one perceives what the spiritual and soul forces develop in the blood, as one perceives the outer world through the outer senses.[323]

At another point Steiner clarified that the processes he had indicated take place by means of the organs of the metabolic–limb system. "And the blood circulation is necessitated by the organs."[324] The bodily oriented effectiveness of the human "I" and soul are developed in the physiological activities of the organs. The higher elements of our being shape and make use of the enlivened bodily configuration of the human being. These higher elements incarnate themselves into the organs of the human being and thus determine the circumstances inside the blood circulation, particularly by means of the metabolic–limb system. Steiner tells us that all metabolic processes, and all processes that transform substances, culminate in the formation of the blood (and, finally, in the movement of the blood). The preparation and movement of the blood is the highest level of the individuating nourishment and substance events, in the sense of the physiological development of the "I."[325] In the metabolic organs necessary for this process, the higher elements of our being work entirely from within, in a maximal intensification of the incarnating activity, and in greatest devotion to physical–material events on Earth.[326] The results of this devotion, Steiner tells us, become perceptible in the heart by means of the processes of the blood. This is true in principle, and also with respect to the current condition of the body:

> Through the heart, the head . . . subconsciously perceives how the blood feeds itself with processed forms of nourishment; how the kidneys, liver, and other organs function; in fact, the head perceives everything that takes place in the organism.[327]

> The heart is actually the inner organ of perception, by means of which the head perceives everything that takes place in the body.[328]

In the concise, condensed formulation of a medical training course, with an eye to the active, working elements of a human being, this was summed up as follows: "The movement of the blood takes place via the "I" and astral body. . . . The heart is given to see how the astral body and the "I" work in the human being. The heart is thus an entirely spiritual organ of perception."[329]

The perception of events taking place in the body, and the human actions that responsibly shape the concrete metabolic situation, are both made possible with the help of the blood and heart processes. Steiner tells us that they enable the development of consciousness and internalization through a step-by-step process.

"The heart—it transforms what takes place in the metabolic organs and converts it into sensory content" (R. Steiner, notebook).[330] The blood-related, blood-concerned heart organ "vibrates" on the feeling and sensitivity level during experiences and events.[331] In connection with this, however, the heart takes part organologically in reflecting the "sensory content" into the sphere of human consciousness—the "sensory content" that was perceived and transformed in the metabolic–limb sphere. Steiner says of various bodily organs that, with their "reflecting" help, both the visualization needed for memory and the resulting renewed awareness of specific soul-spiritual tasks[332] can take place. For example, with the help of the lungs, the recapitulation of abstract trains of thought can be accomplished. Steiner ascribed a general helpful role to the heart in the formation of imaginative pictures in the memory, as Aristotle and Thomas Aquinas had also done.[333] With respect to the heart, Steiner said the following on July 2, 1921, in Dornach:

> Now, to be sure, something is reflected on the heart that is no longer merely a matter of memory and custom. Instead, it becomes spiritualized when it reaches the outside wall: life. The prickles of our conscience are thrown back by the heart, which can be interpreted entirely as a physical phenomenon; prickles of conscience that stream into our consciousness are the content of our experiences, reflected by the heart. This teaches us about the spiritual knowledge of the heart.[334]

The processes of life become "spiritualized" as they complete their "reflection" on the outside wall of the heart.[335] In other words, they become connected, in their inner essence, with the human being's spiritual core. Thus, they are accessible to our consciousness and gain access to the realm of the individual moral conscience.

For the heart, as for other central human organs of memory, Steiner asserted that the reflecting of physiological experiences into the consciousness, which took place in the heart, constitutes only one aspect of its organological memory work. The deeper and more extensive memory of the human being does not restrict itself to current phenomena of consciousness in imaginative images or "memories." Instead, said Steiner, the deeper memory consists of the ordering of our existence not only in terms of our experiences (what has already been lived), but also in terms of the life and activities that are taking place now. Memory, in the sense of a spiritualizing internalization, creates real forces—forces that belong to the future and prepare for a future incarnation that will grant us the opportunity to balance our fate:

> If we look into the heart, we see forces gather there from the entire metabolic–limb system. Moreover, because everything connected with the heart and heart forces is spiritualized, what comes into the heart from our outer lives and actions is also spiritualized. In addition, no matter how paradoxical and unusual it sounds for a human being who is so clever in terms of the present, it is nevertheless true: the forces being prepared in the heart are karmic structures—the structures of karma. It is outrageously foolish to speak of the heart as a mere pump. The heart is the organ that carries what we call karma into the next incarnation, out of and mediated by the metabolic–limb system. The metabolism of the human being is not the mere test-tube seething, bubbling, and boiling presented by modern physiology. With every step you take, a metabolic exchange takes place. That metabolism is not merely a chemical process to be investigated with the tools of physiology and chemistry. It is colored by moral considerations while carrying a moral nuance. That moral nuance is actually stored in the heart and carried over into the next incarnation.... The heart system, as an organ, is connected to the elements of warmth. It is constructed entirely from

warmth elements. Thus, this element, which is the most spiritual, is also the element that gathers up the karmic material into these uncommonly fine structures of warmth, which we also have in our "warmth organism."

When you look into your heart, you can perceive rather well what you will undertake in your next life. You can see only traces, of course—not a fully executed likeness. One can thus say, and not only in general, in abstracto, what will take place karmically in the next life is prepared in this life. One can practically point out the volume [in the Book of Life] in which the karma is worked out for the times to come.

These are the matters that must be considered very concretely if one really wants to study spiritual science.[336]

The heart is an organ of balance and equilibrium of one's past and future human existences. In this sense, it is the "organ of fate." In its connection with the metabolic–limb system, the heart participates in the preparation of the after-death and reincarnative existence. The heart works toward its own metamorphosis and further development, which take place with help from God and the hierarchies.[337] "It is in the heart that the activity of the blood takes place, and in which the activity of the blood is taken into the entire human self [individuality]."[338]

*

The karmic forces of the future are transformed in the warmth structure of the heart. These forces are taken up into its etheric warming space, which is formed out of the cosmos with the most intensive concentration. During a lecture on developmental physiology, Steiner explained that people are able to inscribe individual actions (by means of the soul-body at work), and also intended actions (by means of the "I" at work), into this etheric warmth space following the time of puberty, which he called the "earthly maturity."[339] With an emphasis on astral and etheric events,[340] Steiner said:

> Starting at the time of sexual maturity, all human activity begins in the etheric heart, taking a detour through the astral body. The etheric heart is the organ that arose from the reflection of the stars and the cosmos. Everything begins there.
>
> This is an extraordinarily important occurrence because, when you observe all of this, you find the union of what the human being does on Earth with the cosmic. If you think in terms of the etheric world, you find a compact form of the cosmos in the heart. At the same time, if you think in terms of the astral world, you see in contracted form all that is undertaken by the human being. The human being and the cosmos, with all of its cosmic events, find their connection in the heart. In all of the human body, only in the area around the heart do we find such a close correspondence between the astral body and the etheric body. Through birth, the human being has brought a reflection of the entire world into the etheric body. In fact, it is the case that this entire world, the essence of which is within us, takes into itself and permeates itself with everything the human being does. Through these connections there is an opportunity; every deed in every human life from this point on becomes part of the essence of these reflections of the cosmos.
>
> When human beings pass through the portal of death, we have laid aside the physical body. We take everything with us into the further [next] spirit–soul life in this etheric–astral form in which the heart swims. Since we become increasingly larger spiritually, we can give up our entire karma to the cosmos. After all, the substance of the entire cosmos is there inside, contracted into the heart, in the etheric body....
>
> When we observe the development of the human being, we can actually tell ourselves that, in the region of the heart, there is a conjoining of the cosmic with the earthly. The cosmic, in its cosmic configuration, is taken into the etheric.

There it prepares itself to accept and take in everything we do. We go forth and step into a new cosmic existence when we have gone through the portal of death. We take with us what has formed itself through an inner penetration of the etheric with human deeds. [341]

This is how the human heart becomes and remains an "organism for the development of karma."[342] Where your treasure lies, there, too, lies your heart...(Luke 12:34).

*

Rudolf Steiner characterized the Christ being as the "Lord of Karma."[343] In the future development of the Earth and humanity, Christ is the working spiritual power who will take an ever more active role in the ordering of individual fates and their overarching connection with each other. He has also brought about the general karmic enabling of the human being. According to Steiner, Christ became active in this sense even before his earthly incarnation: "He is the one who sent the very possibility of karma to the human beings before he stepped forth onto the Earth."[344] This was before his earthly life enabled us spiritually to accept our individual fate. Not until the mystery of Golgotha did human beings learn to love their karma.[345]

Rudolf Steiner spoke only once about the means by which the godly Christ being was able to help all of humanity qualify for karma. He spoke about this at a lecture course when the Christian Community was first established. In that course he referred to the sacrificial ritual of the priest-kings. Though pre-Christian, the ritual was apparently connected with and anticipated the coming Christ being. Like Melchizedek, the priest-kings achieved a new physiological situation for the incarnated human spirit–soul with the help of the bread and wine substances (and the principles of salt and phosphorus at work in them, respectively). "It is true that the human being, whose body contains the correct proportion of salt and phosphorus, stands upon the Earth in the correct way and is connected with the Earth quite strongly; but the human being also contains the necessary etheric and astral lightness to be free from earthly forces within its being."[346] Steiner said that what took place in this ritual act enabled a revolutionary new equilibrium of incarnation. This took place through the combining of both principles inside the human body:

> Standing before the mystery of Golgotha, human beings became capable of taking their good and bad deeds with them into the new bodies, which they received in their next earthly life. These actions had been carried out in their previous lives on Earth. In other words, human beings were in a position to develop karma for the first time by means of this important step. Nothing of the moral acts of one earthly life would have been extended into another, future life unless this had taken place. What needed to be carried over had to be carried in this way, from body to body, so that there could be karma, a worldly fate, of the human being.[347]

Then, many centuries later, the Christ being joined himself with the fate of the Earth and with human beings by devoting and sacrificing himself to them. Witnesses from the Gospels tell us that this was achieved in the sense of a real heart force—an effective, working presence in the center of the human being. Here we find the developing "organism for forming the karma" changing, and carrying forward our earthly existence into a macrocosmic spiritual existence. "The Christ impulse was taken into temporality, because he is connected with what has come to be, and that which is fleeting; and because he transforms the time-bound into the eternal."[348] Though Steiner did not explain it directly, the further development of the human heart made it into the central organ of Christ's one-time deed of becoming human. In addition, it made the human heart into the instrument of continuing individual development. Most likely this took place first in this epochal approach of the historic turning point (the coming of Christ). Out of this developmental process arose a new spiritual physiology of freedom. What had earlier been made possible in principle, by the sacrifice of the priest-kings, now became the responsibility of each individual.

For each of us this means an individually redeeming acceptance of responsibility for our own actions and lives, for the fate of the self and the world.[349]

*

According to Rudolf Steiner, the Christ was the spirit of the Sun. Steiner characterized the "secret of the Sun as the secret of Christ himself."[350] The freedom sphere of the Sun continues its crucial work, helping with the formation and functionality of the blood and heart system.[351] The freedom sphere is connected intrinsically to the "warmth structures" that are capable of incorporating the karma-developing forces that developed out of the metabolic–limb system. The warmth process and the physiological gold process[352] immanently connected with the Sun sphere are at the foundation of the entire process of developing and shaping the heart. The warmth is the "spiritual element." The internalization of the future substantive forces takes place in the warmth activities. Here, too, we find the meeting and uniting of the earthly with the cosmic, the physical with the moral, which characterizes the heart organ. "Every moral event that takes place in a human life and, on the other hand, every physical thing that happens is connected in the human heart." These things determine the heart's way of working as the "organ of karma development." Steiner tells us that the heart was formed from cosmic warmth movements. The heart perceives and takes in warmth processes throughout its life,[353] and it lives physiologically from these processes, in physiology and pathology (in health and in sickness).[354]

The individuality, the human "I," works in this bodily heart warmth, in its morality and will intentions. Rudolf Steiner formulated this just as Thomas Aquinas would have:

> When we look at the human heart, we see everything concentrated there that connects the human being with the forces that constitute the will-related nature of one's thoughts—not the content of those thoughts so much as the volitional nature of one's thoughts, or what one wishes to do in spirit.[355]

In the heart, final decisions cross the path of the individual. These are the intentional decisions of the will about the existential path of our thinking and willing. According to Rudolf Steiner, the forces and functional organization of the human being are spiritually resisted. The thinking and willing, nerve–sense, and metabolic–limb systems exist in a relationship with the past and future. These forces are also potentially in a relationship with spiritual beings that tend to make use of their one-sided nature, declaring themselves complete and perfect. In the end, those beings take pains to dissolve the bonds between what has been and what is now taking place, between what is time-bound and what is eternal. They even try to dissolve entirely the individual fate of the human being.[356] The power to set ourselves against these powerful beings is given to us as free and responsible individuals. We can bind ourselves[357] with the Christ forces centered on the heart in a very real sense—even in the physiology of our bodies. This will complete the process of spiritualization of our thinking and willing on a path of heart-centered inner training.[358] This is a sign of the arrangement uniting both the opposite activities of the soul into the spiritual center of our own existence: the heart.

This process is also a sign of the higher, fate-determining "I" and the intentionality and Christ-power working within the "I" ("Not I, but the Christ in me"). In this sense, Rudolf Steiner tells us that it is still possible, despite all threats of the epoch, to recognize the "good" (so throughly discussed in the writings of Aristotle and Thomas Aquinas) that is at work in human beings and can be found there. We must recognize this "good" and allow it to be effective in shaping[359] the world. "People do not believe this yet, but they will believe it someday. What can work only as the Christ-power within the human heart now will someday effectively penetrate the entire cosmos.[360]

*

In the ritual and sacramental actions of esoteric Christianity, human beings can devote themselves to a present, effective Christ and be filled completely with his existence ("May you be in my heart"). Such ritual and sacramental activities are capable of encouraging and strengthening the processes sketched out in this chapter. They culminate in the Easter celebration of the Act of Consecration of Man. The processes of breathing and the blood, which are conveyed with words in this ceremony, are united in the mystery of the heart. This is also true of the ritual for the second seven years of life, the Sacrament of Confirmation, which focuses on the heart and takes place at the time of "earthly maturity" (and the development of a "karma-forming organism"). These rituals are an unmistakable sign of the sacramental physiology of the heart organ. This was first introduced and made visible by Rudolf Steiner at the beginning of the twentieth century, as he continued and intensified the work of Aristotle and Thomas Aquinas. Shortly before his death, Steiner wrote the following sentences from his sickbed:

Blood in the heart, striving toward the breath in the lungs, is humanity's striving for the cosmos. The breath in the lungs, striving toward the blood in the heart, is the cosmos forgiving humanity.

Blood striving for the heart is the refined process of dying. The blood, carrying carbon dioxide out of the body, is portraying the refined process of dying.

The human being streams into the cosmos on an ongoing basis in the flow of the blood. This is an event that shapes itself radically after death by seizing the entire physical being through the blood....

The Christ mystery is the revelation of the great miracle that takes place between the heart and the lungs. The cosmos becomes the human being and the human being becomes the cosmos. The Sun carries the human being out of the cosmos and onto the Earth. The Moon carries the human being from the Earth into the cosmos. In larger terms, what streams from the lungs to the heart is the human correlate of the descent of Christ onto the Earth; what moves from the heart to the lungs is the human correlate of the human being carried into the spirit world by the Christ impulse after death. Thus the secret of Golgotha lives between the heart and the lungs in each human being, in a very human, organ-related sense.

EPILOGUE

"And the Word lives in my heart"

The Heart in the Verses, Mantras, and Therapeutic Meditations of Rudolf Steiner

Preface

"One would have to write many books on these verses, if one wanted to explore the full range of implications in them. Not only is every word full of meaning, there is also the symmetry of the words, the way they are divided among the lines, the intensification from line to line, and many other elements, as well. Only lengthy, patient devotion to the matter can exhaust all that lies therein."

—Rudolf Steiner[361]

In his lecture courses, Rudolf Steiner developed the concept of a spiritual physiology connected with the human heart. He also shaped the words of the religious and sacramental texts of the Christian Community that revolve around the human heart. This was not all that Steiner accomplished in this regard. Many individuals sought him out and asked him for meditative exercises to help them on their own paths toward esoteric knowledge. The heart played an important, often central, role in these exercises. Some of these particular mantras are included in the following section, together with a number of meditations that Steiner gave directly to patients to be used as part of their therapy.[362] We no longer know the precise circumstances under which these words were written or the details of the personal situations of the recipients. Meditative contemplation of the shape and form of these words helps reveal the deeper mystery of the human heart organ. The background behind Steiner's instructions, given in his lectures, has been developed in this text. The anthropological and Christological views expounded by Aristotle and Thomas Aquinas are also very helpful in this respect. They show how we can seek a physiological interpretation of each individual statement of these "language creations" that is concrete and precise. These mantras, appearing at first glance so simple and uncomplicated, exceed every intellectual preconception when experienced through meditation. They take us directly into the highly effective spiritual sphere of the heart, into the developing spiritual world of warmth, in which the fate of the human being and Christ's healing "sun force of grace" can live.[363]

For Ita Wegman:

The hearts interpret the karma

When the hearts learn

To read the word

That forms

Human life

When the hearts learn

To speak the word

That forms

Human life*

*   Written Feb. 27, 1924. CW 40 (English trans.: *Calendar 1912–1913*.
Great Barrington, MA: SteinerBooks, 2004), p. 307. Also appears in
Wer war Ita Wegman. Eine Dokumentation [Who was Ita Wegman?: A
documentary], vol. 1. Dornach, 2000, Illust. 23.

Für Johanna Mücke

Im Herzen
Lebt ein Menschenglied
Das von allen
Stoff enthält,
der am meisten geistig ist;
Das von allen
Geistig lebt
In der Art, die am meisten
Stofflich sich offenbart.
Daher ist Sonne
Im Menschen — Weltall
Das Herz;
Daher ist im Herzen
Der Mensch
Am meisten
In seines Wesens
Tiefstem Quell. —

For Johanna Mücke:

In the heart

Lives a limb of the human being

Which holds the most spiritual

Of all materials;

Which lives

Spiritually

In the sense which

Reveals the most

Materially.

The sun is therefore

The heart

In the human universe;

In the heart

More than anywhere else

The human being is

In the deepest source

Of his being.*

*   Written Oct. 29, 1924. CW 268 (not available in English), p. 108.

Für Frau Henriette Wegman

zum 27. November 1924:

Schau ich in die Sonne,

Spricht ihr Licht mir strahlend

Von dem Geist, der gnadevoll

Durch Weltenwesen waltet.

———

Sonne du Strahlentragende,

Deines Lichtes Stoffgewalt

Zaubert Leben aus der Erde

Unermesslich reichen Tiefen.

———

Fühl' ich in mein Herz,

Spricht der Geist sein eignes Wort

Von dem Menschen, den er

Liebt durch alle Zeit und Ewigkeit

Herz, du Seelentragendes

Deines Lichtes Geistgewalt

Zaubert Leben aus der Menschen

Unermesslich tiefem Innern.

Sehen kann ich, aufwärts blicken

In der Sonne hellem Rund:

Das gewalt'ge Weltenherz.

Fühlen kann ich einwärts schauen

In des Herzens warmem Leben:

Die beseelte Menschen = Sonne

Rudolf Steiner

For Henriette Maria Wegman:

If I look into the Sun,
Its light speaks to me, shining
Of the spirit which, full of grace,
Rules through world beings.

O Sun, bearer of radiance,
The power of your light's substance
Conjures forth life out of Earth's
Immeasurably rich depths.

If I feel into my heart,
The spirit speaks its own word
Of the human being
Whom it loves through all time and eternity.

O Heart, bearer of the soul,
The spirit of your light
Conjures forth life out of the human being's
Immeasurably deep inner being.

Looking upward, I can see
In the Sun's brilliant sphere
The mighty world heart.

Looking inward, I can feel
In the heart's warm life
The ensouled human-Sun.*

---

*   Written Nov. 1924. CW 268 (not available in English), p. 109.

Mein Herz

Nimm' auf des Christus ~~Kraft~~ gnade

Erwärme meine Seele

Geist in meinem Blute

   Erleuchte meinen Geist

   Dass ich werde

~~Gesund~~

Stark und gesund

Zur Arbeit für die Welt

———————

Meine Seele   Mon âme

Empfinde des Kristus Grade   ~~Sens~~

   Von   Tu dois sentir la grâce de
~~In~~ meinem Herzen   Christ
                                   de
                            ~~Dans~~ mon coeur

Christus trägt mich   me
                              Christ tient

In des Geistes Land   Dans le pays de l'esprit

   Und giebt mir   Et me donne

Kraft zum rechten Leben   La Force pour la vraie vie

For morning meditation:

My heart

Take up the mercy of Christ

Warm my soul

Spirit in my blood

Illuminate my spirit

That I may become

Strong and healthy

To work for the world.

For evening meditation:

My soul

Sense the mercy of Christ

From my heart

Christ carries me

Into the land of the spirit

And gives me

Strength to live rightly and truly.*

* Written ca. 1924 in French and German. CW 268 (not available in English), pp. 174–175.

For a young, tired, and weakened female patient:

> In the beginning was the Word
>
> And the Word was with God
>
> And God was the Word
>
> And the Word lives in my heart.[*]

---

[*] Hilma Walter: *Die sieben Hauptmetalle* [The seven precious metals]. *Krankengeschichte* [Case history]. Dornach, 1999, p. 255.

I think about my heart

It enlivens me

It warms me

My firm trust rests

In the eternal Self

That works within me

That carries me.[*]

*   CW 268 (not available in English), p. 18.

For an exhausted, sleepless female patient with tuberculosis:

My heart

Carrier of my soul

Be a home to my Godly being

Living within me

Guiding me

Giving me light

Bringing me warmth

Through time and eternity.*

*   Written in 1924. Hilma Walter: *Die sieben Hauptmetalle* [The seven precious metals]. *Krankengeschichte* [Case history] #9, p. 318. Also in CW 268 (not available in English), p. 173.

For a patient with stenocardia:

Light of the sun

Working before me

Becoming warmth

Penetrating my heart

Streaming through me

I exist

In warmth*

*   *Meditationen für Patienten* [Meditations for patients] A 27; also in
       CW 268 (not available in English), p. 163.

In me the power of warmth

I feel the power of warmth,

Which permeates me

Permeates from my head right through my heart

Through my entire body

I feel myself entirely warmed, through and through.[*]

For a patient with a blood disorder, high blood pressure, and
"blood pounding too hard against the breathing system"
(Rudolf Steiner):

> Within me I feel myself
>
> Godly power takes hold of me
>
> Within the sphere of my existence
>
> I take hold of Godly power
>
> In the middle of my heart
>
> And I find my spirit.
>
> Granting peace, peace, peace
>
> To my God-seeking soul.*

---

*   *Meditationen für Patienten* [Meditations for patients].
    Krankengeschichte [Case history] V / 47.

For a sleepless female patient with a chill, pounding heart, and digestive difficulties:

I sink deep into my inner self

I take the power of my heart

And send it into my hands

I take the power of my heart

And send it into my feet.*

---

*   *Meditationen für Patienten* [Meditations for patients]. *Krankengeschichte* [Case history] II / 44.

For a young, emaciated female patient who tires quickly,
with digestive difficulties and a "troubled astral life":

For morning meditation:

> In my heart
> Lives the strength
> Which enlivens me.
> If I take hold of that strength
> With my will
> It will carry me
> In health
> Through life.

For evening meditation:

> If I look around me
> I see the acts of the light
> Of the sun
> If I look within myself
> I see the spirit will
> Of my soul.
> I am in the spirit
> The spirit is in the light.*

---

*   Hilma Walter: *Die sieben Hauptmetalle* [The Seven precious metals].
Krankengeschichte [Case history] #113, p. 319.

For a sick person with chronic knee pain, but normalized organic test results:

I take the pain

From the left side of my body

I take the pain

From the right side of my body

I carry the pain upward

And transform it in my heart

Because I am strong in the center of my being.*

---

*　　*Meditationen für Patienten* [Meditations for patients].
Krankengeschichte [Case history] I / 15.

For a restless female patient with heart troubles, sleep difficulties, and dizziness. The first line is recited while focusing on the left foot, the second while focusing on the right foot, the third while focusing on the left hand, and the fourth while focusing on the right hand:

My "I" carries me

My "I" holds me

My "I" protects me

My "I" defends itself

Strength to carry my burdens

Strength to carry on

Protection and defense

I bind these four

Into One

In my heart*

*   Written in 1924. *Meditationen für Patienten* [Meditations for patients] A 24; also in Ludwig Engel: *Patientenvorstellungen in Koberwitz* [Imaginations for patients in Koberwitz] which appeared in *Rundbrief der Medizinischen Sektion* [Newsletter of the Medical Section]. No. 19 / 1996, pp.. 224–25; and CW 268 (not available in English), p. 183.

For a 12-year-old child with epileptic episodes
and one-sided paralysis:

> In my heart I find strength
>
> In my head I find sense
>
> When I remember this
>
> I can fortify myself.
>
> In all my limbs I do this, do this with all my power.[*]

---

[*]   *Meditationen für Patienten* [Meditations for patients] III/102.

Ich fühle in meinem Kopf
Warme Liebekraft
Ich fühle in meinem Herzen
Leuchtende Gedankenmacht,
Die warme Liebekraft
Vereint sich mit der
leuchtenden Gedankenmacht
Davon werden stark
meine Hände
Zu gutem menschlichem Wirken.
Ich fühle mich

Bergsma

Photocopy of the verse opposite in Rudolf Steiner's handwriting.
(Ita Wegman Archiv, Arlesheim)

In my head I feel

The warm power of love

In my heart I feel

The illuminating process of thought,

The warm power of love

Unites itself with

The illuminating process of thought

Through this

My hands become strong

For doing good works for others.

I feel myself.*

*   CW 268 (not available in English), p. 164.

For a 15-year-old girl with epileptic episodes:

I sit

I stand up

I take three steps

I stand firmly on my left foot

With my left leg

I stand firmly on my right foot

With my right leg

I lean on this pillar of strength

My heart is strong and supple.*

*   *Meditationen für Patienten* [Meditations for patients].
Krankengeschichte [Case history] III/104.

Rezept für ....

Es scheinen die Sterne

Es ist Nacht

Es füllt Ruhe den Raum

Alles schweigt

Ich fühle die Ruhe

Ich fühle das Schweigen

In meinem Herzen

In meinem Kopf

Stuttgart, den...................................

Gott spricht Christus spricht.

Photocopy of the original verse in Steiner's handwriting on a sheet from a prescription pad. (Stuttgart, 1924)

For a sleepless boy with severe eye injuries:

The stars shine

It is night

Silence fills the room

Everything is silent

I feel the peace

I feel the silence

In my heart

In my head

God speaks

Christ speaks.*

---

*   Nik Fiechter: *Eine Heilmeditation für ein Kind* [Healing meditation for
     a child]. In *Mitteilungen aus der anthroposophischen Arbeit in Deutsch-
     land* 131/1980, p. 43; also in Antonij Degenaar: *Krankheitsfälle und
     andere medizinische Fragen, besprochen mit Dr. Rudolf Steiner* [Cases
     of illness and other medical questions, discussed with Dr. Rudolf Steiner].
     Krankengeschichte [Case history], pp. 15f. (without the text for medita-
     tion); and in CW 268 (not available in English), p. 171.

For a very ill male patient:

O spirit of God, fulfill me

Fulfill me in my soul;

My soul be given great power,

Great power be given unto my heart

My heart, seeking you,

Seeking with deep longing

Deep longing for health

For health and courageous strength,

Courageous strength into my limbs is streaming

Streaming like a noble gift of God

God's gift from you, O spirit of God,

O spirit of God fulfill me.*

*   Written in 1924. *Meditationen für Patienten* [Meditations for patients]
     AI; also in CW 268 (not available in English), p. 181.

Herzen, die lieben
Sonnen, die wärmen
Ihr Wegespuren Christi
In des Vaters Weltenall
Euch rufen wir aus eigner Brust
Euch suchen wir im eignen Geist
O, strebet zu ihm.

Menschenherzen – Strahlen
Andachtwarmes Sehnen
Ihr Heimatstätten Christi
In des Vaters Erdenhaus
Euch rufen wir aus eigner Brust
Euch suchen wir im eignen Geist
O, lebet bei ihm.

Strahlende Menschenliebe,
Wärmender Sonnenglanz
Ihr Seelenkleider Christi
In des Vaters Menschentempel
Euch rufen wir aus eigner Brust
Euch suchen wir im eignen Geist
O, helfet in ihm.

Facsimile of the original in Steiner's handwriting. (Dornach, 1925)

*For the spiritual circle of friends of a very ill male patient,
for communal mediation:*

Hearts which love
Suns which warm
Traces of Christ's path
In the universe of the Father
We call you out of our own breast
We seek you in our own spirit
O reach for him.

Rays of the human heart
Longing warm with devotion
Resting places of Christ
In the Father's earthly home
We call you out of our own breast
We seek you in our own spirit
O live with him.

Human love beaming
Bright sun warming
Soul clothing of Christ
In the human temple of the Father
We call you out of our own breast
We seek you in our own spirit
O help in him.[*]

---

[*] *Meditationen für Patienten* [Meditation for patients] A9; also in Peter
Selg: *Krankheit und Christus-Erkenntnis* [Seeing Christ in sickness and
healing], Dornach, 2003, p. 50 (facsimile); and in CW 268 (not available
in English), p. 194.

For a dying person:

Before me

Far in the distance

Stands a star.

It comes ever closer

Spirit-being,

Send me starlight

In your love.

The star dives

Into my own heart.

It fills my heart with love

The love in my heart

Becomes in my soul

The power of love.

I know that

With this love

I can overcome

The burden of my body.*

---

*   *Meditationen für Patienten* [Meditations for patients] A6; also in CW
268 (not available in English), pp. 90–91.

To meditate for someone who has died:

May the warm life of my heart

Stream toward your soul

To warm you if you are cold

To cool you if you are hot

In the spirit worlds

May my thoughts live in yours

And your thoughts live in mine.*

---

* Written in 1924. *Notizbuch* [Notebook], 1924; CW 268 (not available in English), p. 219.

153

Notes

1   W. U. Klünker, in *Das Goetheanum* [The Goetheanum], no. 14/2004, p. 12. (For more on the positive valuation of and necessary corrections to Klünker's own work on Thomas, see endnotes 126, 189, and 227, among others, in this volume.)

2   In a sense, it would indeed be interesting to take an even broader look at these matters. That goes without saying. However, a more extensive exploration of the history of these ideas would have taken us beyond the scope of this book. Its specific intention and spiritual substance are dedicated to a central incarnation motif of Rudolf Steiner's lifelong work. The description you will read on the following pages is not primarily the developmental history of a specific idea of the heart. Nor does it tell of the world's reaction to that idea. It describes, instead, the threefold form of a groundbreaking project in spiritual research.

3   "I believe that Rudolf Steiner would be pleased with a book like this." *Das Goetheanum* [The Goetheanum], issue 14/2004, p. 13.

4   Rudolf Steiner: *Menschliches Seelenleben und Geistesstreben im Zusammenhange mit Welt- und Erdentwicklung* [Human soul life and spiritual striving in connection with the development of the world and the earth]. *Gesamtausgabe* [Complete edition], vol. 212 (not available in English). Dornach ²1998, p. 126 (Rudolf Steiner's writings will be cited according to the number assigned to them in the Complete Edition in German [or CW, the Complete Works], referring to the most recent edition of each volume. Page numbers refer to the German editions).

5   Rudolf Steiner, CW 74 (English trans.: *The Redemption of Thinking: A Study in the Philosophy of Thomas Aquinas*. Hudson, NY: Anthroposophic Press, 1983), p. 108.

6   Ibid., p. 101.

7   Josef Pieper (*Thomas von Aquin: Leben und Werk* [Thomas Aquinas: Life and Work]), among others, spoke indirectly about the commonalities of the views of Goethe and Thomas Aquinas with regard to the cognitive theory of a selfless awareness of reality. Karl Schlechta completed a profound study on the important relatedness of the contextual and epistemological work of Goethe and Aristotle thirteen years after Rudolf Steiner's death. (*Goethe in seinem Verhältnis zu Aristoteles: Ein Versuch* [Goethe's relationship to Aristotle: an attempt]. Frankfurt, 1938). These placed the more limited preliminary studies of Peter Petersen in a broader context (*Goethe and Aristotle*. Hamburg, 1914).

A decade after Schlechta, Adolph Meyer-Abich said that "Plato or Aristotle...would have conducted natural research just as he [Goethe] had, had the humanities been at the same point in their time" (*Biologie der Goethezeit* [Biology in Goethe's era]. Stuttgart, 1949, p. 24). With regard to Goethe's own background, in terms of fate, see Rudolf Steiner's lectures from June 1 and 9, 1924, CWs 239 and 240 [English trans.: *Karmic Relationships: Esoteric Studies*, vols. 5 and 6. London: Rudolf Steiner Press, 2011, 2009]. In addition, we should not overlook the fact that Steiner had already pointed out similarities in the approaches of Aristotle and Goethe in his writings on Goethe's worldview, published in 1897: "If Western philosophy had built upon a proper understanding of Aristotle's [idea-realistic] view, it would have protected itself from a situation in which Goethe's world view appeared to be an aberration." In this text Steiner had also mentioned the false understanding of Aristotle held by various Christian intellectuals in the Middle Ages, holding up Thomas Aquinas as a most positive exception to the rule: "Thomas Aquinas, the important Christian intellectual, was the first to attempt to weave the thoughts of Aristotle into the Christian development of ideas to the extent that this was possible in his era." (CW 6 [English trans.: *Goethe's World View*, Spring Valley, NY: Mercury Press, 1985], pp. 34–5).

8   Ibid., p. 92.

9   Ibid., pp. 92f.

10   Paul Celan, *Gesammelte Werke* [Collected Works], vol. 2. Frankfurt, 1986, p. 50.

11   Cited in Josef Pieper, *Thomas von Aquin: Leben und Werk* [Thomas Aquinas: Life and Work].

12   Ibid., p. 34.

13   Ibid., p. 84.

14   Ibid., p. 73.

15   Ibid., p. 71.

16   See also the excellent doctoral dissertation by Thomas Fuchs: *Die Mechanisierung des Herzens. Harvey und Descartes—der vitale und der mechanische Aspekt des Kreislaufs* [The Mechanization of the Heart. Harvey and Descartes—The Living and Mechanical Aspect of the Circulation of the Blood]. Frankfurt, 1992.

17   To read more about Steiner's early thematic work on the heart in his anthroposophical and physiological writings, see the outstanding overview written by Herbert Sieweke in 1948: *Die Ausgestaltung der Herzanschauung im Lebenswerke Rudolf Steiners* [The Shaping of Rudolf Steiner's View of the Heart] (found in the *Ärzte-Rundbrief* [Physician's Newsletter], year 2, vol. I/2, pp. 24–38) and Peter Selg: *Vom Logos menschlicher Physis. Die Entfaltung einer anthroposophischen Humanphysiologie im Werk Rudolf Steiners* [On the Logos of Human Physiology. The Unfolding of an Anthroposophical Human Physiology in the Work of Rudolf Steiner] (Dornach, ¹2000, esp. pp. 164f., 226ff.,

524ff., and 687ff.). Peter Selg first brought up several points of view on the subject in his essay "'Es keimet die Seele in des Herzens Schrein.' Das Herz als Schicksals-Organ" ["The Soul Germinates in the Shrine of the Heart." The Heart as the Organ of Destiny], and developed these points more fully in the volume you hold in your hands. (Found in Peter Selg: *Krankheit und Christus-Erkenntnis* [Illness and the Knowledge of Christ]. Dornach, 2003, pp. 109ff.)

18 Also see the extensive publication by Georg Berkemer and Guido Rappe: *Das Herz im Kulturvergleich* [The Heart: A Cultural Comparison] (Berlin, 1995). Rudolf Steiner's teachings on the heart are not mentioned at all in this work, nor are the preliminary Aristotelian and Thomistic works, written on genuinely European soil. Nor will you find any consideration of Steiner's contributions in the historically focused monographs on the heart cited in endnotes 34, 274, and 275. Neither their spiritual connection to the Christology of the New Testament nor their anthropological aspects, which were introduced by Aristotle and Thomas Aquinas (and completely suppressed and supplanted in the meantime), were ever noticed or adequately appreciated.

19 These same [things] focus, for the most part, on advice for the advanced scholarly study of [pastoral and] medical human anthropology, and enhance the portrayals of the current text somewhat, thematically, without unduly overloading the main text (particularly with regard to the lesser-known anthropological viewpoints in the thinking of Aristotle and Thomas Aquinas). Very seldom, on the other hand, do we find a reference in them to the spiritual-scientific interconnections between the positions of Aristotle and Thomas Aquinas and the further work done by Rudolf Steiner on the same issues. Such references are seen, in fact, only when they are absolutely logical and necessary for a more complete understanding of the content. For anyone who is truly familiar with Steiner's work, the thematic and content-related connections between the extensive physiological and anthropological (but also epistemological and methodological) viewpoints of Aristotle and Thomas and those of Steiner's anthroposophical anthropology, formulated many centuries later, are highly apparent, detailed, and profuse. Should these readers wish to explore individual themes more extensively from Steiner's point of view, such as the formation of human experience and memory, or the concept of warmth, I would like to direct them to the corresponding chapters of my book, *Vom Logos menschlicher Physis. Die Entfaltung einer anthroposophischen Humanphysiologie im Werk Rudolf Steiners* [On the Logos of Human Physiology. The Unfolding of an Anthroposophical Human Physiology in the Work of Rudolf Steiner] (Dornach, ¹2000). It seemed crucial to me to call attention to some notable publications on the biography and work of Aristotle and Thomas Aquinas in several of these endnotes. These would be helpful for further independent study on these subjects. On the whole, however, the straightforward and accessible text of this

work can stand on its own and may be studied as an independent text, resisting the temptation to become distracted by a myriad of different individual viewpoints.

20   On Easter in the year 1269, six years before his death, Thomas Aquinas wrote: "During the construction of the spiritual building there are manual laborers, so to speak, who care for souls by administering the sacraments and performing similar tasks. It is actually the bishops who are paving the way for this foundational work, however, as they command and decree how each man should be carrying out his work. For this reason, they are called Episcopi, or 'those who preside.' In this same way, theologians are laying the foundational stones as they do research and teach others how they should convey the teachings on the well-being and salvation of the soul. In an absolute sense it is better and more productive (if done with good intentions) to teach the Holy Scripture than to devote oneself to saving the soul of this or that particular person. It is for this reason that the apostle says, 'Christ sent me not to baptize, but rather to proclaim the Gospel' (I Cor. 1:17), although baptizing would contribute more to the salvation of souls; and in II Timothy 2:2 the same apostle says, 'To the believers you should recommend those who are able to teach others'" (*Quodlibet I*, vol. 7, no. 2 [publication of the Society of Online Christian Theology and Philosophy]). In these words, though they may seem disconcerting at first glance, the self-image of the master, Thomas Aquinas, is expressed: a man who bore great respect for the pastoral work and lives of his fellow priests; yet who lived his whole life, even to the point of exhaustion, occupied with spiritual research and teaching. He turned down every offer of higher office within the Dominican order, always careful to avoid neglecting or endangering his own essential work. He was convinced of its value and importance. (For more on this topic, see Jean-Pierre Torrell: *Magister Thomas* [Master Thomas]. Freiburg, 1995.) It should also be taken into consideration that (as he wrote in a commentary on Dionysius) Thomas himself held this to be the greatest pastoral deed one could perform for another human being: leading someone from an errant path into the way of truth [*ab errore ad veritatem* (see *Commentaria in Dionysii. De divinis nominibus* [Commentary on Dionysius. Divine names] 13, lecture 4, no. 1006). We should think a bit more deeply about how effective Thomas was in advancing the spiritual and cultural development of the western world, because of his single-minded devotion to his cognitive work and teaching. We would see how crucial his spiritual intention was, and take note of how very much we owe to this man. This would place the ostensibly problematic radical nature of his statements in an entirely different light—one worth considering in future topics of debate, as well. At the beginning of the 1980s, anthroposophic physician and lecturer in neurology and psychiatry, Gerhard Kienle (1923–1983), was still planning to establish a theological professorship at the private university he founded at

Witten-Herdecke. He often brought up the idea of the essential work to be done at the university. Not only were Christian Community priests to be trained, but they would then be able to take up theological and Christological foundational work done by Steiner and expand upon his work, conceptually, placing it in a broader spiritual-scientific context, and making it accessible to all of modern humanity. (For more on Gerhard Kienle, see Peter Selg's volume *Gerhard Kienle. Leben und Werk* [Life and work], 2 vols. Dornach, 2003.) In the words of Rudolf Steiner, "We dare not trust the illusion that it will ever really be possible to carry on a religious movement that is truly separate from contemporary cultural life; specifically, truly separate from the scientific beliefs held by a particular culture at a particular time" (CW 345, p. 25 [Lectures and Courses on Christian Religious Work, vol. 4; not available in English]).

21   "That is the ultimate goal we are trying to attain: the ability to take the Bible literally. One could almost say: He who cannot yet take the Bible literally has no true comprehension of the passages that he cannot take literally. To be sure, this is the case with many people in these modern times" (CW 346, p. 59 [English trans.: *The Book of Revelation: And the Work of the Priest*. London: Rudolf Steiner Press, 2008]).

22   The passages from the Gospels (here and throughout this volume) are taken from the translation done by Heinrich Ogilvie (Stuttgart, 1996). Crucial passages are also cited from the Latin Vulgate (according to Nestle-Aland: *Novum Testamentum Graece et Latine* [Greek and Latin New Testament]. Stuttgart, 2002). In various modern translations [of the Gospels] into German, we see mentions made of the "heart" that cannot be found in the original Greek and Latin texts. (This happens only very seldom with Ogilvie's translation; for instance in Luke 22:15.) If it is conceivable that the concept of the heart bears a spiritual-physiological foundation within itself that goes far beyond the metaphorical, such unexplained "appearances" of the word in the translations are highly problematic.

23   In his speech on Pentecost (Acts 2:26), fifty days after Christ's death, Peter reminded his listeners of the words of David (Psalm 16:8ff.), though Peter was referring unambiguously to Christ: "I see the Lord always before my face, for he is on my right hand, that I should not be moved. Therefore did my heart rejoice, and my tongue was glad; moreover also my flesh shall rest in hope" (*Providebam Dominum coram me semper, quoniam a dextris meis est, ne commovear. Propter hoc laetatum est cor meum, et exsultavit lingua mea*).

24   In Mark, as in Matthew, the word of Christ is repeated, that Moses would consider an official divorce only in cases of an objectively provable "hardening of the heart" of the husbands in question; and in cases where the wives had been abandoned, or where abandonment could no longer be prevented. "And the Pharisees came to him, and asked him, Is it lawful for a man to divorce his wife? tempting him. And he answered and said unto them, What did Moses command you? And

they said, Moses suffered to write a bill of divorce, and to leave her. And Jesus answered and said unto them, For the hardness of your heart he wrote you this precept. But from the beginning of the creation God made them male and female. For this cause shall a man leave his father and mother, and cleave to his wife; And the two shall be one flesh: so then they are no more apart, but one flesh. What therefore God hath joined together, let not man put asunder (Gen. 1:27 and 2:24). And in the house his disciples asked him again of the same matter. And he said unto them, Whosoever shall divorce his wife, and marry another, commits adultery against her" (Mark 10:2–11; compare also Matt. 19:8).

25   Before Matthew was chosen (which meant a decision not to choose Joseph), the Apostles prayed to Christ with these words: "And they prayed, and said, Thou, Lord, who knowest the hearts of all men [*Tu, Domine, qui corda nosti omnium*], show which of these two thou hast chosen, that he may take part in this ministry and apostleship, from which Judas by transgression fell and departed, that he might go to his own place" (Acts 1:24,25).

26   It is possible for ungodly forces (according to the testimony of the Gospel of Luke) to "take away" or even "destroy" the words in our hearts, which were originally godly and spiritual, so that no inner connection arises between these positive words and the human will (*"deinde venit Diabolus et tollit verbum de corde eorum, ne credentes salvi fiant"* [Luke 8:12]).

27   According to the testimony of three writers of the Gospels (Matthew, Mark, and Luke), Christ answered the question (about which "law" takes priority) by referring to the words of the Old Testament from Deut. 6:5: "And thou shalt love the Lord thy God with all thy heart, and with all thy soul, and with all thy might [*Diliges DominumDeum tuum ex toto corde tuo et ex tota anima tua at ex tota mente tuaet ex tota virtute tua*]" (Mark 12:30, as well as Matt. 23:37 and Luke 10:27).

28   A passage in Matthew indicates that, because of the processes of the heart, not only actions that we have already performed, but even *intended* actions and efforts have a decided effectiveness: "Ye have heard that it was said by them in ancient times, Thou shalt not commit adultery: But I say unto you, That whosoever looketh on a woman to lust after her hath committed adultery with her already in his heart [*Omnis, qui viderit mulierem ad concupiscendum eam, iam moechatus est eam in corde suo*]" (Matt. 5:27,28). Physical actions and soul-spiritual processes are not only completed with the help of the heart, but have an actual, decisive affect on the heart, which is suggested in Luke 21:34: "And take heed unto yourselves, lest at any time your hearts be overcharged with surfeiting, and drunkenness, and the cares of this life (*attendite autem vobis, ne fortegraventur corda vestra in crapula et ebrietate et curis huius vitae*), and so that day of destruction come upon you unawares. For as a snare shall it come on all them that dwell on the face of the whole Earth."

29   In light of this, we should also take into consideration that Christ, with a humble heart (Matt. 11:29), merged his fate with that of the earth, in[to] whose heart (*in corde terrae*) he penetrated for the three days in Golgotha (Matt. 12:40). The disciples working with him were taken up into his loving heart-sphere during those three years on earth. The parting speeches of John tell us of this central, heart-focused phenomenon (see John 14:1 and 14:27: "Let not your heart be troubled, neither let it be afraid"; and John 16:7 and 16:22: "I will see you again, and your heart shall rejoice"). As the season of Pentecost began, it marked the beginning of a period of enhanced effectiveness for these disciples. This effectiveness was largely carried by the Christological Logos forces of the heart. It soon experienced an even broader expansion. The Acts of the Apostles' account of Peter's speech on Pentecost explicitly mentions that their words touched the hearts of the people of Jerusalem who were present that day (Acts 2:37).

30   For more on the subject, see the excellent and not yet fully appreciated work by Gerhard Kienle: *Die ungeschriebene Philosophie Jesu. Entwurf zu einer Rekonstruktion* [The Unwritten Philosophy of Jesus. An Attempted Reconstruction] (reprinted in Peter Selg's *Gerhard Kienle: Leben und Werk* [Gerhard Kienle: life and work], vol. 2. Dornach 2003, pp. 387–458). In this work, Kienle establishes the extent to which the New Testament builds upon the philosophical thought of Ancient Greece, and serves as a logical extension of that philosophical direction in an epistemological, scientific, and anthropological sense.

31   CW 312, pp. 115f. (English trans.: *Introducing Anthroposophical Medicine*. Great Barrington, MA: SteinerBooks, 2010).

32   See also Konrad Gaiser: *Platons ungeschriebene Lehre* [The unwritten teachings of Plato]. Stuttgart, 1962.

33   Even the historical portrayal written by Paolo Bavastros in the anthroposophical book *The Human Heart* does not differ from more conventional papers on this topic in any significant way in its references to ancient "views" (*Das Herz des Menschen* [The human heart]. Stuttgart, 1999, ed. by Paolo Bavastro and Hans Christoph Kümmell, pp. 16–26).

34   Ernst Wilhelm Eschmann presented a remarkable and original outline of pre-Christian "heart-thought" in his 1966 monograph entitled *Das Herz in Kult und Glauben* [The heart in cultural thought and belief]. The book describes the insights about the heart achieved in ancient, spiritually advanced civilizations. With regard to Babylon, for example, Eschmann shows (in a fascinating way) how the hearts of humans, gods, and animals were ascribed a vital, central meaning in the early Sumerian epics. This began with Ishtar's descent into hell, three to four thousand years BCE, and is also to be found in the epic of Gilgamesh, which appeared later. Gilgamesh's heart, rejoicing over Enkidu, placed demands that were too heavy, according to the elders of Ur. Doubts crept into his heart when he glimpsed the giants keeping watch. Later,

his heart was "full of lamentations" following the death of Enkidu, and became a site filled with the fear of death and pointless struggles ("my heart's blood was spilled in vain"). In the end, however, his heart was able to affirm his earthly, active destiny, coping with obstacles and achieving mastery over his path in life, including his kingly tasks, up to and including the building of the wall in Ur: "Gilgamesh's heart beat, full of pride." At decisive points in the Babylonian texts, the heart appears as the sensing, knowing center of soul-spiritual life. In early Indian literature, mention was made of the prayers of the people "penetrating into the hearts" of the gods, and how those prayers were borne by the comprehension and insight of the hearts of humanity. The love of one human for another was understood and expressed as the anointing "of one heart with many hearts." Over and above that, in the oldest religious texts of China, the heart figures as the foremost among the physiological organs in the human being. This is shown with a clarity and complexity we rarely see elsewhere. The heart is shown to be the ruler of the body, as well the origin and location of consciousness and spiritual life. In addition, the heart provides the body with its will and driving forces; a process in which the organs of the metabolic system (such as the liver, stomach, and kidneys) also take part, and are also assigned specific roles. The understanding of the heart shown in the Egyptian mysteries reaches yet another step deeper. A heart prayer from the second millennium BCE took on lasting form when inscribed on a stone scarab. The scarab had been set in the place of the heart (which had been removed) in the embalmed body of a deceased person. The text: "O heart, that I received from my mother! O heart, integral part of my being! Do not testify against me, or oppose me before the judges, or take a stand against me when I face the Master of the Scales [when the weight of wrongdoings in my heart is weighed against a feather after my death]. You are the spirit in my body. Do not let our name sink down. Do not tell lies against me before the god." Here the heart organ is clearly shown to be connected with the selfhood of the person, and stands as a symbol of the individual, eternal, immortal self. "Mastering the heart in the afterworld ensures the resurrection of the body, which was the primary wish and hope of the ancient Egyptians, and the reason for their extensive, careful preparations and practices before and during their burial ceremonies" (Eschmann, p. 16). This same information is contained in various figures of speech of the ancient Egyptian language. Someone who was on the wrong path, spiritually or morally, was said to have a "confused" heart; or it was said of him that "his heart was not with him." In the early Indian Vedas and Upanishads, there was already thought to be a corresponding spiritual dimension to the heart. As Eschmann very convincingly worked out, the heart is spoken of as a spiritual organ in these texts. The human being can start a "fire" in the heart, in the spiritual-physiological sense; and in doing so, bring himself as a sacrifice to his higher self (and thereby also to the deities). According to the Vedas and Upanishads, the central core of divinity possessed its true center of incarnation within the human heart. The organ itself then takes on a creating, transforming, and forming character. There, in the "ether of the heart," the divine lives "in deepest slumber" in a "hollow space" sheltering the universe. It is there that the human being and the world become one. "Manas, the spiritual power of the divine, divided into infinitely tiny pieces within our individual bodies and throughout the world, generates warmth in the body. Out of this arises the breath, and from the breath the Om-sound is created in the heart. It rises up to the throat and the lungs, becoming progressively more powerful with each step, until it becomes the 'sound of the heart' and 'matrix' of the world; the voice at the center of everything, the 'womb,' literally 'mátrikam'" (Eschmann, pp. 55f). In addition, in Eschmann's cultural-historical studies, he makes note of the fact that from very early times, the heart was seen to stand in significant relationship to the sun; "and that is equally, surprisingly true in the most disparate cultures, no matter how far distant they might have been from one another." To exemplify this, he wrote, "Ishtar, whose love was scorned by Gilgamesh, sent the Bull of Heaven to earth as revenge, where it destroyed the fields and oppressed the people. Gilgamesh and his friend slayed the bull, tore out its heart, and brought it as a sacrifice to the sun god. On the most important holiday in ancient Mexico, the priest stood on the highest temple pyramid and tore the living heart out of a prisoner of war or sacrificed slave, and held it up to the sun. The connection of the heart to the sun appears in its mildest, healing form when its metal, gold, was and is used to heal sick or weakened hearts" (Eschmann, p. 23). To examine the larger cultural-historical context of the questions and issues about the heart raised by Eschmann, and their relationship to the history of consciousness, see (in addition to other texts) the extensive work already brought up in endnote 15: *Das Herz im Kulturvergleich* [The heart: a cultural comparison] (Berlin, 1995) by Georg Berkemer and Guido Rappe. In that work, additional aspects of the historical views on the heart from China, Japan, India, and Egypt; and also from Timor and the Aztecs, are introduced and discussed in a preliminary way in light of the phenomenology of the body proposed by Hermann Schmitz, a philosopher from Kiel. To my knowledge, there has never been a systematic, exhaustive study of the anthropology of the heart as portrayed in the Old Testament, although I consider this to be an urgent task.

35   On this topic, see also the excellent work by Bruno Snell, *Die Entdeck-ung des Geistes. Studien zur Entstehung des europäischen Denkens bei den Griechen* [The discovery of the spirit. Studies on the origin of European thought] (Hamburg, 1946); by Wolfgang Schadewaldt, *Die Anfänge der Philosophie bei den Griechen* [The beginnings of philosophy among the Greeks] (Frankfurt, 1978); and by Karl-Martin

Dietz, *Metamorphosen des Geistes. Das Erwachen des europäischen Denkens* [Metamorphoses of the spirit. The awakening of European thought] (3 vols., Stuttgart, 1988–1990).

36   As cited by Wilhelm Capelle (ed.) in *Die Vorsokratiker* [The Presocratics]. Stuttgart, 1968, p. 234.

37   "He who lets himself be initiated into the mysteries should not learn something, but rather experience something. He should let himself be put into a mood which makes him receptive, assuming that he is capable of that in the first place" (Aristotle: *Fragmentum* [Fragment] 15; cited by J.-M. Zemb: *Aristoteles* [Aristotle]. Hamburg, 2002, p. 147). When studied from our current state of academic knowledge and awareness, it is apparent that Plato and Aristotle were initiated into the Elysian mysteries, at the very least. According to Lauenstein (*Die Mysterien von Eleusis* [The Elysian mysteries]. Stuttgart, 1987, pp. 12ff.), thirteen of Plato's forty written works grant us a deep and substantial glimpse into the Elysian world ("And [Plato] alludes to it in nearly every work" [Zemb, p. 12]). Aristotle wrote a text on that subject specifically, but it was lost in medieval Byzantium. Rudolf Steiner, on the other hand, stressed Plato and Aristotle's training in the Elysian and Chthonian [pertaining to the underworld, from Greek khthonios, of the earth] mysteries, which led them to a deep and esoteric knowlege of the natural world (see CW 232 [*Mystery Knowledge and Mystery Centres.* London: Rudolf Steiner Press, 1997], lecture of Dec. 15, 1923). He also pointed out Aristotle's familiarity with the Samothracian mysteries of the Cabiri (CW 232, as above, and CW 233, lecture of Dec. 27, 1923, and CW 233a ["Mystery Sites of the Middle Ages"; not available in English], lecture of Apr. 22, 1924). Steiner also emphasized that Aristotle's individuality from the most recent previous incarnation had been initiated into the high mysteries of Ephesus (see CW 233 [*World History and the Mysteries.* London: Rudolf Steiner Press, 1997], lecture of Dec. 26, 1923 and CW 233a, lecture of Apr. 22, 1924). We see the resonances of these decidedly concrete initiation experiences used to great effect in many of Aristotle's teachings. Concerning Aristotle's cosmology and teachings on the elements, see the remarks in CW 233, lecture of Dec. 27, 1923; for more on the concepts of form and matter, see the remarks in CW 233a, lecture of Jan. 12, 1924. With regard to the cathartic aspect of Greek tragedy, see the early interpretations in CW 126 [*Occult History: Historical Personalities and Events in the Light of Spiritual Science.* London: Rudolf Steiner Press, 1982], lecture of Dec. 29, 1910. There are many other related lectures, as well.

38   "The heart, the knot of the veins and the fountain of the blood that races through all the limbs was set in the place of guard; that when the might of passion was roused by reason, making proclamation of any wrong assailing them from without, or being perpetrated by the desires within; quickly the whole power of feeling in the body, perceiving these commands and threats, might obey and follow through every turn and

alley; and thus allow the principle of the best to have the command in all of them. But the gods, foreknowing that the palpitation of the heart in the expectation of danger; and the swelling and excitement of passion caused by fire; formed and implanted as a supporter to the heart, the lung, which was, in the first place, soft and bloodless; and also had within it hollows like the pores of a sponge; in order that by receiving the breath and the drink, it might give coolness and the power of respiration and alleviate the heat. Wherefore they cut the air channels leading to the lung, and placed the lung about the heart as a soft spring; that, when passion was rife within, the heart, beating against a yielding body, might be cooled and suffer less; and might thus become more ready to join with passion in the service of reason" (Plato: *Timaeus.* Trans. by B. Jowett in 1871).

39   Plato developed his theory on motion in the major dialogues *Laws* and *Timaeus.* An excellent interpretation of these central aspects of Plato's philosophy was written in 1962 by Konrad Gaiser in his professorship treatise (*Platons ungeschriebene Lehre* [Plato's unwritten theory]. Stuttgart, 1962, pp. 173–201).

40   Aristotle, *Über die Glieder der Geschöpfe* [On the limbs of the creatures]. In *Werke* [Works], vol. 3, p. 65. Ed. by Ernst Grumach and Hellmuth Flashar, Darmstadt, 1985.

41   The monumental work of Ingemar Düring offers the best available guide to the life and entire collected works of Aristotle. It offers an extensive, scientifically meticulous, nevertheless exceptionally readable evaluation of the collected works (Ingemar Düring, *Aristoteles. Darstellung und Interpretation seines Denkens* [Aristotle. The Presentation and Interpretation of His Thought]. Heidelberg, 1966). Werner Jaeger's pioneering publication *Aristoteles. Grundlegung einer Geschichte seiner Entwicklung* [Aristotle. Fundamentals of the History of His Development], although now outdated with regard to some individual details, is still of great importance. The first edition appeared in Berlin during Rudolf Steiner's lifetime, in 1923. The volume attempted not only to introduce the development of the history of ideas as found in the views of Aristotle; but also to show the unusual intensity of the situation in which he found himself at Plato's Academy; and to illuminate the range of ideas to which he subsequently devoted his life's work. "As everywhere, we will achieve true insight only when we observe the development of things from their origins onward" (Aristotle). In considering the theory of the heart developed by Aristotle, and the aspects of natural philosophy connected with it in the narrower sense, we must refer to his original writings, particularly to *De anima* [On the Soul]; *Historia animalium* [Natural History of Animals]; *De generatio animalium* [On the Origin of Animals]; *De partibus animalium* [On the Limbs/Parts of Animals]; *De somno et vigilia* [On Sleep and Waking]; *De sensu et sensato* [On Sensing and the Objects Sensed]; *De memoria* [On Memory and Remembrance]; *De longaevitate* [On Longevity and

the Brevity of Life]; *De juventute et senectute, de vita et morte* [On Youth and Old Age, Life and Death]; *De respiratione* [On Breathing]; and *De insomniis* [On the Interpretation of Dreams]. The citations that follow in the rest of this text are taken from the translations into the German done by Willy Theiler (*Über die Seele* [On the Soul]. In *Aristotle. Philosophische Schriften in sechs Bänden* [Philosophical Writings in Six Volumes], vol. 6. Hamburg, 1995), Eugen Dönt (*Über die Wahrnehmung und die Gegenstände der Wahrnehmung* [On Sensing and the Objects Sensed]; *Über Gedächtnis und Erinnerung* [On Memory and Remembrance]; *Über Schlaf und Wachen* [On Sleep and Waking]; *Über Träume* [On Dreams]; *Über Traumdeutung* [On the Interpretation of Dreams]; *Über die Länge und Kürze des Lebens* [On Longevity and the Brevity of Life]; *Über Jugend und Alter, Leben und Tod* [On Youth and Old Age, Life and Death]; *Über die Atmung* [On Breathing]. In *Aristoteles. Parva Naturalia.* Stuttgart, 1997), Jutta Kollesch (*Über die Bewegung der Lebewesen* [On Movement in Living Beings]; *Über die Fortbewegung der Lebewesen* [On the Gait of Living Beings]. In *Aristoteles. Werke* [Works], ed. by Ernst Grumach and Hellmuth Flashar, vol. 17: *Zoologische Schriften* II [Zoological Writings II]. Darmstadt, 1985), Paul Gohlke (*Über die Glieder der Geschöpfe* [On the Limbs/Parts of Animals]; *Über die Zeugung der Geschöpfe* [On the Generation of Animals]. In *Aristotle. Die Lehrschriften*, vols. 8/2 and 8/3. Paderborn, 1959) and Friedrich Stack (*Naturgeschichte der Tiere* [Natural History of Animals]. Frankfurt, 1816).

42   At the time of Aristotle's arrival at the Hain akademos in Athens, there was a radical shift in the use of scientific methodology at Plato's Academy, characterized by a renewed and strengthened interest in the world of individual sciences and their empirical basis. Writing on the subject, Werner Jaeger said, "The Academy, which Aristotle entered in 367, was no longer in the age of the Symposium, around whose table the important heads of the arts and sciences, and representatives of Hellenistic youth would gather in an outburst of enthusiasm, to take in the great mystery of the birth of the spirit out of the Eros, straight from the mouth of the seeress. The essence of Platonic philosophy could no longer be sufficiently represented by the symbol developed in the earlier works of the central form of the philosophy of Socrates. The content and method both far transcended the complexity of the issues addressed by Socrates. What Socrates had meant to Plato and the early Platonic School was accessible only to Aristotle through his reading of earlier texts. The living presence of the Socratic spirit was no longer to be found in the Academy in the decade following 360 BCE. Phaidon and Gorgias, Politeia and Symposion towered high over the bustling reality of the school like silent gods; classical witnesses of a bygone era, a past phase in the life of the master. Anyone who had been tempted to travel long distances to enjoy Plato's personal presence found himself quite surprised. Deep in the bosom of the school,

no mysteries were celebrated. Great energy for the reshaping of things shines out from these works, and a new seriousness. Aristotle did find this in the Academy. But Plato's classical teachings on ideas; singularity and plurality; appetite and aversion; on the state, the soul, and virtue; were not seen as untouchable, sacred matters by the students. Instead, they were ceaselessly subjected to a precise differentiation of the concepts, and a painstaking investigation of their logical sustainability. They were constantly tested, defended, and remodeled. Of vital importance was the fact that the students took part in this collective thought-work. The figures and myths of the Dialogues had been, and remained, Plato's most individual, unrepeatable creation. The discussion of concepts, on the other hand, was the driving force upon which the school was built, in addition to the religious inquiry being done by the Academy. Only these two elements of Plato's spirit and intellectual work could be transferred to others. The more students he attracted, the more they outweighed the artistic side of his nature. This was the cause of the repression of the poet in Plato, and the triumph of his dialectic side. The change he underwent was set in motion by these two opposing forces; but it was the school itself that drove him inexorably in this direction. This change was taking place just as Aristotle entered the Academy. The development of the late Platonic dialectics, with all of its far-reaching consequences, was crucial for the course taken by Aristotle's mind and spirit. Thanks to the discoveries made in the recent research done on Plato, we can follow these gradual developments in the important dialogues on methodology, which Plato wrote during this time; the Theaitetos, Sophistes, Politikos, Parmenides, and Philebos, with chronological exactness. The leading dialogue of this group, the Theaitetos, was written shortly following the death of this famous mathematician, whose memory Plato was honoring.... Around 367, Eudoxos of Kyzikos came to Athens with his school, to work together with Plato and his students, discussing problems which were of concern to both parties. That was a momentous event, and from then on we see members of the School of Math and Astronomy, such as Helikon, Athenaios, and others, working cooperatively with the Academy" (Werner Jaeger, *Aristoteles. Grundlegung einer Geschichte seiner Entwicklung* [Aristotle. Fundamentals of the History of His Development]. Berlin, 1955, pp. 12ff/15).

43   Even during his lifetime, Aristotle was characterized as "the Reader." This was at a time when a book was considered to have been "published" if it had been read aloud by an anagnostes [*lector*] before the audience gathered in the Academy's auditorium. Most of Plato's students almost exclusively heard (rather than read) books. In contrast to this, Aristotle grappled with the written texts intensively; read with great inner activity and participation; and exercised his power of judgment as he read. He made marginal notes and prepared collections of excerpts.

44   Many views on natural philosophy from the pre-Aristotelian era, which had arisen out of the old wisdom of the mysteries, are available to us now only in the form of summaries composed by Aristotle. Aristotle thus became a prime source of historical information by recapitulating the old insights, and increasingly, also the traditional "opinions" of his predecessors. As he did so, he carefully separated the good from the bad, never restraining himself from expressing his well-founded critical responses to the texts. In this matter, as always, his interesting intellectual disposition and habits were apparent in some of the incisive, restrainedly humorous introductory remarks he wrote to accompany his own texts. Thomas Aquinas and Rudolf Steiner followed this tradition quite consistently later. Aristotle's treatise *Über die Atmung* [On Breathing] began with these words: "A few of the early natural philosophers have indeed spoken on the subject of breathing. Some gave no explanation, however, of how breathing serves, or helps, living beings. Others expressed themselves on the topic, but spoke incorrectly, and had only the most minimal knowledge of the facts. They maintained, moreover, that all animals breathe; but that is not correct. We must first examine the words of these researchers, *so as not to awaken the impression that we are making empty accusations against them, without letting them speak for themselves*" (I 471b; italics added by Dr. Selg). In his own time, 1,500 years after Aristotle, Thomas Aquinas recapitulated the whole of Greek and Christian thought (see also the beginning of the chapter on Thomas Aquinas in this volume). He treasured the opportunity to examine and analyze other philosophical lines of thought. He saw this work as enabling him to seek truths that reached beyond personal needs or goals. Thomas saw his writings as continuing the work begun by Aristotle, and reflecting Aristotle's idea of gratefully honoring the person holding the oppositional viewpoint in each scientific discussion. "For this reason, Aristotle told us that we must love both him whose opinion we share, and him whose opinion we reject. Both have sought the truth and aided us in our own search for truth" (*Commentaria in Metaphysicam Aristotelis*, vol. 2, lecture 1). Thomas Aquinas often represented not only his own view but also the opposing view in his own theses, generally doing a better job of it than his true opponents. "Often enough he exposes the power of these opposing arguments. He frequently formulates the antagonistic objections in such a way that they gain greater persuasiveness through Aquinas's formulation" (Josef Pieper, *Thomas-Brevier* [The Human Wisdom of St. Thomas Aquinas: a Breviary of Philosophy from the Works of St. Thomas Aquinas]. Munich, 1956, p. 25). And: "It can certainly happen, when one is in the process of reading the summation written to argue against the heathen, that one unsuspectingly reaches a chapter in which Thomas described the arguments of the opposing viewpoint. From the theological standpoint, these might well be the views of heretics. It can also happen, that one can acknowledge the value of

these opposing arguments, and is tempted to consider them irrefutable, for Thomas formulated these arguments so ingenuously" (Josef Pieper, *Thomas von Aquin. Leben und Werk* [Thomas of Aquinas. His Life and Work]. Munich, 1990, p. 49). Rudolf Steiner also reiterated the philosophical and theological-theosophical history of consciousness of humanity, and developed the form and character of his lectures and writings to connect to this tradition, while still allowing careful examination and analysis. Frequently he chose to address topics of spiritual science for which he normally advocated, taking the opportunity to point out all the possible objections to the topic under discussion, as had Aquinas before him. For example, Steiner spoke in Prague on March 19, 1911, in a lecture titled "How Should One Best Refute Theosophy?" not resuming the discussion until six days later. This time he called his lecture, "How Should One Best Defend Theosophy?" This change caused deep and lasting irritation in an attendee of the first lecture: "Theosophical Lectures of Dr. Rudolf Steiner, Berlin. Rhetorical effect: Comfortable discussion of the objections of opponents. The listener is astonished at the powerful opposition, and develops great concern, immersing himself deeply in these objections and arguments, as if there were nothing else. The listener becomes convinced that the objections cannot be overcome, and would be more than happy to hear even the briefest description of ways to defend the ideas" (Franz Kafka: *Tagebücher* [Diaries] *1910–1923*. Frankfurt, 1983, p. 40).

45 Aristotle insinuated repeatedly that the specific knowledge of the medical field held by physicians themselves would be essential for the formulation of a comprehensive and detailed theory of medicine. Still, it is remarkable to see how intensively and often the subject of the healing arts takes a central role in his thinking. Working from the basis of his ideas on physiological anthropology, he occupied himself, naturally enough, with the processes within the human being that make us sick, and those that make us healthy. He had already spent a great deal of time exploring the dynamics of this transistion (from sick into healthy, and vice versa) in his work *Physics*; see for example 230a and numerous other passages. He emphasized repeatedly that the field of medicine should concern itself with inquiries into the initial reasons (*aitia*)— the true causes of the processes of sickness and healing. In order to do this, their reflections would need a valid philosophical foundation. "The natural philosopher must also consider the initial causes of health and sickness in his observations. Neither health nor sickness is experienced by non-living beings. For this reason, most natural philosophers explore medical questions only late in their work. The physicians who conduct their work in a philosophical manner, on the other hand, tend to start out by examining these questions of nature" (*Über die Wahrnehmung und die Gegenstände der Wahrnehmung* [On Perception and the Objects of Perception], 436a). Aristotle was one of the scientists he himself described, who, when it came to medicine, "are perhaps

not in the field ourselves, but who seek to determine the true causes of things and to gain knowledge and insight" (*Über Traumdeutung* [On the Interpretation of Dreams], 463a). He knew very well that the "wisdom of nature" played a substantial role in the discussion of the causes of illness and the processes of healing: "To express oneself on the causes of health and illness is not only the business of the physician, but also the concern of the natural philosopher, up to a certain point" (*Über die Atmung* [On Breathing] XXI, 480b; see also *Über die Glieder der Geschöpfe* [On the Limbs/Parts of Animals] II, 53a; and *Über die Länge und Kürze des Lebens* [On the Duration and Brevity of Life], 464b). Despite his pronounced and consciously exercised reticence in medical matters, he arranged to have anatomy and anthropological physiology, at the very least, taught within the framework of his Athenian School. These classes were taught with the help of corresponding illustrations and teaching materials (see Jaeger, *Aristoteles* [Aristotle], p. 359). His reticence in writing on such matters is based at least partially on the fact that he differentiated the practical arts of healing (in their therapeutic context, one of deliberately taken actions) from theoretical medical knowledge. "And we see that he who is merely in possession of the knowledge of the pharmacological arts does not heal; because there is something which has the power to achieve a certain end in keeping with the laws of science; but it is not science itself which is taking action" (*De anima* [On the Soul], 433a). In his lectures he often made it clear, using illustrative examples, what well-founded knowledge he possessed of symptoms and disease patterns, and the forces at work in specific illnesses; in epilepsy, for example, which he described as being connected with the processes of sleep and waking (see *Über Schlafen und Wachen* [On Sleep and Waking], 457a). He also knowledgeably discussed the effects of specific individual natural substances upon the human being. The older literature, at any rate, took it as a given fact that the healing done by Alexander the Great (as reported by Plutarch as well as Diodorus, Justinus, and Curtius) was based on medical instruction Alexander had received under the tutelage of Aristotle. Concerning this subject, Plutarch wrote, "Aristotle, I believe, had infused Alexander with a love of pharmacology. He was interested not only in the theoretical aspects of this science, but gave his ailing friends real and practical assistance by prescribing certain remedies and a very specific diet for each of them" (cited in Norbert Geier, *Alexander und Aristoteles* [Alexander and Aristotle]. Halle, 1856, p. 68). Even today, it seems eminently sensible to examine the theoretical and fundamental aspects of medical science formulated by Aristotle. This would include the almost casually expressed remark that a physician must necessarily ascertain the desired and intended state of health of the patient, which the physician will strive to help the patient achieve, "in thoughts or in some perceptible manner" before starting any therapy; and before taking any effective steps toward that goal for the patient. (See *Über die*

Glieder der Geschöpfe [On the Limbs/Parts of Animals] I, 39b.) This line of inquiry would also include Aristotle's question, "Do natural beings with long lives necessarily also have healthy constitutions? Or do short lives and sickness have nothing to do with one another? Or is it the case, with some illnesses, that a connection exists between a sickly constitution of the body and a short lifespan? And in the case of other illnesses, is it possible to live a long time, despite being ill?" (*Über die Länge und Kürze des Lebens* [On Longevity and the Brevity of Life], 464b).

46   Cited by Otfried Höff, *Aristoteles* [Aristotle]. Munich, 1999, p. 16.

47   The instructional writings and lecture manuscripts still available to us that discuss biological questions comprise more than a third of the entire surviving oeuvre.

48   "One must see with absolute clarity that, when one is speaking of any particular organ or vessel, one does not direct one's attention to the specific individual part, but the relation of the part to the entire form. It is the house that is truly important; not the bricks, mortar, or timber. And in the same manner, the principle focus of natural research is not on individual parts, split off from the whole, but on the structure of the whole body; for the individual parts cease to exist when divided from the being as a whole" (*Über die Glieder der Geschöpfe* [On the Limbs/ Parts of Animals] I, 5).

49   According to Rudolf Steiner, Aristotle achieved great historical importance by transferring older Greek mystery wisdom into an "intellectual consciousness" (CW 60, p. 289 [not available in English]), working through it conceptually. In the fourth century before Christ, Aristotle was functioning not as an initiate, Steiner tells us; but rather as a scientist still standing in a living relationship with the old rituals of initiation (CW 52, pp. 37 and 149 [not available in English]). He set into motion a "culture of thinking" (CW 61, p. 354 [not available in English]) anchored in the human being in a nearly physiological sense. Steiner spoke in a late lecture on Aristotle's difference from Plato in this regard: "One should try at least one time to discover the difference between the reading of Plato and the reading of Aristotle, on the basis of inner, spiritual experience based on meditation. When a modern person reads Plato with a true, correct intellectual-spiritual sensitivity and a particular meditative basis, one will feel afterward, as if one's head were somewhat higher than the physical head; as if one had emerged somewhat out of one's physical organism. This happens to everyone who reads Plato on any but the coarsest level. It is different with Aristotle. One could never have the experience of leaving one's body while reading Aristotle. But if one reads Aristotle after doing a certain meditative preparation, one will have the feeling that one is working in the physical human being right that moment. The physical human being betters itself and makes progress by reading Aristotle. One is working. This is not logic that one merely contemplates. This

is instead a logic which works within us" (CW 233, pp. 107f. [*World History and the Mysteries*]).

50   *Metaphysik* [Metaphysics] I, 980a. There is an unfortunate and widespread opinion that Aristotle always had an eye out for the technical applicability of the processes of nature, in stark contrast to the search for pure knowledge. To some extent, this is because of his frequent use of technical and practical examples from the world of handcraft to explain his ideas, particularly with regard to his theory on causation (see *Physik* [Physics] II 3). Nevertheless, this false idea rests on a complete misinterpretation of his entire cognitive approach and view of the universe [*Kosmos*]. With regard to this, Ingrid Craemer-Ruegenberg made these very accurate observations: "What takes place in the realm of the manufacture and use of things is of only secondary importance to Aristotle. It accounts for the reconstruction of natural conditional relationships and their use in connection with the determination of specifically human aims. The natural takes absolute priority [with Aristotle]. The technical use of nature is nothing other than the deliberate exploitation of processes that already occur in the natural world. Precisely because of this, the reassignment of technical connections and relations from nature is not anthropomorphism, in Aristotle's view; but rather a simple methodological and didactic ruse. We are simply more familiar with daily human experience than we are with the natural order of things, to which our daily experience conforms. An idea was popularized as the result of reinterpretations of Aristotle made during medieval times. It suggested that Aristotle interpreted the world and its events according to a model of technical production. We see, then, that this idea is completely erroneous" (Ingrid Craemer-Ruegenberg: *Die Naturphilosophie des Aristoteles* [The Natural Philosophy of Aristotle]. Freiburg/Munich, 1980, p. 41).

51   *Über die Glieder der Geschöpfe* [On the Limbs/Parts of Animals] I, 45a.

52   *Physik* [Physics] 193b 12.

53   *Über die Glieder der Geschöpfe* [On the Limbs/Parts of Animals] I, 45b 11.

54   Ibid. IV, 10.

55   *De anima* [On the Soul] II, 412a.

56   Ibid. II, 412b.

57   Ibid. I, 411b.

58   For more on the subject, see also Steiner's statement that people initiated into the ancient mysteries were led to a deepened experience of the embryonic processes of life and experience. "An awareness and consciousness emerged about the way of life experienced by the human being during the embryonic period.... One passed through the time of embryonic experience up to birth. Through this a sense arose, in the way memories always arise, of the human being sensing himself emerging from a spiritual world, still half belonging to a spiritual world. These were the mysteries of birth; and among other things,

one understood, during the time when the mysteries were flourishing, what the human being could experience by means of such an initiation" (CW 343, p. 25 [not available in English]). This was a fact that continued to resonate (at least in the background) for Aristotle; and very likely helped to shape and determine both his perspective and the questions he sought to answer.

59   In the sixth book of his *Geschichte der Tiere* [History of the Animals] (VI, 37b), Aristotle reported on the developmental stages of the chicken, because the process can be seen and grasped with the naked eye. His classical embryological description was unsurpassed in its macroscopic precision of detail for more than 2,000 years, until the embryologist Carl Ernst von Baer published his findings in the 1820s. Aristotle wrote, "After three days and three nights [of the incubation of the egg] the heart is visible in the egg white as a blood-red spot. This jumps and moves itself, giving clear signs that it is alive. Somewhat later, the entire body is formed, and the individual parts differentiate themselves. The head and the starkly protruding eyes can be recognized particularly well. On the tenth day all of the organs are clearly visible, including the stomach and the intestines. On the twentieth day, the young chicken makes noises and moves itself about within the eggshell. If you open the egg on this day, you will find that it already has feathers. The head lies over the right thigh along the edge, and one wing lies on the head." (For more on the subject, see also the impressive essay by Franz Büchner: *Aristoteles im Lichte moderner Biologie und Pathologie. Ein Beitrag zur Lehre vom Menschen* [Aristotle in Light of Modern Biology and Pathology. A Contribution to the Theory and Teachings on the Human Being]. In Wolfgang Kullmann [ed.]: *Aristoteles und die moderne Wissenschaft* [Aristotle and Modern Science]. *Freiburger Universitätsblätter* [Journal (lit. "pages") of Freiburg University], no. 73, 1981, pp. 33–43).

60   *Über die Zeugung der Geschöpfe* [On the Generation of Animals] II, 40a.

61   Ibid. II, 35a.

62   Ibid. II, 40a.

63   Ibid. II, 41b.

64   *Über die Glieder der Geschöpfe* [On the Limbs/Parts of Animals] III, 66a.

65   *Über die Atmung* [On Breathing] VIII, 474b.

66   Ibid. II, 47b. "The heart is [the] source and starting point for the veins" (*Über die Glieder der Geschöpfe* [On the Limbs/Parts of Animals] III, 65b).

67   *Über die Glieder der Geschöpfe* [On the Limbs/Parts of Animals] III, 66a.

68   *Tierkunde* [The Study of Animals] III, 2.

69   Aristotle occupied himself very intensively with the substance of blood itself. He often maintained that blood cannot really be properly

studied except within a living, ensouled organism. When the life processes cease, blood becomes entirely different. Among other things, he dedicated himself in his studies to a closer analysis of the coagulation process under physiological and pathophysiological conditions. He was familiar with the significant substances that were important to these processes, and described the existence and functionality of blood fibers 2,000 years before their "rediscovery" by the Italian physician and anatomist Marcello Malpighi, made while he was working with a microscope.

70   With regard to this, see also the interesting study made by Jochen Althoff, *Aristoteles' Vorstellung von der Ernährung der Lebewesen* [Aristotle's Conception of the Nourishment of Living Beings]. In Wolfgang Kullmann (ed.): *Aristotelische Biologie* [Aristotelian Biology]. Stuttgart, 1997, pp. 351–364.

71   In his remarks on *Über die Glieder der Geschöpfe* [On the Limbs/Parts of Animals], Aristotle made reference to the blood-rich nature of the liver. "The liver is (next to the heart) the richest in blood of all the internal parts of the body" (III, 73b). With this in mind, he stressed its importance for the human constitution as a whole, and for the organism's potential for health.

72   Ibid. III, 14.

73   Ibid.

74   In a number of his works on natural science, Aristotle pointed out the great importance of the spatial polarities within the human organism, and the constellations of forces at work in the various regions of the body (above and below; front and back; right and left). He repeatedly emphasized that the corresponding relationships within plants (with regard to the polarity of "above and below") was the opposite, or the reverse, of that found in the human being. We see an example of this viewpoint in *De anima* [On the Soul]: "Above and below are not at all the same among the various beings and in the universe as a whole. The head of living beings corresponds to the roots of the plants...." (II, 416a). At another point he offered a more extensive explanation, differentiating between human beings, animals, and plants; and defining an "upper" region that takes in nourishment and a "lower" region that excretes and distributes nourishment: "Thus we see that things are exactly opposite [with these spatial orientations] with regard to plants and animals. This is particularly true with regard to human beings, more so than with any other living beings, because of their upright stance. The upper portion of the human being is oriented toward the upper portion of the universe. With other forms [of animal life], the upper portion is in the middle. With regard to plants, on the other hand, which cannot move about, and take their nourishment from the earth, this upper portion is necessarily always oriented downward. The roots of the plants correspond to the part of the animal we call the mouth" (*Über Jugend und Alter, Leben und Tod* [On Youth and

Old Age, Life and Death] I, 468a). See also the corresponding explanations in *Über die Fortbewegung der Lebewesen* [On the Gait of Living Beings] IV, 705b.

75 See also *Über die Glieder der Geschöpfe* [On the Limbs/Parts of Animals] II, 47a and 48a.

76 See also *Über die Atmung* [On Breathing] XIII, 477a.

77 *Über die Glieder der Geschöpfe* [On the Limbs/Parts of Animals] II, 50a. As Aristotle emphasized in *De anima*, the process of nourishment actually consists of a transformational internalizing of substances that were originally "opposed" or "antithetical" to the organism (416a).

78 *Über Jugend und Alter, Leben und Tod* [On Youth and Old Age, Life and Death] III, 469a.

79 Ibid. IV, 469a.

80 Ibid. III 469a. See also Althoff [endnote 67], pp. 354ff., concerning Aristotle's view of the differentiated nourishment and growth qualities that are intrinsic to the digestion of substances.

81 According to Aristotle, the continual building and rebuilding of the bodily substances takes place at different stages of the transformation of nourishment. The sense organs, he tells us, take on substance at the final, or highest, stage (see *Über die Zeugung der Geschöpfe* [On the Generation of Animals] II 6, 744b, as well as other passages). See below for more on the relationship between the heart processes and sensory processes.

82 Ibid. IV, 469b.

83 *Über die Zeugung der Geschöpfe* [On the Generation of Animals] II, 44a.

84 *Über die Glieder der Geschöpfe* [On the Limbs/Parts of Animals] II 6, 77a. When keeping the larger view of matters in mind, with regard to the physiological basis of human thought activities, we must consider that Aristotle often stressed that the real thinking spirit (nous poetikos) does not enter into a physiological unity with the body. The thinking spirit requires no specifically physiological processes in order to become efficacious. This is in contrast to the processes of sensory perception, which are primarily conducted by the body. (See, for example, *De anima* [On the Soul] III 4, 429b.) The actual thinking, actively creative spirit, Aristotle tells us, is essentially choristos; that is, completely free and independent of the mortal body, in which it operates "from the outside," to a certain extent (*thyrathen*); as if entering through a door, not combined with any bodily processes, and immortal in and of itself (*aphthartos*). On the other hand, Aristotle also recognized and described a "passive" spirit (*nous patheikos*), absorbing and receiving, suffering through experiences, and perishing along with the body. Aristotle repeatedly rewrote [in the passage above, for example] lists of specific physiological requirements or conditions that help the body achieve the development of higher spiritual capacities, in the sense that they enable this development physiologically. Aristotle did not

explicate these complex relationships more specifically in the lecture manuscripts that are still available to us today. For more on this philosophical discussion, there are several useful sources to consult. Among them is the overview provided by Karl-Martin Dietz (*Metamorphosen des Geistes. Das Erwachen des europäischen Denkens* [Metamorphoses of the Spirit. The Awakening of European Thought], vol. 3, pp. 137ff.); and the remarkable explications by Heinz Herbert Schöffler, in *Die Akademie von Gondischapur. Aristoteles auf dem Wege in den Orient* [The Academy of Gundishapur. Aristotle on the Way to the Orient]. Stuttgart, 1980, pp. 18–24, "Die Psychologie des Aristoteles [The Psychology of Aristotle]"). Nevertheless, Aristotle indicated the possibility of a subtle relationship between the substantive spirituality of the thinking human soul and its bodily organizational structure, although he did not consider this part of the spirit, and saw it as affecting the spirit only indirectly. More than 2,000 years later, these subtle relationships stood at the very center of Rudolf Steiner's anthroposophical and physiological research. With this background in mind, Steiner's concept of the "I"-organization; that is, his extensive deliberations on the relation of the body to the thinking spirit, can be seen in the context of its expansive historical background, both intellectual and spiritual; and make it possible for us to develop a deeper understanding of the subtle Aristotelian references and alleged contradictions. Steiner expressed this in *Die Philosophie der Freiheit*, CW 4 [English trans.: *Intuitive Thinking as a Spiritual Path: A Philosophy of Freedom*. Hudson, NY: Anthroposophic Press, 1995] in these words: "Only when one has struggled to recognize the truth about the intuitive nature of thought, gained through unbiased observation, can one succeed in finding a clear path to an accurate concept of the close association of the human body and soul. One recognizes that this union cannot bring about any change in the nature and essence of thought. At first this appears to contradict the obvious state of affairs. In the course of normal human experience, thought arises only by means of this associative relationship between the soul and the body. This appearance [of thought] asserts itself so strongly that its true meaning can only be glimpsed by those who have recognized that this body-soul union plays no role in the nature and essence of thought. Such a person will no longer be able to avoid realizing just how unusual this relationship is between the human body-soul arrangement and human thought. This relationship of body to soul has no effect upon the nature of thought. In fact, it retreats into the background when the activity of thinking is in progress. It gives way, surrenders its own activity, and leaves space free—which is then occupied by thinking. A double responsibility then rests upon the essential processes taking place in the activity of thinking: first, thinking represses the individual and customary activity of the human organism; and secondly, it replaces this activity with its own activity. For the first of these two, the organizational structure of the body, is itself the result of thought activity. And it is the result of the particular part of thought which prepares for the appearance, or manifestation, of thought. From this one is able to learn in what sense thinking has a counter-image, or double, within the close association of the body and the soul. When one has learned this, one cannot be led astray with regard to the true meaning of this counter-image" (pp. 116f. and see also Peter Selg, *Vom* Logos *menschlicher Physis* [The Logos of Human Physiology], pp. 252ff. and 428ff.).

85   *Über die Zeugung der Geschöpfe* [On the Generation of Animals] II, 43b.

86   For more on the subject, please see endnote 84, as well.

87   With regard to the assistance from the brain, missing from the actual sensory processes: according to Aristotle, sensory processes are carried out by the individual sensory organs in collaboration with the heart. The brain is not part of this cooperative effort. With regard to this phenomenon, Aristotle wrote these very direct words in *Über die Glieder der Geschöpfe* [On the Limbs/Parts of Animals]: "And the brain does not participate in any sense perception activities" (II, 56a).

88   See for example *Über Schlafen und Wachen* [On Sleeping and Waking] III, 456b.

89   *Über die Glieder der Geschöpfe* [On the Limbs/Parts of Animals] III, 73b.

90   *Über Jugend und Alter, Leben und Tod* [On Youth and Old Age, Life and Death] IV, 469a.

91   See also *De anima* [On the Soul] III, 425a.

92   *Über Schlafen und Wachen* [On Sleeping and Waking] II, 455a.

93   Aristotle once wrote these words on the mechanics of the sense of hearing and its collaboration with the heart (or better said, with the rhythmic system of the blood and the heart). This deviated from the general style of Aristotle's related statements, arising from the idea that movement impulses are taken up into the blood: "Precision [in the realm of the senses of hearing and smell] means, that we must first become aware of all the differences in the sensations at hand, to hear and smell from a distance. The apparatus of sensory perception is also essential in the judgment of these differences. The same is true for sight; according to whether we see things clearly, or if we see only the membrane that surrounds things. Pathways lead from all of these senses to the heart, as I discussed in my work on perception. In places where there is no heart, the pathways lead to a corresponding substitute for the heart, instead. The path for hearing ends in the place where instinctive breathing brings about the pulse in some beings; and in others, where inhaling and exhaling take place. This is true because the sensory apparatus for hearing belongs to the realm of the air. In this way, we can understand what is being said as if what was heard were being repeated. For just as the movement penetrates the sensory apparatus, so too does it emanate from the voice, as if the two were cast in the

same mold, so that one is repeating what one has heard" (*Über die Glieder der Geschöpfe* [On the Limbs/Parts of Animals] V, 81a).

94   Ibid. II, 56b.

95   *Über die Träume* [On Dreams] II, 460b.

96   Ibid. III, 461a.

97   Ibid.

98   "On the whole we can say that the perceptions of the individual senses concur with the central processing authority; unless the perception contradicts a bit of highly reliable perceived data. A sensory impression arises, no matter what, even in these contradictory instances. But we do not always agree with it, unless the central processing authority is restricted in some way, or is not responding correctly [for example, when we are sleeping, or when we are ill]" (P. Selg. ibid. 461b).

99   For more on Aristotle's fundamental and groundbreaking anthropological differentiation between activities of memory and remembering, see *Über Gedächtnis und Erinnerung* [On Memory and Remembering], chaps. 1 and 2. In *De anima*, Aristotle had already implicitly differentiated the two activities; and in addition, he wrote: "Perhaps it is better not to say that the soul feels compassion, or that it learns, or thinks; but rather that the human being does these things along with the soul; not in the sense that the activity is within the soul, but rather, that the activity moves toward the soul, then emerges from it. For example, perception arises and moves toward the soul; and remembrance, on the other hand, moves from the soul to the activities or residual conditions in the sense organs."

100   *Über Gedächtnis und Erinnerung* [On Memory and Remembering] I, 451a.

101   *Über Schlafen und Wachen* [On Sleeping and Waking] III.

102   Ibid. II, 455b. According to Aristotle, the actual sensing ability and consciousness activity of a living being, as well as his (mostly) daily change from a waking body to a sleeping one, are all connected. These abilities first came into being in the animal world (where animals took on perceiving and desiring soul capacities, in contrast to the vegetative sphere). In his work *Über Wachen und Schlafen* [On Waking and Sleeping], Aristotle wrote, "Earlier, in other places [that is to say, in *De anima* (On the Soul), book 2], we differentiated the so-called parts of the soul, and determined that the capacity to nourish can exist without other capacities; but no other capacity can exist unless the capacity to nourish is also present. From this we can clearly see that no living being that takes part only in growing and decaying, such as a plant, sleeps or wakes. This is because of the fact that plants have no soul component capable of perception.... In the same sense, it is clear that there is no species of living being that is always awake or always asleep. Each living being always experiences both conditions. It is also true for all beings that possess a natural function, that they lose their functional competence when they try to exceed the allotted time for exercising

that function; that is, their eyes can no longer see, and they must cease their attempts.... If there is an organ whose function is perception, it will also lose its functional proficiency and become unable to carry out its function, if it exceeds the time during which it was able to exercise its function in a coherent, cohesive manner. The state of waking is thus determined by the ability to freely exercise the skill of perception" (*Über Wachen und Schlafen* [On Waking and Sleeping] I 454a). Later in the work: "Because without perception there is neither sleeping nor waking. What possesses perception also possesses the capacity to mourn and rejoice, and consequently also the capacity to desire. Plants have nothing of the sort" (Ibid. I, 454b). For more on the decrease in the vital powers of regeneration, with the appearance of the perceiving and desiring aspects of the soul in the organism, see also the discussion in *Über die Länge und Kürze des Lebens* [On Longevity and the Brevity of Life], chap. VI.

103   Ibid. II, 456a.

104   *Über die Glieder der Geschöpfe* [On the Limbs/Parts of Animals] III, 66a.

105   *Über die Zeugung der Geschöpfe* [On the Generation of Animals] II, 43b.

106   In a zoological work, Aristotle wrote the following on the relationships between the structure and nature of the heart and the soul-characterological nature of some living beings: "Non-sensitive animals have a hard, thick heart, while sensitive animals have a softer heart. Those with large hearts are cowardly, while those with small and medium-sized hearts are braver. This is due to the fact that the effect of fear is already present ahead of time in those; because warmth does not correspond to the size of the heart, and the minimal warmth in a large area is extinguished easily, leaving the blood colder. The rabbit, deer, mouse, hyena, donkey, panther, and weasel have large hearts; as well as all animals, as a rule, that are noticeably fearful or act ferocious because of fear" (*Über die Glieder der Geschöpfe* [On the Limbs/Parts of Animals] III, 67a).

107   Ibid. II, 52b.

108   *De anima* [On the Soul] I, 408b.

109   Ibid. I, 403a and 403b. In this passage, Aristotle wrote on the relationship between soul life and bodily life; that is to say, the relationship between form and substance, *eidos* and *materie*. He exemplified this (not by chance) with the heart, and formulated his thoughts thus: "It appears that all of the emotions are connected with the body: bravery, meekness, fear, sympathy, daring, and additionally even joy, love, and hatred. The body experiences something right along with these emotions. A sign [of this]: from time to time, powerful and distinct emotions can arise, although one is not agitated or fearful; and one can be affected by minor, weak emotions when the body is flying into a rage and reacts as if one were furious. Moreover, it is clear that even

when nothing to arouse fear is taking place, human beings can experience the emotions of someone who is afraid. When this happens, then the emotions are clearly *Logoi* (conceptual conditions) affecting matter. Thus even the definitions are formulated in this way; for example, becoming enraged is a conditioned activity of the body, body part, or capacity, [caused] by this particular object and due to this particular purpose. For this reason, it is the task of the physicist [the natural philosopher] to undertake a theoretical examination of the soul; either each soul, or such a soul. A physicist and a dialectician would deal with each emotion in a different manner; for example, in determining the nature of anger. One of them would define it as a striving for retaliation for pain, or similarly; and the other would define it as a seething of the blood, which flows around the heart and is warm. One gives an account of the effects of the emotions upon matter; and the other gives the form and concept, because the concept belongs to the thing itself, and must necessarily act upon matter, if it is to be [real]. Thus there is a concept of the house as a place of protection that prevents damage due to rain, wind, and heat. Another concept of the house names stones, bricks, and timber; and yet another definition again mentions the form of the house with a specific purpose in mind. Which of these is given by the physicist [natural philosopher]? The one that concerns itself with matter, without knowing the concept or the one that concerns itself with the concept? Or more likely the one which concerns itself with both? But then who gave the first two definitions above? Or is there no one who investigates the characteristics of matter which are separable and inseparable from it? The physicist is more likely to occupy himself with all of the accomplishments and emotions befitting such a body and such matter." For more on the way emotional processes are grounded in the body, specifically, in human blood, see also *Tierkunde* [Zoology] I, 3.

110   Aristotle draws attention to the meaning of each substance in the blood for the specific, qualitative nature of the processes of sensation, temperament, and thought, in his remarks on the differences within a single organism; and also with regard to the differences between various individual animal species. In his lecture manuscript *Über die Glieder der Geschöpfe* [On the Limbs/Parts of Animals], he wrote, "Thicker, warmer blood gives more strength. Thinner, colder blood is more appropriate for feeling and thinking. We can recognize this difference in animals that have a substitute for blood. Bees and similar beings are much more sensible than some animals with blood; and among these, the animals with colder, thinner [finer] blood are more sensible than would be practical for bravery and understanding to be found within a single creature" (II, 48b).

111   *Über die Glieder der Geschöpfe* [On the Limbs/Parts of Animals] III, 69a (ital. added by Dr. Selg).

112 A succinct summary of this is to be found in Höffe, *Aristoteles* [Aristotle]. Munich, 1999, pp. 110–117.

113 *Über die Glieder der Geschöpfe* [On the Limbs/Parts of Animals] III, 65a.

114 *Über die Bewegung der Lebewesen* [On Movement in Living Beings], VII 701b.

115 As Aristotle described in his work *Über die Zeugung der Geschöpfe* [On the Generation of Animals], the "instinctive pneuma" has the character of "warm air" on one hand; and at the same time, the substance to be found in the *pneuma* corresponds to the element of the stars; that is to say, to the ether (II, 736a and b). In the end, all completed actions take place by means of, and with the intervention and help of, the warmth element. Aristotle substantiated this claim in *Über die Bewegung der Lebewesen* [On Movement in Living Beings] with these words: "What we are striving to achieve, or striving to avoid, turns out to be the initial step in the activity. This necessarily follows the thoughts we have on these things, and the perception we have of their warmth or coldness. We should avoid things that do not bring us happiness, and strive for what is pleasant. Both the unpleasant and the pleasant are connected with a certain sense of cold or warmth. In minor matters, however, this consideration escapes our notice (VIII, 701b).

116 Ibid. X, 703a.

117 *Über die Atmung* [On Breathing] XX, 479b.

118 Ibid. 480a.

119 "The apparatus of breathing is the lung, which receives the impulse to move from the heart" (*Über die Glieder der Geschöpfe* [On the Limbs/Parts of Animals] III, 69a).

120 *Über die Bewegung der Lebewesen* [On Movement in Living Beings] XI.

121 *Über die Glieder der Geschöpfe* [On the Limbs/Parts of Animals] III, 67b.

122 Ibid. III, 66a.

123 See also endnote 87.

124 For more on this, compare the lecture manuscripts *De caelo* and *De generatione et corruptione* as well as *Meteorologica*. "He who immerses himself nowadays in the meager number of manuscripts we still have available from Aristotle will see how powerful his insight was in describing the connection between the human being and the cosmos" (Rudolf Steiner, CW 233 [*World History and the Mysteries*], p. 76). Building upon work done by Plato, Aristotle argued for the essential spirituality of the celestial bodies, and their autonomous cosmic physicality, free of earthly regulation. He attempted to describe this on the basis of the independent existence of the etheric; the life pneuma of the earthly organism as being commensurate with the etheric warmth element of the stars. In so doing, he placed special emphasis on the (circular) movement impulses that are an intrinsic part of

the cosmic-etheric element. In the process, he repudiated several old theories most emphatically; among them, the idea that the universe had arisen out of elemental chaos; and the theory of the evolution of living beings in the [later] Darwinian sense. He wrote about the meaning of the cosmic influences on earthly movement phenomena in his treatise *Über die Zeugung der Geschöpfe* [On the Generation of Animals], for example. "In certain proportions, warming and cooling bring about development and decay. These processes are regulated by the orbit of the heavens. The movements of the sea and the air, and everything within them, are determined by the path of the sun and the moon. Everything that has life, from the highest organism to the lowest, stands under this influence. Nature measures the extent of development and decay by the number of movements made by those two stars" (IV, 10, 777b). Individual statements on the meaning of these cosmic connections for the physiology of the human heart cannot be found in the teaching manuscripts still available to us today.

125 *Über Werden und Vergehen* [On Development and Decay] 336a.

126 On this subject, see also (among other sources) the brief but very informative chapter "Das Gebet" ["The Prayer"] in the Aristotle monograph by J.-M. Zemb, *Aristoteles* [Aristotle]. Hamburg, 2002, pp. 147–152.

127 On the adventuresome earlier history of this edition of the "body of works" of Aristotle, published by Andronikos of Rhodes, see Ingemar Düring, *Aristoteles. Darstellung und Interpretation seines Denkens* [Aristotle. The Presentation and Interpretation of His Thought]. Heidelberg, 1966, pp. 32–43; and Hellmuth Flashar, *Aristoteles* [Aristotle]. In Hellmuth Flashar (ed.), *Grundriss der Geschichte der Philosophie. Die Philosophie der Antike* [An Outline of the History of Philosophy. Ancient Philosophy]. Vol. 3: *Ältere Akademie. Aristoteles—Peripatos*. [Older Academy. Aristotle—Peripatos]. Basel/Stuttgart, 1983.

128 *Expositio et Lectura super Epistolas Pauli Apostoli* 5, I.

129 In my opinion, both of the classic publications from Josef Pieper are still the finest introductions to the life story, work, and situation of Thomas Aquinas. *Thomas von Aquin. Leben und Werk* [Thomas of Aquinas. Life and Work]. Munich 1958 and *Scholastik. Gestalten und Probleme der mittelalterlichen Philosophie* [Scholasticism. Important Figures and Issues in Medieval Philosophy]. Munich, 1960. Two further volumes offer additional well-chosen material to round out the biographical overview: Josef Pieper's *Thomas-Brevier* [The Human Wisdom of St. Thomas Aquinas: a Breviary of Philosophy from the Works of St. Thomas Aquinas] (Munich, 1956) and the texts compiled by Eugen Rolfes, *Die Philosophie des Thomas von Aquin* [The Philosophy of Thomas Aquinas] (Hamburg, 1977). The most up-to-date, thorough, and scientifically-based biography of Thomas Aquinas, with an integrated bibliography containing short summaries of all of his writings, was published by Jean-Pierre Torrell in 1995 in German, as well [as French]: *Magister Thomas* [Master Thomas] (Freiburg). Books

of an introductory nature on his life and work include the very read-able work by the Aquinas specialists Martin Grabmann, *Thomas von Aquin. Persönlichkeit und Gedankenwelt* [Thomas of Aquinas. His Personality and The World of His Thought] (Munich, 1935), and M.-D. Chenu, *Das Werk des Heiligen Thomas von Aquin* [The Work of Saint Thomas of Aquinas] (Heidelberg, Graz, Vienna, Cologne, 1960) and *Thomas von Aquin in Selbstzeugnissen und Bilddokumenten* [An Illustrated Biography of Thomas of Aquinas, Consisting of Excerpts from His Work] (Hamburg, 1960). Only certain written works of Thomas Aquinas have been translated into German, and the quality of the translations varies widely. [The edition of the *Summa theologica* by Joseph Bernhart, a translation and commentary of certain por-tions of the work, is particularly problematic in this regard (3 vols., Stuttgart, 1985).] With regard to the anthropological dimension of Thomas's thought, which is of greatest interest to us within the frame-work of this study, the complete edition of the *Summa theologica* (in Latin and German) is the most useful. Volumes have been appearing in succession since 1933 (more than thirty to date) and contain exten-sive, historically systematic commentary. The study of the magnificent Summa contra Gentiles is also very helpful (translated into German by Helmut Fashel. 6 vols. Zurich, 1942–1960). Very useful are also the dense *Compendium Theologiae* (translated into German by Hans Louis Fäh. Ed. by Rudolf Tannhoff. Heidelberg, 1963) and the *Sen-tenzen* [Aphorisms], translated by Josef Pieper (Munich, 1965), as well as numerous highly interesting individual works that have appeared in German in recent decades for the first time. Among these are the two early works *De ente et essentia* (translated by Franz Leo Beer-etz. Stuttgart, 1979) and *De principiis naturae* (translated by Richard Heinzmann. Stuttgart, Berlin, Cologne, 1999). Also very helpful are the papers that appeared as part of the very worthy translated edition published by the Friedrich von Hardenberg Institute for Cultural Stud-ies in Heidelberg. Particularly interesting for the theme of this book is the volume of that study entitled *De unitate intellectus contra averrois-tas/De motu cordis*. Stuttgart, 1987). Last, a special recommendation should be given to the volume Thomas von Aquin, *Prologe zu den Aris-toteles-Kommentaren* [Thomas of Aquinas: Prologue to the Aristotle Commentaries], published in 1993 in German and Latin by Francis Cheneval and Ruedi Imbach (Vittorio Klostermann, Frankfurt), who wrote a meticulous introduction to the work. With regard to second-ary literature on the topic being pursued here, I recommend that you read the work by the Dominican psychology professor, American Rob-ert Edward Brennan, *Thomistische Psychologie. Eine philosophische Analyse der menschlichen Natur* [Thomistic Psychology: a Philosophic Analysis of the Nature of Man] (Heidelberg, Graz, Vienna, Cologne, 1957). To a more limited extent, I recommend the publication by the Roman Catholic existential philosopher Gustav Siewerth, *Der Mensch und sein Leib* [Man and His Body] (Einsiedeln, 1953), part of which addresses Thomas Aquinas's teachings on the heart (although it then loses itself increasingly in pseudo-lyrical, churchly excesses written in "existential" language). Further, the relatively prosaic but actually first-rate publications by Wolf-Ulrich Klünker, *Selbsterkenntnis der Seele. Zur Anthropologie des Thomas von Aquin* [Self-Awareness of the Soul. On the Anthropology of Thomas of Aquinas] (Stuttgart, 1990); and Klünker together with Bruno Sandkühler, *Menschliche Seele und kosmischer Geist. Siger von Brabant in der Auseinandersetzung mit Thomas von Aquin* [Human Soul and Cosmic Spirit. Siger of Brabant in Conflict with Thomas of Aquinas] (Stuttgart, 1988); the idiosyncratic collection of texts and interpretations by Roman Boos (*Thomas von Aquin. Übersetzungen, Aufsätze, Vorträge* [Thomas of Aquinas. Translations, Essays, Lectures] (Schaffhausen, 1959); especially the essay called "Der Pulsschlag der Geistesgeschichte in der Herzlehre Thomas von Aquino" ["The Pulse of Intellectual History in *Thomas of Aquinas's* Teachings on the Heart"]), the study by Rudolf Steiner's excellent student and colleague, physician Eugen Koslisko, *Zum Werk des Thomas von Aquino über die Bewegung des Herzens* [Thomas of Aquinas's Work on the Movement of the Heart] (in Natura [*Journal of the Medical Section of the Anthroposophical Society*, which he edited from 1926–31—Tr.], vol. 1. 1926–27, pp. 168–177) and certain isolated aspects of the publication by Heinz Herbert Schöffler, *Das Herz als Sinnesorgan. Perspektiven zu einem geisteswissenschaftlichen Organbild* [The Heart as a Sense Organ. Perspectives from the Humanities on the View of the Heart] (Stuttgart, 1975; chap. 5: "Das Herz als Sinnesorgan bei Aristoteles, Thomas von Aquin, und Rudolf Steiner" [The Heart as Sense Organ in the Work of Aristotle, Thomas of Aquinas, and Rudolf Steiner], pp. 70–90).

130 See the outline summarizing the history of the reception of the Aristotelian "body of work" in the years following the publication of the Roman edition by Andronicus of Rhodes [active around 60 BCE—Tr.] (in Francis Cheneval and Ruedi Imbach, *Thomas von Aquin: Prologe zu den Aristoteles-Kommentaren* [Thomas of Aquinas: Prologue to the Aristotle Commentaries] (Vittorio Klostermann, Frankfurt, 1993), pp. xiv–xli), based largely on the more extensive account by Flashar. We know today that the Arabic reception left a strong imprint upon the understanding of Aristotle's works, which lasted until the onset of the Christian-Scholastic examination of his works in the thirteenth century. There had been intensive efforts to produce studies and commentaries in the first centuries after Christ, to be sure, in the circle of Neo-Platonists working with Plotin's student Porphyrius. This work was carried out by Themistius and Simplicius in Athens, Constantinople, and Alexandria. Some tentative first efforts were also undertaken among the early Christians working with Clement of Alexandria and Origen, although most of these early responses to Aristotle were

rejections of his theories. After the sixth century CE, the writings of Aristotle were almost completely forgotten in the cultural realm of the Latin language during medieval times. At exactly the same time, however, among the Nestorian Christians in Syria and Persia, huge efforts at translating and studying Aristotle's works were underway. This work was relocated to Antioch and Harran after the Arabs conquered Egypt and the Levant. At the beginning of the ninth century, an expanded Academy was created in the capital of the new Arabian world, Baghdad, a city founded in 762 CE. The new Academy set itself the task of bringing every known field of study to the Arabian cultural region. They translated Greek, Syrian, and Persian texts. By the tenth century, the entire *Corpus Aristotelicum* was available in the vernacular, and the debate of Islam with Aristotelian thinking had begun; a debate carried out largely by Averroes, a physician from Cordoba (Ibn Rushd, 1126–1198), in the decades before Thomas Aquinas began his own work on the subject.

131   "One has understood nothing about Scholasticism, it seems to me, if one has not perceived that it was a matchless learning process above all else; an educational event of unprecedented magnitude that lasted several centuries. If the grand inheritance from the ancient world, heathen as well as Christian, was to be successfully appropriated, the first task had to be the organization of the discovered material. It had to be organized in terms of its potential to be taught and learned. This, it must be expected, would first of all involve the very prosaic work of organizing, sorting, and classifying, which would bring a meaning to the mass of material that lacked meaning prior to that. And the writings of medieval Scholasticism were missing the magic of personal directness. There was no way of avoiding this. Textbooks leave very little room for the originality of their authors to show. Learning can be achieved only this way, in the average case. And if learning the content of the traditional treasures was the most pressing historical task in those centuries when the world order of ancient times was collapsing, then the didactic nature of Scholasticism was not only unavoidable, but absolutely imperative. Who can say whether we might have had a direct intellectual and spiritual link to the work of Plato, Aristotle, and Augustine, if that patient effort at an elementary understanding had not taken place first? And the mastery of such an immense inventory on the part of the learning and teaching Scholastic presupposes a completely unusual degree of intellectual autonomy and independence, as well as a highly-developed sense of one's relationship to the world," *Scholastik*. "Gestalten und Probleme der mittelalterlichen Philosophie" [Scholasticism. Important Figures and Issues in Medieval Philosophy]. Munich ⁴1998, pp. 28f.).

132   See Rudolf Steiner's extensive deliberations in the context of his *Esoterische Betrachtungen karmischer Zusammenhänge* [Esoteric Views of Karmic Connections] for more information on the process of

the "immersion" of Aristotelian thought into Christianity taking place within the Dominican order, as well as the greater spiritual context of these events (lectures on the subject in CW 237, 238, and 240 [*Karmic Relationships: Esoteric Studies*, vols. 3, 4, and 5. London: Rudolf Steiner Press, 2009, 1997, 2011] are particularly appropriate).

133   Throughout his years in Athens, Aristotle was a stranger born elsewhere. He lived with a certain amount of danger, and had to flee Athens just one-and-one-half years before his death, because of an accusation that was raised against him (a charge of Godlessness, *asebia*).

134   *Summa theologica* II-II 188, 6.

135   Thomas Aquinas considered teaching to be a substantial element of the care of souls. In light of this, he argued for the necessity of giving up a certain portion of contemplative withdrawal [from the world] in order to reserve time for teaching. In his *Quaestio disputata de caritate*, he wrote the following words on the subject: "Some sense such joy in this time set aside for the unencumbered contemplation of God. This being the case, they do not want to lose this freedom, to leave the contemplative life—not even to help with the salvation of another person, in the service of God. But others reach such a high level of love, that they are willing to give up the contemplation of God, even though they experience the greatest joy in this pursuit, in order to serve God. This was the perfection found in St. Paul...and this is the perfection that is peculiar to...preachers as well" (II ad 6).

136   *Summa theologica* I 117, I ad 7. A corresponding passage is also to be found in *Quaestiones disputatae de veritate*: "It is said of the physician that he heals, although he works only from the outside. Nature alone is active from inside; and one says also, that humans teach the truth, although they are only proclaiming something externally; while God is teaching the human being from within" (I–II, I ad 1).

137   Numerous clerical regulations, enacted after 1210, were supposed to restrict the distribution of Aristotelian writings, in order to prevent the undermining of Christian dogma through heathen philosophy. But these regulations remained just as unsuccessful as the official clerical condemnation of numerous Aristotelian theses; as well as a number of theses from Thomas Aquinas himself, which were still being condemned by the Bishop of Paris, in 1270 and 1277, four years after Thomas's death.

138   See *De unitate intellectus*, as well as the monograph by Wolfgang-Ulrich Klünker and Bruno Sandkühler: *Menschliche Seele und kosmischer Geist. Siger von Brabant in der Auseinandersetzung mit Thomas von Aquin* [Human Soul and Cosmic Spirit. Siger of Brabant in Conflict with Thomas of Aquinas] (Stuttgart, 1988).

139   Cited by Josef Pieper in *Thomas-Brevier* [The Human Wisdom of St. Thomas Aquinas: a Breviary of Philosophy from the Works of St. Thomas Aquinas]. Munich, 1956, p. 12.

140   Taking the same stance, Thomas Aquinas repeatedly defended Plato against accusations made by Aristotle. Thomas stated that Aristotle, in seeking to dissociate himself from his great spiritual teacher, did not always take note of and consider Plato's actual intentions, the *veritas occulta*. Instead, Aristotle often noticed only the apparent sound of the words (*sonus bonus*); and let himself be guided by that in his explications, an approach that was not productive. This was done more often and polemically in his earlier works. As Aristotle got older, he grew to value Plato's work, and softened his earlier, harsh judgment. (For more on this, see Josef Pieper, *Thomas von Aquin* [Thomas of Aquinas], p. 67, and the corresponding references in Thomas Aquinas's commentaries on Aristotelian metaphysics [*Sententia super Metaphysicam* 3, II; no. 471], his commentaries on *De anima* [*Sententia Libri De anima* I, 8; no. 107] and in his *Sententia super Librum De caelo et mundo* [I, 22; 3,6]).

141   Albertus Magnus: *Kommentar zur aristotelischen Physik* (Commentary on Aristotelian Physics). Cited by Josef Pieper in *Scholastik* (Scholasticism), p. 169.

142   Jean-Pierre Torrell: *Magister Thomas* [Master Thomas], p. 253. Thomas, it was said in later centuries, almost "baptized" Aristotle. His references to Aristotle in central Christological topics could take on a provocative, free-spirited air, characterized by a fine, subtle sense of humor. For example, in a work containing observations on the Eucharist, he wrote about the actual presence of Christ in the altar sacrament, and added: "And because Aristotle tells us that it is a very special aspect of friendship 'to eat together with friends' (Nikomachische Ethik [Nicomachean Ethics] 9, 12), God promises to reward us with his physical presence" (*Summa theologica* III, 75, 1).

143   In his *Summa contra Gentiles* (4, II), Thomas described this order itself in the following way: "In simple beings, because of the different nature of their existence, we find that they have a different way of expressing their existence. As we look at beings of ever-higher orders, we see them carrying out this expressive process internally. Of all things that exist, things lacking souls occupy the lowest level. There can be no expressive activity carried out among these things except by the effect or action of one, taken upon another.... Among ensouled, living bodies the next highest level is held by the plants; and in these the expressive action does begin from within. The fluids inside the plant are converted into seeds; and then the seed, when sunken into the earth, grows into a new plant. Here we find the first level of life, for to be alive is to move oneself to action.... The life of plants is still imperfect. The expressive actions of plants begin from the inside; but what is expressed in the action moves outside the plant and in the end, is entirely external to the plant. First a blossom is formed from the sap of the tree, and then the fruit, which is still bound to the tree, yet is outside [external to] its bark. When the fruit is ripe, it separates itself from the tree entirely; it

falls to the ground and its power to reproduce produces another plant. If one watches this very carefully, one will see that the impetus for this expressive action comes from outside the plant, for the inner sap of the tree is drawn out of the earth through the roots, from which the plant draws its nourishment. Above the level of the plants stands animal life, higher because it has a soul that can sense. Their way of expressing their being does begin outside the animals, but it ends inside them. The further they progress, the more inwardly focused they become. An object is sensed, and an impression of the object is created in the senses. From here it presses through to the imagination, and then to the storehouse of the memory. But in all of these expressive actions, the beginning [impulse] and the end [result] lie in different areas. A sensory cognitive faculty cannot be directed at itself. This level of life is much higher than plant life, to be sure, as the activity of animal life does take place more inside; but it is still not a perfect level, because the beginning and end take place far apart. The highest and most perfect level is the life of spiritual and intellectual recognition. The intellect focuses upon itself, and can perceive itself. But even in intellectual life we must differentiate between various levels. The human intellect, although it can perceive itself, takes the beginning of its perception from outside itself. It cannot perceive without a sensory image. The intellectual life of angels is more perfect; for they do not reach the point of self-recognition from outside themselves, but perceive themselves through themselves. Still, their lives do not reach the final, highest levels; because their intellectual image of themselves, although it is entirely internal, is not one with their being. Perception and being are not one and the same. Only God has attained this highest level of perfection, for in him one cannot differentiate between perception and being."

144   Thomas interpreted the concept of the "world" (*mundus*) in various ways, and drew attention to nuances of meaning with a threefold division within the framework of the Gospels. In his exegesis of the Prologue of John, he wrote the following in his fifth chapter: "Sometimes he uses the word *world* (*mundus*) in reference to the Creation; for instance, when the evangelist...says [John 1:10], 'Through this, the world came to be.' Sometimes the name [world, mundus] is also used in reference to the perfection of the world, which it is trying to attain through Christ, as for example in I Cor. 5:19, 'Through Christ, God has reconciled himself with the world.' Sometimes it is also used in reference to perversity, as in I John 5:19, 'The whole world lies in a terrible state.'" Josef Pieper wrote the following on the subject: "This was of great concern to Saint Thomas: that the first sense of 'world' ('world' as Creation) not be equated with or confused with the third ('world' as the shape taken on by the elements of the Creation that had become perverted); the world of the Creation does *not* lie in a terrible state" (Josef Pieper: *Thomas-Brevier* [The Human Wisdom of St. Thomas

Aquinas: a Breviary of Philosophy from the Works of St. Thomas Aquinas]. Munich, 1956, p. 32).

145 *Summa contra Gentiles* 2, 87.

146 *Summa theologica* III 6, I ad I.

147 *Quaestiones disputatae de veritate* 14, 10 ad 9.

148 *Summa theologica* I 63, 9.

149 See Thomas's exegesis on the Prologue of John in *Lectura super Ionannem*. Translated into German by Josef Pieper (*Thomas von Aquin. Das Wort* [Thomas of Aquinas. The Word]. Munich, 1955) and Wolf-Ulrich Klünker (*Thomas von Aquin. Der Prolog des Johannes-Evangeliums* [Thomas of Aquinas. The Prologue of the Gospel of John]. Stuttgart, 1986). According to Josef Pieper, Thomas's study of the Prologue represents "the most magnificent formulation of the teachings on the Logos" to be found in all of Western theology (ibid., p. 7). However, as contemporary research has shown, we must assume that it was not Thomas Aquinas himself, but rather Reginald of Piperno, who set the corresponding Parisian Lectures (ca. 1270–1272) down on paper upon request: "This is what I, Brother Reginald of Piperno, member of the Dominican Order, on the request of some of my fellow Brothers; and as specifically mandated by His Worthiness the High Chaplain of Saint-Omer, have gleaned (and, I hope, not diminished) from Brother Thomas Aquinas, as one who collects the remaining grapes after the official harvest" (cited by Jean-Pierre Torrell in *Magister Thomas* [Master Thomas], p. 213). Thomas maintained a lifelong intellectual and spiritual interest in John [the Evangelist], and experienced him as a perpetual example of the contemplative human being. According to Thomas, John took as his theme the "Godliness of Christ," while the three remaining evangelists pursued the theme of the "Secrets of the Human Existence of Christ." In Thomas's introduction to his commentaries on John, he wrote, "The eagle is the symbol of John. The other three evangelists were occupied with the question of what Christ had brought about in his human existence. They are portrayed by symbols of beings that walk upon the earth; by the human being, the bull, and the lion. But John, like the eagle, soars over the fog of human impotence and gazes into the light of unchangeable truth, *looking up with the steady eye of his heart*" (cited in Pieper, *Thomas von Aquin. Das Wort* (Munich, 1955); emphasis added).

150 *Compendium theologiae I*, 201. In a different location (in the *Quaestiones disputatae de veritate*) Thomas wrote: "The emergence of everything created by God would not have been complete, if the emergence had not been matched by a return to God [*Imperfectus esset creaturarum a Deo exitus, nisi reditio in Deum exitum adaequaret*]" (20, 4).

151 *Summa theologica* I, 2 prologus.

152 Ibid. III 2, 9 ad 3.

153 Ibid. I 75, 4.

154 Ibid. I 75, 5 ad 2.

155   Ibid. I 75, 1.
156   Ibid. I 75, 5.
157   Ibid. I 75, 5 ad 2.
158   Ibid. III 2, 1 ad 2.
159   Ibid. I 75, 4.
160   Ibid. I 76, 1.
161   Ibid. I 76, 7 ad 3. "For Thomas, this means that the soul carries out
      the entire physical, vegetative, sensitively organic shaping of the body.
      This means that the soul penetrates the body in unbroken continuity
      right down to the most basic of the first, completely unformed sub-
      stances, which (as "purely receptive" material) are awakened, con-
      structed, ensouled, and embodied. To be sure, the reforming does not
      completely transform the being; the true essence of the pre-existing
      physical and animal-like bodily nature maintains its influence, pre-
      venting us from saying that the soul "is" the body. But it is permitted,
      and necessary, for us to say, that the body and soul form one single
      being, built according to a basic form, pervasive and vigorous; whose
      nature is, by and large, determined by this inner penetration by these
      two basic forms of existence: body and soul" (Siewerth: *Der Mensch
      und sein Leib* [Man and His Body] (Einsiedeln, 1953, pp. 11f.). "The
      substance is present in the plant, which is transformed by the forces
      streaming onto the earth. This is the living substance; the substance of
      life. It stands in a reciprocal arrangement with the lifeless substance.
      One should imagine that the living substance is continually being sepa-
      rated from the lifeless substance within the plant. The shape of the
      plant is the result of the forces streaming onto the earth. This creates a
      flow of substances. The lifeless transforms itself into the living; and the
      living transforms itself into the lifeless. The organs of the plant take
      shape within this flow. In the case of animals, the sentient substance
      arises from the living substance just as the living substance arises from
      the lifeless substance among the plants. A two-way exchange of sub-
      stances is present. Within the etheric, life is not brought to the point of
      being fully formed. This is achieved in the stream, and the formation
      slides into the flowing life stream through the astral organization. In
      the human being, this too is achieved in the flowing stream. The sen-
      tient substance is drawn into the realm of a still broader entity. One
      could call this the "I"-organization. The sentient substance transforms
      itself yet again. A three-way flow of substances arises. Within this, the
      inner and outer form of the human being arises. In this way, it becomes
      the bearer of self-aware spiritual and intellectual life. Right down to
      his smallest component parts, the human being, in the form he takes
      on, is the result of this 'I'-structure" (Rudolf Steiner and Ita Wegman:
      *Grundlegendes zu einer Erweiterung der Heilkunst nach geisteswis-
      senschaftlichen Erkenntnissen* [English trans.: *Extending Practical
      Medicine: Fundamental Principles Based on the Science of the Spirit.*
      London: Rudolf Steiner Press, 1996], CW 27, pp. 92ff.).

162   *Summa theologica* I 75, 7 ad 3.

163   Ibid. I 76, 2 ad 6.

164   *Quaestio disputata de spiritualibus creaturis* 2 ad 5.

165   *Sententia Libri de Anima* 3, 8, lect. 13. In another passsage, Thomas
wrote, "It is said that the soul is supposed to be everything, because it
is designed to know and recognize everything. In this manner, it is possible that the perfection of the entire universe could be present in the
existence of a single being. So the philosophers consider this the highest form of perfection to which the soul can aspire. The entire order of
the universe and its causes are written in this perfection" (*Quaestiones
disputatae de veritate* 2,2). And in the Summa theologica he formulated it as follows: "Beings that perceive differentiate themselves from
those that do not perceive; because beings that do not perceive have
nothing but their own form. A perceiving being, on the other hand, is
capable of carrying the form of other beings, as well as its own. This
is true because an image of the perceived object resides within the per-
ceiver. It is clear that the existence of the non-perceiving being is more
limited and constrained. The existence of the perceiving being has
greater breadth and capacity. For this reason, the philosopher [Aristo-
tle] says that the soul is of the greatest importance—is everything, in a
sense" (I 14, 1).

166   *Summa contra Gentiles* 3, 22.

167   See also endnote 34.

168   *Summa theologica* I 75, 3 ad 3.

169   *Quaestiones disputatae de veritate* 12, 3 ad 2. In the *Summa theologica* (I 76, 5) Thomas wrote the following on the subject: "The [human]
spirit–soul occupies the lowest level among spiritual beings, according
to the natural order of things, to the extent that they possess none of
the knowledge of the truth that is a natural characteristic of angels.
Instead, they are faced with the necessity of gathering this knowledge
from scattered sources along the path of sensory awareness."

170   "For this reason, once the soul has left the body, we give the corpse
the name "animal," or "human being," only in the sense that we call
painted wood or carved stone an animal. And it is the same with the
hand and eye, flesh and leg, as the philosopher [Aristotle; *De anima* 2,
I] says. A sign of this is the fact that no part of the body can perform its
particular, characteristic task any longer, while everything that retains
its characteristic purpose also retains the reality corresponding to that
description. Thus the soul must be present in the entire body, and in
each part of the body (*unde oportet animam esse in toto corpore, et in
qualibet ejus parte*)" (I-II 76, 8).

171   The particular capacity of the human being, insofar as he is a human
being, is thinking (*intelligere*); because he transcends (*transcendit*) all
other sentient beings by means of this capacity" (Ibid. I-II 76, 1).

172   In the words of Rudolf Steiner, formulated later: "The human body has
a structure appropriate for thinking" (*Theosophie. Eine Einführung*

in übersinnliche Welterkenntnis und Menschenbestimmung [English trans.: *Theosophy: An Introduction to the Spiritual Processes in Human Life and in the Cosmos.* Hudson, NY: Anthroposophic Press, 1994], CW 9, p. 28).

173   *Summa theologica* III 2, 2 ad 2.

174   "It is sensible, that the subordinated natural effective forces determine the preceding life forms and capacities. The most effective force of all, God himself, creates the ultimate form of life: the soul endowed with a spirit" (*Compendium theologiae* I, 93).

175   See also endnote 34.

176   Gustav Siewerth wrote on the Thomist–anthropologic understanding of the sense organs and the activities carried out by them. In his explication of the viewpoints Thomas had developed on the subject, Siewerth wrote that the senses existed "in [a state of] possibility," "empty," and "needy." It was not possible for them to emerge from the state of possibility into effective action (that is to say, perception) by means of any internal impulse. "The sense organs, and humans right along with them, take the action necessary to fulfill their sensory nature entirely from the outside, from the world, from other things. Since a sense exists within a body, however, its organ is not allocated only one single spot. It expands itself within a space. It has taken the substance; that is to say, the outwardly determined receptivity possessed by all natural things, and formed and developed this inside itself. As such, each sense is a capacity that has opened up a space for itself and stands open to the spatial growth and extending of all beings. Within its own space, it can perceive these spatially extended objects only as something external. But there is only one space, in which each part is connected with the other, and external with relation to the others. The sense receives and deduces spatial references and expanded reality only by being opened up by the space and being resolved to be externalized by it. Therefore it would be incomplete to say that the senses convey the qualities and images of natural things through their receptiveness. The senses can receive these things only because they themselves are originally part of the expressive, world-forming spatial action. Because they are fully realized in their lives, they come to be part of this spatial action 'outside' in the world. Through the spatially organized sensory body, the human being is primarily not conscious and within himself when he is engaged in sensory perception. Instead, he is 'carried out' into the world. He is 'in the world,' and encompasses the world by which he is simultaneously emcompassed. Here at the source it is quite easy to see how false (or half-true) it is to say that the human being receives things through a subjective capacity. The human is receiving, only because he is a fully realized 'existing in the world' (Heidegger) presence; because he has been carried out into the world as a being who exists there. Insofar as he 'has' the world, he is received by it and encompassed by it. The world is open in its light-action [to

do with sight]; its sounding air-action [to do with hearing]; and in its touching-movement-action [to do with touch] for the senses in their worldly, extended presence. In this enlightened openness, the human can only open himself to further worldly things, to things that belong to the world" (Siewerth: *Der Mensch und sein Leib* [Man and His Body], Einsiedeln, 1953, pp. 29f.). 700 years after Thomas's death, the young Rudolf Steiner began his debate with the contemporary theory of the senses. Under the influence of Descartes, Humes, and Kant, it had twisted itself into the opposite of the Aristotelian-Thomistic view. It spoke only of the "subjective" way of reacting to the "stimuli" of an ultimately unrecognizable and unfathomable environment. Rudolf Steiner published a text in March 1925, just weeks before his death, in which he wrote: "Through the [spiritual and imaginative] viewpoint it is apparent that human beings have not bound themselves intensively to their sensory system. It is not the human being who lives in this sensory system, but rather the environment. The environment built itself into the nature of the sensory organization. And for this reason the imaginative and observing human being considers the sensory organization to be part of the exterior environment. A part of the exterior environment that stands closer to the human being than the natural environment [the external world around us] stands; but nevertheless exterior to us. It differentiates itself from the rest of the external environment only in the sense that the human being in this environment can do nothing else but plunge himself consciously into it by means of sensory perception. The sensory organization is an eternal world; but the human being stretches his soul-spiritual nature into this external world, having brought his nature with him out of the spiritual world as he stepped into his earthly existence. With the exception of the fact that the human being fills his sensory organization with his soul-spiritual nature, this organization is part of the external world, just as it is the external world that is perpetually expanding around the human being. In the end, the eye belongs to the world, rather than to the human being; in the same way that a rose, perceived by a human being, belongs to the world, and not to the person. In the age the human being has just experienced in cosmic evolution, perceptive beings appeared who said, 'Impressions of color, sound, and warmth are not in the world, but in the human being. The color red,' they said, 'was not outside in the environment surrounding the human, but only the effect of something unknown upon the person.' But the truth is the exact opposite of this view. It is not the color that belongs to the eye of the human being; but the eye that belongs to the world, along with color. The human being does not allow the earthly environment to stream into himself during his life on earth. Instead, he *grows out* into the external world between birth and death" (Rudolf Steiner: *Anthroposophische Leitsätze* [English trans.: *Anthroposophical Leading Thoughts: Anthroposophy as a Path of Knowledge*. London:

Rudolf Steiner Press, 1998], CW 26, pp. 231ff.; see also Peter Selg, *Vom Logos menschlicher Physis* [The Logos of Human Physiology], pp.63ff., 174ff., 261ff., 438ff.).

177   *Summa theologica* I 75, 3 ad 2.

178   Ibid. I 87, 1.

179   Ibid.

180   Speaking on this subject in the *Quaestiones disputatae de veritate*, Thomas wrote: "The most perfect beings in the realm of existence, such as the spiritual beings, revert to their own nature when their return journey is completed. Because they recognize something outside themselves, they step outside themselves, in a certain sense. In recognizing that they recognize, they begin their return journey; for recognition lies in the middle between the one who recognizes and the object that is recognized. Each return journey is completely accomplished when they recognize their own nature. For this reason we can say that each being that knows its own nature returns to its nature at the end of its completed return journey" (I, 9).

181   "None of the senses perceives itself or its activity. The eye neither sees itself, nor perceives the fact that it is seeing. The knowing spirit, however, recognizes itself; and recognizes that it recognizes itself" (*Summa contra Gentiles* 2, 66).

182   *Summa contra Gentiles* 10, 8.

183   For more on this subject, see also the summarizing discussion, with the corresponding text passages, in Wolf-Ulrich Klünker: *Selbsterkenntnis der Seele. Zur Anthropologie des Thomas von Aquin* [The Self-aware Soul. On the Anthropolgy of Thomas of Aquinas], pp. 70–80 ("Die Existenz der Seele nach dem Tod" [The Existence of the Soul After Death]).

184   "It is essential to say that the human soul recognizes all things in the eternal images of existence; by dint of their participation, we recognize everything. The light of knowledge that lives within us is nothing else but a likeness in which we participate, showing the uncreated light, which contains the eternal images." (*Summa theologica* I 84, 5).

185   See Wolf-Ulrich Klünker, loc. cit., pp. 37ff. ("Habitus-Bildung als Entwicklung des Ich" [Building Habits as Self-Development]).

186   *Quaestiones disputatae de veritate* 24, 2.

187   "*Ubicumque est intellectus, est liberum arbitrium*" (*Summa theologica* I 59, 3). According to Thomas Aquinas, human freedom is experienced in the motion of recognizing; but not fully realized until the stage of acting is reached. As Thomas had already pointed out in one of his early works (the commentary on the aphorisms of Petrus Lombardus) the content of the activity of recognition is defined by the existing reality of things; whereas the defined goals of the will forces lie in the freedom of the human being, who decides independently (or at least *can* decide independently) what its use should be, on the basis of its own perceptive work. To this extent freedom is experienced in the sense

of individual activity in the realm of the motion of recognition. But only in the realm of moral action does this lead to independent, freely chosen positions: The will is more the master of its actions (*domina sui actus*) than of its cognitive power, because it is compelled by the truth of the matter. For that reason, a person is called good or bad according to the effectiveness of the will; because the effectiveness of the will is the effectiveness of the human; because it is left to the discretion of his strength, but not according to the effectiveness of his cognitive power, over which he is not the master (*Scriptum super libros Sententiarum* 2, d. 7, 2, I ad 2).

188   This is how Thomas began the foreword (*prooemium*) of his *Über die Einheit des Geistes, gegen die Averroisten* (*De unitate intellectus, contra averroistas*) with unexpectedly sharp words: "As all people naturally long to recognize truth, there dwells in them an inherent desire to avoid and refute errors, insofar as it lies within their power. Among the various errors, an especially grave one is deceiving oneself about the spirit. We are born to recognize the truth through the spirit, and to avoid errors. To be sure, an error about the spirit has become established in the minds of many for a long while. This error originated with the teaching of Averroes. Averroes took a great deal of trouble to prove that the spirit that Aristotle designated as a possible (*possibiles*) spirit was a being that had separated itself from the body and could not be united with the form of the body. Averroes referred to this with the inappropriate name "material" (*materialis*) spirit. In addition, Averroes claimed that this possible spirit could be the essential spirit for all human beings. We have written against this viewpoint many times. Because the effrontery of this false teacher continues, as he opposes the truth (*sed quia errantium impudentia non cessat veritati reniti*), we have taken it upon ourselves and decided to write yet another piece against these errors, to refute the error we have named with absolute clarity" (173, Ed. Klünker).

189   Ibid. 232.

190   *Summa contra Gentiles* 3, 144.

191   *Summa theologica* I 75.

192   According to Jean-Pierre Torrell, there are 126 handmade copies of the manuscript of *De motu cordis* alone, and 33 verifiable printed editions (Torrell, *Magister Thomas* [Master Thomas], p. 228). The first German translation of the work dates from the year 1926, and was done by the anthroposophic physicians Eugen Kolisko and Eberhard Schickler (in *Natura. Zeitschrift zur Erweiterung der Heilkunst nach gesiteswissenschaftlicher Menschenkunde* [Natura: Journal for the Expansion of the Healing Arts according to the Knowledge of the Human Being Gained through Spiritual Science], vol. 1, 1926, pp. 86–93). An in-depth interpretative study by Kolisko followed a short time later in the same journal (ibid., pp. 168–177; Kolisko's motivation to study and translate *De motu cordis* may have come from Rudolf

Steiner himself). A second German translation (with the Latin text in parallel columns, and a short section of notes) was published in Stuttgart in 1987 by Wolf-Ulrich Klünker. Klünker and Torrell appear to have been entirely unaware of the work of Kolisko and Schickler (see Torrell's bibliography of Thomas's works and translations, *Magister Thomas* [Master Thomas], p. 228). The editors of Klünker's edition, Karl-Martin Dietz and Thomas Kracht, used these words in their foreword: "The short work *Über die Bewegung des Herzens* [On the Movement of the Heart] *appears here for the first time in German translation*, as was the case with *De unitate intellectus*, clarifying additional aspects of Thomas's anthropology and teachings on the soul" (ital. added by Dr. Selg).

193   *Summa theologica* II-II 122, 2. In the notes for the twentieth volume of the complete edition of *Summa theologica*, the editors wrote that Thomas had been an adherent "of the notion now proven to be fallacious" whereby "the heart is the most important element for the life and development of the organism." Actually, "natural science of the modern era" would teach "us" something else, and would show that "in each stage of development, the most important element of that stage develops first," such as the embryonic layers before the actual organs (pp. 324f.). Actually, the heart and circulatory system, active since the end of the third week of life, doubtlessly constitute the first functioning organ system of the entire organism. It ties the furthest periphery of the embryonic environment with the developing center, and precedes (significantly earlier) all of the organologic formations that will follow. The heartbeat or rhythmic contraction of the heart itself starts on the twenty-second day and follows (by five days) the appearance of the first blood vessels and the resultant onset of the movement of the blood.

194   *Scriptum super libros Sententiarum* 2.14, I. I ad 2.

195   *Summa theologica* I 18, I ad I.

196   *Scriptum super libros Sententiarum* 3.13, 2, I ad 5.

197   *Summa theologica* I 44, 5; see also I 20, I and I-II 17, 9 ad 2.

198   *De motu cordis* 454 (Klünker ed.).

199   *Summa theologica* I 18, 1.

200   *Lectura super Ioannem* I 3.

201   *De motu cordis* 453 (Klunker ed.). Eugen Kolisko and Eberhard Schickler translate this as: "Nothing is more intrinsically important to the ensouled living being than the movement of the heart; for when this ceases to take place, life ceases" (*Natura*, loc. cit., p. 87).

202   Ibid. 454.

203   Summa theologica I-II 17, 9 ad 2.

204   *De motu cordis* 458.

205   With reference to Aristotle, Thomas wrote on the subject in *De motu cordis*: "I designate the movement of the heart as the natural movement of the sensory being, because (as the philosopher [Aristotle] explained in the book De *Motu Animalium* [On the Movement of

Sensory Beings]) it must be assumed that the sensory being exists in the same way that a good and lawfully directed state exists. When the systematic order is carefully set up in a state, it is not necessary that the absent ruler be present for every single event that takes place. Instead, each does his work, as arranged and decreed, and later this is done out of habit. Among sensory beings, nature accomplishes the same thing" (Ibid. 458).

206   Ibid. 459.

207   Ibid.

208   *Summa theologica* I 18, I ad I.

209   *De motu cordis* 460.

210   Ibid.

211   Ibid. 462.

212   Ibid.

213   In *De motu cordis*, in reference to the heart, Thomas spoke of the effective *"anima sensitiva"* (see also endnote 340).

214   In the chapter of his Thomas publication called *Der Ort der substantiellen Einheit des Menschen* [The Point of Substantial Unity in the Human Being], Gustav Siewerth wrote things that, though very probably consistent with Thomas's work, nevertheless are not to be found in any identifiable extant works by Thomas Aquinas. These passages have to do with the role and status of the heart in Thomist anthropology: "There must be an inner basis for unity and life; a root of existence, from which the divided, hierarchical, ordered organization [of the human being] arises; in which development takes place, and to which one always returns. Without a doubt, this is the basis for the heart and root, the center of life of the individual, in which he has unity and existence as part of his nature; in which nature streams into the personal self-awareness; or in which this feels and experiences itself to be part of human nature. Here the vegetative and the sensory life have a unified root, the basis of life itself, so that everything—spirit, soul, and body—nurtures itself from this deep source, adjusts to it, and floods across its boundaries, one flowing into the other. Everything the human being is, is brought about by his heart, that foundation and deep abyss of our nature; it is more the basis of our unity than the 'purely spiritual,' the 'purely soulful,' and our sensory and vegetative aspects; because it pervades all of these realms and unifies aspects of our being and essence 'substantially and substantively'" (Siewerth: *Der Mensch und sein Leib* [Man and his body]. Einsiedeln, 1953, p. 15).

215   *Summa theologica* I-II 17, 9 ad 3.

216   See the corresponding statements in *Quaestio disputata De anima* and *Quaestio disputata De spiritualibus*, in which Thomas, in connection with the Aristotelian statements in *Über Wachen und Schlafen* [On Waking and Sleeping], drew connections between the changes in the sense activities within the sleeping-waking rhythm and the heart-centered warmth processes (see R. Boos, *Thomas von Aquin.*

Übersetzungen, Aufsätze, Vorträge [Thomas of Aquinas. Translations, Essays, Lectures]. Schaffhausen, 1959, p. 94).

217 Thomas wrote this as part of the—in the narrower sense—Christological explanations of the *Summa theologica* on the question: "Did Christ's soul have unlimited power over his body?" This is the third of the possible answers listed: "By its very nature, everything that was imagined by the soul [*imaginatio*] influences the body; and in fact all the more so, when the imaginative power of the soul is stronger. The soul of Christ had imaginative power (and every other power of the soul) at the highest level of perfection. Accordingly, it must also have had unlimited power over the body." The general anthropological phrasing of this: "The body, because of its nature, is subject to the influence of strong imaginings: for example, when someone imagines he is falling from a high beam. Because these imaginings are apt to cause localized activity, as [Aristotle] suggested in *De Anima*. The same thing can happen when imagining warmth, cold, and other things that bring about change in the body. As is natural, agitation (*passiones animae*) can arise from these imaginings. As a result, the heart begins to move more strongly (*secundum quas movetur cor*); and by means of the agitation of the spirit (*per commotionem spirituum*), this spreads throughout the entire body, causing alterations as it spreads" (III 13, 3 ad 3). Carrying these thoughts further, Thomas Aquinas subsequently alleged, in blanket terms, in his two treatises *Quaestio disputata de anima* and *Quaestio disputata de spiritualibus*, that it is always the heart-centered effectiveness of the spirit in the human being that underlies the body's activities and capacities for action (for more about the larger anthropological dimension of this matter, see the interpretation by Boos, loc. cit., pp. 94ff. and below).

218 In *De motu cordis*, Thomas spoke repeatedly of the meaning of the *anima sensitiva* for shaping (and the subsequent manner of functioning) the heart. Although not expressed so specifically, we could question if it is not indeed this dimension of the human soul that constitutes the heart in a certain sense, if only in a way open to the higher life of the anima intellectiva (see below).

219 "The word *passiones* can be translated into German only with great difficulty. It denotes 'conditions' into which the soul can fall because it experiences or suffers something from outside itself. The soul is not itself active, but rather an impression is brought about within it. In this sense, the soul remains passive even with regard to its 'moods and perceptions'" (Klünker, loc. cit., note 156, p. 168).

220 *Summa theologica* I-II 24, 2 ad 2.

221 Ibid. I-II 48, 2.

222 Ibid. and I-II 44, I ad I.

223 Ibid. I-II 44, 3 ad 3.

224 Ibid. I-II 44, 2 ad 3.

225 Ibid. I-II 31, 3 ad 3 and I-II 33, 1 ad 3.

226 Ibid. I–II 28, 5.

227 Thomas spoke in this way about the "rising" and the "heating up" of the blood surrounding the heart, and the "Spiritus" in conditions of anger (or its collective climb in the direction of the heart). He described the opposite movement appearing in conditions of fear, and in reference to this he noted, "Among those experiencing fear, on the other hand, the Spiritus moves downward, instead, because of the cold, which thickens the blood. This coldness arises out of the imagined failing of one's strength [!]. As a result, warmth and life forces in the area around the heart do not increase, but are instead more likely to flee from the heart" (I–II 44, 1 ad 1). With reference to the ways we experience joy and love, it is not truly clear whether Thomas had concrete physiological processes in mind when he spoke about the "expansion" of the heart (*dilatatione cordis*) in joyful circumstances (I–II 31, 3 ad 3 and I–II 33, 1 ad 3) or with reference to love and the adaptation (necessary, according to Thomas) to the beloved object. In a lengthy discussion, he determined the following (among other things): "For this reason, a hardening or hardness of the heart (*cordis congelatio vel duritia*) is a condition that contradicts love. In contrast to this, melting implies a softening of the heart, through which the heart offers itself as well-suited, so that the loved one can enter (*sed liquefactio importat quandam mollificationem codis, qua exhibet se cor habile ut amatum in ipsum subintret*)" (I–II 28, 5).

228 Ibid. I–II 48, 4 ad 3.

229 *Summa theologica* III 8, 1 ad 3.

230 Wolf-Ulrich Klünker writes a closing remark at the end of his edition of *De motu cordis:* "In explaining the commandment 'Thou shalt love the Lord thy God with all thy heart,' Thomas lists aspects of his understanding not mentioned in the foregoing discussion: 'In this commandment, the heart is not regarded as a part of the body, because loving God is not an activity of the body. For this reason, one needs to understand the word *heart* in a spiritual sense (*spiritualiter*). But the heart, understood in the spiritual sense, is the soul (*anima*) itself, or something soulful.... The strength of a person is primarily dependent upon the heart, whether it is understood in the spiritual or physical sense.... We should take note of the fact that love is an activity of the will (*voluntas*), designated by the term heart. For just as the bodily heart is the cause (*principium*) of all bodily activity, so, too, is the will the cause of all spiritual activity'" (*Summe der Theologie* [Summary of the Theology] II–II q. 44, a. 5). At first, Klünker's words appear to offer very little help in achieving an understanding of Thomas's view of the heart. It does not seem to bring us any closer to understanding. In this particular form, as a remark, it is barely comprehensible. With regard to the text, it is not exactly comprehensive (and seems to cover only arbitrarily chosen segments). Textually it is decidedly problematic. Klünker gathered aspects of the discussion that Thomas

had brought up in an *articulus*, aspects upon which he had given lectures. Klünker did not state the sources of these statements, however, and in this form they simply cannot be taken to constitute a position authorized by Thomas Aquinas, or even a position traceable back to Thomas's original texts. To an extent, they even contain opinions that Thomas had rejected. (For more on the construction and structure of an *articulus* (and the Scholastic forms of the *quaestio, disputatio,* and *disputatio quodlibetalis* connected to it), see M.-D. Chenu: *Das Werk des Heiligen Thomas von Aquin* [The Work of Saint Thomas of Aquinas]. Heidelberg, Graz, Vienna, Cologne, 1960.) The important fifth *articulus* of the forty-fourth *quaestio* ("The Commandments of Love," "De praeceptis caritatis") out of the second part of the second book of the Summa theologica, cited only in part by Klünker, is cited here in its entirety: Article 5 (II-II 44, 4). "Is it fitting to add 'with all thy soul, and with all thy strength,' to the words, 'Thou shalt love the Lord thy God with all thy heart'? (Deut. 6:5) 1) For *heart* does not mean a part of the body in this context, since to love God is not a matter for the body; and therefore 'heart' should be understood here in a spiritual sense. The heart, understood spiritually, is either the soul itself or some part of the soul. Therefore it is superfluous to name both [heart and soul]. 2) A person's strength, whether understood to be spiritual strength or bodily strength, depends (above all) upon the heart. After the words, 'Thou shalt love the Lord thy God with all thy heart,' it was therefore unnecessary to add, 'with all thy strength.' 3) In Matt. 22:37 we read: 'With all thy mind,' which is not expressed here. Therefore it seems that this commandment is not given in an appropriate form in Deut. 6. *The authority of the Bible stands in opposition to this (sec contra). Answer (respondeo):* This commandment is transmitted to us using different words in different passages. In Deut. 6 three things are listed: 'with all thy heart,' and 'with all thy soul,' and 'with all thy might.' In Matt. 22:37 we find two of these named: 'with all thy heart' and 'with all thy soul,' while 'with all thy strength' is omitted, but 'with all thy mind' is added instead. Yet in Mark 12:30 we find all four listed: 'with all thy heart,' and 'with all thy soul,' and 'with all thy mind,' and 'with all thy strength.' Moreover, these four are mentioned in Luke 10:27, where in place of 'strength' or 'force' we read 'with all thy power[s].' Accordingly these four have to be explained, since the fact that one of them is omitted here or there is due to one implying another [whether it is mentioned or not]. We must consider, therefore, that love is an act of the will, which is here denoted by the word 'heart'; because just as the bodily heart is the source of all the movements of the body; so too, the will, especially in regard to the final goal, which is directed toward the object of love, is the source of all the movements of the spirit. There are three principles of action which are moved by the will; namely, the intellect or understanding, which is denoted by 'mind'; the baser capacity for striving, denoted by 'soul'; and the external power signified by 'strength,' 'capacity,' or 'might.' For this reason we are commanded to direct our whole inner focus toward God, and this is what is meant by the words 'with all thy heart'; to subordinate our intellect or understanding to God, and this is expressed in the words 'with all thy mind'; to allow God to regulate our capacity for striving, which is meant by the words 'with all thy soul'; and to be obedient to God in our external actions, that is to say: to love God with all of our 'strength,' 'capacity,' or 'might.' Chrysostom, on the other hand, interprets 'heart' and 'soul' in the opposite sense; and Augustine associates 'heart' with our thoughts; 'soul' to our life; and 'mind' to our intellect or understanding. But some say 'with all thy heart,' that is to say, with the intellect or understanding; 'with [all] thy soul,' that is to say, with the will; and 'with [all] thy mind,' that is to say, with the memory. Or, according to Gregory of Nyssa, 'heart' signifies the vegetative soul; 'soul' the sensing soul; and 'mind' the intellectual-spiritual soul; because everything that nourishes us, everything we perceive with our senses, and everything we understand must be focused upon God. From this we can draw our response [*responsio*] to the [above] objections [*objecta*]."

231   *Summa theologica* I 34, 1.

232   Ibid. I, 27, 1.

233   Ibid. I 34, 1.

234   *De Natura Verbi Intellectus*, cited in Pieper *Thomas-Brevier* [The Human Wisdom of St. Thomas Aquinas: a Breviary of Philosophy from the Works of St. Thomas Aquinas]. Munich, 1956, p. 95.

235   In a certain sense, the one who is perceiving, or aware, steps out of himself during the activity of perception, and returns (steps back into himself) with the existential picture (or forms) of what was perceived. "The knowledge within us is a reflection of our soul through objects" (*Quaestiones disputatae de veritate* 2, 1 ad 6). Thomas wrote the following subsequent thoughts in the *Summa theologica*: "Perception exists, to the extent that the perceived [thing] exists in the perceiving [person]. Love, though, exists insofar as the one who is loving unites himself with the beloved reality" (ibid. I 108, 6 ad 3). And: "Perception is complete, when the one who is perceived becomes one in his essence with the one who is perceiving. Love causes the real thing that is loved to become one, in a certain sense, with the one who is loving. Thus love has more unifying power (*est magis unitivus*) than perception" (ibid. I-II 28, 1 ad 3). It stands closer than pure heart perception to the pole of human existence occupied by the will and carried by sympathy.

236   *Summa theologica* I–II 28, 2.

237   Ibid.

238   Ibid. II-II 24, 7. On the Holy Spirit as "love of the Father and the Son" (*amor Patris et Filii*), see (among other passages) also III 3, 5 ad 2; I 45, 6 ("God the Father created the world through his word, which is the Son, and through his love, which is the Holy Spirit [*Deus pater operatus est creaturam per suum Verbum, quod est Filius, et per suum*

Amorem, qui est Spiritus Sanctus]"). Also see the corresponding explications in *Summa contra Gentiles*, in which Thomas wrote: "The Holy
Spirit goes forth in love [*procedit per modum amoris*], in which God
loves himself" (4, 20).

239   *Expositio et Lectura super Epistolas Pauli Apostoli.* 5, 1.

240   See the passages on warmth in the chapter on Aristotle, and endnote
115.

241   *Summa contra Gentiles* 4, 20.

242   See *Summa theologica* II–II 24, 3: "It is better, that the human being
not only wants what is good, but brings it about by external actions.
In the same way, it is part of the perfection of the moral good, that the
human being is moved to the good not only by the will, but also by
the sensory striving. According to Psalm 84:3: 'My heart and my flesh
rejoiced to the living God,' and here we understand 'heart' to mean
intellectual-spiritual striving [*ut cor accipiamus pro appetitu intellec-
tivo*], and 'flesh' to mean sensory striving."

243   Ibid. III 66, 11.

244   According to Thomas, the heart's activity or capacity with regard to
believing stands in a close relationship to perception, as he understood
this in the sense of a free, willed activity directed at an extrasensory
object of perception—as an "imperfect perception" (*Fides enim imper-
fecta est cognitio*, in *Compendium Theologiae* 2, 1). He also saw this
as an anticipated, affirming agreement, which for its part is the prerequisite for future processes of perception, and as a deliberately assenting
thinking process, attentive and careful in and of itself. ("And this is
peculiar to the one who believes: that he thinks with assent [*et sic proprium est credentis, ut cum assensu cogitet*]" *Summa theologica* II–II
2, 1.) In the *Summa theologica*, Thomas wrote more on the subject:
"Each one who learns, must believe that he will achieve perfect knowledge at some point" (II–II 2, 3). And: "Belief is a type of perception, to
the extent that the power to perceive is fixed upon the perceived object
by means of that belief. This "being-fixed-upon-one-thing" does not
arise out of the sight of the one who believes [*non procedit ex visione
eius cui creditur*]" (I 12, 13, 3). On the one hand, many useful insights
on Thomas's Christological anthropology arise from this information,
including the spiritual and physiological role of the "believing heart" in
that anthropology (see also the rest of the text). On the other hand, we
also find aspects in this work of Thomas Aquinas that help us understand Rudolf Steiner's work in the twentieth century. Countless times,
Steiner urged his listeners to work with the results of his research into
spiritual science. Aspects of his work that were not yet accessible to the
perception or thinking of a given individual were to be pursued and
thoughtfully examined with full attention and calm inner acceptance.
This would allow Steiner's work to become the starting point for our
own individual acquisition of knowledge in the future. In the 1904
introduction to *Theosophy*, Rudolf Steiner wrote: "One is looking at

the things of the extrasensory world in the right manner, if one presumes that healthy thought and sensitivity can comprehend everything that can flow out of the higher worlds in the way of true perceptions and knowledge. In addition, if we start with this understanding, and use it to form a solid basis, this can enable us to take an important step toward our own observations and insights. This is true even though other things must also take place in order for us to reach this point. One closes the door to true higher knowledge if one dismisses this path and wishes to force one's way into the higher worlds in some other manner. The principle: to first know and perceive higher worlds, when one has glimpsed them oneself, is an obstacle to this knowledge and perception. The *will* to understand everything through healthy thought first, which one will later be able to see oneself, assists and furthers this ability to see. It brings forth important soul forces, which lead to this 'sight of the seer'" (CW 4, p. 19, emphasis added). Rudolf Steiner, like Thomas Aquinas before him, was not describing a naive approval of spiritual content in the sense of an acceptance of "loyalty and belief." Instead, he was describing the beginning of a spiritual activity leading in the direction of the wisdom of God (*"theo-sophia"*). As Thomas put it: "The beginning of an ascent to God [*principium accendi ad Deum*]" (*Compendium Theologiae* 2, 243). To gain a further understanding of the tasks of Rudolf Steiner's life, we must also consider the particular Michaelic dimension of his work and accomplishments. ("Michael is not the particular spirit who watches over intellectuality, but everything he offers as spirituality enlightens humankind in the form of ideas, and in the form of thoughts; but in the form of ideas and thoughts that encompass the spiritual. Michael wants each person to be a free human being whose concepts and ideas also offer insight into what is revealed to him by the spiritual worlds" CW 240 [*Karmic Relationships: Esoteric Studies*, vol 6. London: Rudolf Steiner Press, 2009], p. 167.)

245 Ibid. III 72, 1.
246 Ibid. I–II 69, 4.
247 Ibid. III 72, 2 ad 2.
248 Ibid. III 57, 2 ad 2.
249 *Summa contra Gentiles* 4, 46.
250 "The word of God penetrates everything with its power, by guarding and carrying all things in existence. Even so, it is still able to unite itself (by means of a relationship of similitude) in a higher and inexpressible way with a spiritually endowed (spiritually gifted) creature who is able to enjoy the word in its true and actual sense, and able to take part in it" (ibid. 4, 41).
251 Ibid. I, 93, 6.
252 See also Boos, *Thomas von Aquin. Übersetzungen, Aufsätze, Vorträge* [Thomas of Aquinas. Translations, Essays, Lectures]. Schaffhausen, 1959, pp. 86f.

253   Thomas's profound observations on the sacraments are found in Part III of his *Summa theologica* and are worthy of thorough study. This constitutes vols. 29–34 in the German-Latin complete edition. The entire thirtieth volume is devoted to the sacrament of the Eucharist. For more on Thomas Aquinas and the Corpus Christi service (*Offizium*), see James A Weisheipl: *Thomas von Aquin. Sein Leben und seine Theologie* [Thomas of Aquinas: His Life and Theology]. Graz, Vienna, Cologne, 1980, pp. 166–173.

254   "*Omnium sacramentorum finis*" (*Summa theologica* III, 73, 3).

255   Ibid. III 75, 2 ad 2. "The celebration of the secret of Christ, God, and perfect human at one and the same time, entirely contained in the sacrament, stands at the center of all things for Thomas. This is true to such an extent that he does not speak of receiving the body or blood of Christ, but rather speaks of receiving Christ [*Christus sumitur,* or even *Deus sumitur*]" (Torrell, *Magister Thomas* [Master Thomas]. Freiburg, 1995, p. 153).

256   The first biographer of Thomas Aquinas was Wilhelm von Tocco. He was also a priest in the Dominican order, and lived in the cloister of Naples along with Thomas in the early 1270s. On this topic, he wrote: "Brother Thomas celebrated Mass each morning in the Nicholas Chapel, and another priest began as soon as he was finished; and as soon as Thomas had participated in this, he removed his (Mass) vestments and gave a lecture at once. As soon as this was finished, he began to write. He dictated to several secretaries at the same time. After this he ate, returned to his room, or dedicated himself to Godly matters until the time of the great silence. After the period of silence he began to write again. In this way, he ordered his entire life around his service to God" (cited in Torrell, loc. cit., p. 257).

257   Roman Boos wrote about Thomas's *verbum cordis* and his religious speech in his interpretative work on Thomas: "Spiritually, Thomas experienced the heart as the cradle of the Word. In theological experience (they still had that back in those days), Thomas experienced the heart as the birthplace of the Godly word in human beings. In experience and perception it was the birthplace of the *verbum cordis,* the word of the heart. In his *Traktat vom Wort* [Treatise on the Word], Thomas succeeded in portraying this experience of forming words in the heart with such an Appolonic fullness of light that even today, after almost seven centuries, one can sense this process in a very real, bodily way. [The harbor city Appolonia, in modern-day Libya, was the birthplace of Erotosthenes. —Tr.] It takes place at the beginning of the Eucharistic process of the bodily purification in the heart, and the illumination of the Dionysian flesh-and-blood human being. In the word of the heart, each thought reaches its target. According to Thomas, human thinking must always arise from the external world through 'perception.' Through 'truth-giving' and 'giving words' it returns to the external world. In the forming of the inner 'word' of naming an object

(which is not necessarily followed by speaking it through the *verbum vocis*, the spoken word), the most sublime will of the human being is entirely active in the service of perception. In the transfigured human body, the instinctual drives of the flesh and blood will also serve us in this way. Christ's body and blood, taken into the body and blood of the human being during the Eucharist, are a promise to the human being that he will someday live as a whole human being in God. For now, he must experience this in his heart between a spiritual give and take: a spiritual taking from the world and a spiritual giving to the world. The most sublime *spiritus vitalis* lives in the realm of the heart, in the *praecordia*, if the *spiritus* of the heart ascends, in the warmth of the enthusiasm of perception, from the heart to the *aorta vocalis*, to the vocal arteries, and they pulse in word-forming movements in the larynx (*in gutture*). Thomas gave this the name *meditationes*. Thomas experienced his larynx as the place of meditation on the truth. (Thomas gave *Summa contra Gentiles* the epigraph: 'My larynx [*guttur*] will meditate on the truth, and the testimony of my lips will destroy the impious [*detestabuntur*].' In the vocal arteries of the breathing tubes, whose 'head' is the place where we form our gutteral sounds, there is no more heavy blood. Only *'spiritus.'* According to Thomas, all thinking ends in the forming of words, and the formation of words is a way of retaining the actions of formative forces. The speaking heart communicates these forces to the *spiritus vitalis* in the esophagus, and all thinking is in the larynx; the truth can be contained in the word. The external air communicates the truth-word, the larynx-word, authentically only if religion takes up the spiritus of the altar, the Holy Spirit, keeping it pure in impure surroundings. Otherwise it serves only to testify against the impious, for the battle, leaving the lips to enter the impure world. *'Guttur'* and *'labia'*—*'ecclesia triumphans'* and *'ecclesia militans'*(!). *Spiritus Sanctus*, the Holy Spirit, infuses itself into this meditation, if the Son, the word of the heavenly Father, lives in it. Standing before the altar, the Holy Spirit steps out over the lips in the religious words that are spoken" (loc. cit., p. 96).

258   *Scriptum super Libros Sententiarum* 4d. 43, 1, 2, 2 ad 2. See also Rudolf Steiner's later statements as he answered theological questions: "If someone merely reads the religious text, it is no longer a religious text. The text must be read [aloud] by another and heard by the person in question. If someone reads the text, it could be a religious text only if he were able to hear it spoken at the same time from the extrasensory world; at that point it would be a religious text for that person. But when someone living on the physical plane merely reads the text, it is not a religious text" (CW 344 [Not available in English], p. 213).

259   "But God illuminates the baptized persons from within, preparing their hearts to accept the teaching of the truth, according to the words: 'It is written by the prophets: all people shall be God's students' (John 6:45)" (*Summa theologica* III 69, 5 ad 4).

260 Ibid. III 67, 5 ad 1.

261 As it was very simply worded in the *Summa theologica*: "The sacrament of Holy Communion, through which the human being's inner self is strengthened, is related to the heart, according to the words: 'May the bread strengthen the heart of the human being' (Psalm 103:4) [*Sacramentum Eucharistiae, quo homo in seipso confirmatur, pertinet ad cor, secundum illud: 'Panis cor hominis confirmat'*]" (III 72, 9 ad 2). In another passage of his observations on the Eucharist, as well (III 75, 7), Thomas refers to this formulation from the Psalms.

262 "Priests are consecrated in order to complete the sacrament of the body of Christ" (Ibid. III 67, 2).

263 *Summa theologica* III 78, 1. The sacramental words of Christ are also effective in a heart-centered manner, to the extent that the consecrated priest does not live in the way he should: "For a tool to be a tool, no matter what sense and power it might have, everything that is not part of the intrinsic concept of the tool is irrelevant. The same is true, for example, if the body of the doctor, the tool of his soul, which understands his work as a physician, is healthy or sick; and if the pipe, through which water flows, is made of silver or of lead. For this reason, those carrying out the offices of the church are able to administer the sacraments, even if they are evil" (ibid. III 64, 5). And even more clearly stated: "The taskmaster works differently with his hand and with his hatchet. In the sacraments, Christ works through the good people as though working through living limbs, and through evil people as if through lifeless tools (*per instrumenta carentia vita*)" (ibid. 64, 5 ad 2).

264 Thomas Aquinas wrote about hope in a commentary on Aristotle's text on *Gedächtnis und Erinnerung* [On Memory and Remembering]. He wrote that hope is the "perception of future events," as opposed to perceiving events of the moment and remembering events of the past (*In Librum de Memoria et Reminiscentia Commentarium*, no. 387, cited in Klünker: *Selbsterkenntnis der Seele. Zur Anthropologie des Thomas von Aquin* [Self-Awareness of the Soul: On the Anthropology of Thomas of Aquinas], p. 64; see above, as well, p. 59). In this sense, the human heart is the organ of hope, and of the future, for Thomistic anthropology. The heart prepares for the future and lives, perceiving, in that future already, together with the spirit-infused will. In this respect, the heart is also the organ of "belief" (see endnote 244), because even now, it accepts cognitive possibilities that belong to the future.

265 Ibid. I–II 106, 1.

266 Ibid. III 87, 1.

267 Cited in Torrell, loc. cit., p. 302.

268 Cited in Pieper, *Thomas-Brevier*, p. 21. [The text of *Os justi* comes from Psalm 37:30–31—Tr.]

269 In 1923, researcher Martin Grabmann made reference to the fact that for the first time, in Thomas, the church had canonized someone for

being a theologian and teacher. He was not canonized for performing miracles, for remarkable visions, or for the unusual extent of his ascetic practices and unusual character traits; but primarily for being a thinker, teacher, and writer. (*Die Kanonisation des heiligen Thomas* [The Canonization of the Holy Thomas]. In *Divus Thomas*, vol. 1 [1923], pp. 241ff.) In this same sense, Thomas was declared an official "teacher of the church" in 1567. He was accepted into the *Codex Iuris Canonici* in 1918, and the way for this had been paved by his inclusion in the 1879 encyclical called *"Aeterni Patris."* His canonization was made "with the specification that the priests of the Catholic Church should receive their theological and philosophical training according to the methods, teachings, and principles of Thomas Aquinas" (Pieper, *Thomas von Aquinas. Leben und Werk* [Thomas of Aquinas. Life and Work], p. 34).

270   "May I remind you of an astonishing fact: Thomas, although such a great teacher, had no 'students' in the narrower sense. He stood alone throughout his life" (Pieper, loc. cit., p. 37).

271   *Summa theologica* I 58, 6.

272   Ibid. III 5, 4 ad 2.

273   CW 11, pp. 176ff.

274   According to Rudolf Steiner (Dornach, December 29, 1923; CW 233 [English trans.: *World History and the Mysteries*. London: Rudolf Steiner Press, 1997]), knowledge of nature, the spiritual science of nature, was carried to Asia by Aristotle, on the journeys of Alexander the Great. There, this study was continued intensively. For the time being, however, it did not make its way to the West, or to Europe ("In all honesty, Europe was unable to bear this deeper knowledge of nature at first. It wanted external knowledge, external culture, external civilization" [CW 233, p. 107]). During the decisive cultural change of the Aristotelian "Renaissance" of the Latin Middle Ages, Steiner tells us, the logical texts of the *Corpus Aristotelium* stood almost exclusively at the center of Scholastic interest. This led to a productive connection between the schools of thought. Nevertheless, "As the basis of Middle European insights, we have ideas that, though unattractive, are propagated by large groups, including even rather primitive peoples. See for example how the seed that Alexander carried over into Asia, then traveled over all possible routes across Arabia, and so forth, finally reaching Europe via the overland route, thanks to the Crusaders. These ideas live everywhere, but they are unattractive, and live in hidden places. Then people like Jacob Böhme, Paracelsus, and countless others come forth and take up these ideas that have reached the wide, primitive sections of the European population in this roundabout way. We have transmitted ancient folk wisdom—far more than one would usually think. It lives among us. And sometimes it streams into the reservoirs of such people as Valentin Wiegel, Paracelcus, Jakob Böhme, and many others, whose names are not heard so often. This [stream of]

wisdom shines upon the tardy Alexandrianism of Europe in Basilius Valentinus and others like him. A truly alchemistic wisdom lives on in the monasteries, which taught more than a few simple transformations of substances. It taught us about the most essential characteristics of human transformations in the cosmos." With a definite autobiographical implication, Steiner said more on the subject in 1923: "He who is no longer terribly young, and who consciously participated in the events from the middle to the last decades of the nineteenth century, already knows, if he gets around a bit (so to speak); he knows how, for instance, the ideas of Paracelsus were circulated among the common country folk. He already knows that the last leftover bits of folk wisdom from the Middle Ages, which Paracelsus and Jakob Böhme used for their work, were still around until well into the 1870s and 1880s.... In the last decades of the nineteenth century, one could still say: Thank God that the last little offshoots of that old natural science are still around, the ideas that Alexander's journeys carried into Asia—even if they are barely recognizable, and corrupted. What remains from the old knowledge of alchemy, from the old knowledge and connections between natural substances and natural forces, which lived on in primitive culture and folk wisdom in a remarkable way—those were the last lingering resonances. Today they are dead. They do not exist any longer. They cannot be found. We know nothing of them" (ibid. pp. 109ff.; on the spiritual background of this effacement or extinction, see ibid. p. 82, just to name one. CW 346, lecture on Sept. 17, 1924). Steiner made statements about the concrete reappearance of aspects of the contents of Aristotle's teachings on the heart. If we re-examine these statements, which appear rather alienating at first, taking into account the now well-documented views on the heart, as well as the practices and rituals concerning the heart that were part of Middle European folk wisdom, we find strong evidence for the connections which Steiner pointed out. We must also examine the religious, artistic, and language-oriented aspects of the question (see for instance the excellent overview in the monograph by Franz Vonessen: *Das Herz in der Naturphilosophie* [The Heart in Natural Philosophy]. Biberach, 1969; and Hubert Schrade: *Das Herz in Kunst und Geschichte* [The Heart in Art and History]. Biberach, 1969; as well as the works listed in endnote 31).

275 Among the ranks of the Dominican Order stood also Albertus Magnus and Meister Eckhart, both of whom spoke of highly spiritual aspects of the heart. (Meister Eckhart, for example, wrote the following on the sacrament of the Eucharist: "We should be transformed in Jesus, and be made one with him, so that everything that is His becomes ours, and everything that is ours becomes His, our heart and his heart becoming one.") Worship of the five wounds of Christ and the emphasis on the wound on the heart of Christ were the result of the work of the Dominicans. These would soon become the quintessential signs of

his Passion and the sacrament at the altar. (This worship of the heart of Christ gave rise to the first groups of Jesus and John, which shows the disciples at the heart of the Lord in medieval paintings.) For more on the religious forms of the worship of the heart of Christ and the heart of God, from the thirteenth century on, see the monograph by Albert Walzer: *Das Herz im christlichen Glauben* [The Heart in Christian Belief]. Biberach, 1967.

276 "It is of greatest importance to know the true reason for the movement of the heart. Without that knowledge, it would be impossible to know anything at all about the theory of medicine. All of the other functions of a living being are dependent upon the movement of the heart" (René Descartes: *Tractatus de Homine* [1632; pub. 1664] cited in Thomas Fuchs, loc. cit., p. 128). According to Fuchs' impressive analysis, Descartes was the first to recognize the possibility (assisted by Harvey's empirical discoveries on the heart and circulation) of applying "a decisive lever for the implementation of a mechanical interpretation of the organism"; and he "integrated this mechanical interpretation into his system of natural philosophy, *albeit with a depiction of the action of the heart which contradicted Harvey's ideas*" (ibid., pp. 12 and 116, emphasis added).

277 On Harvey's views of Aristotle's three works, *De motu cordis, De Motu Locali Animalium,* and *De Generatione Animalium,* see the exceptional analysis by Thomas Fuchs, *Die Mechanisierung des Herzens. Harvey und Descartes—der vitale und der mechanische Aspekt des Kreislaufs* [The Mechanization of the Heart. Harvey and Descartes—The Living and Mechanical Aspect of the Circulation of the Blood]. Frankfurt, 1992. Fuchs was able to work out, very convincingly, that (contrary to Descartes' interpretation of his publications) Harvey saw the heart rhythm as an interdependent relationship of the heart and the blood. In his *Entdeckung des Blutkreislaufes* [Discovery of the Circulation of the Blood], he took as his starting point the embryonic vitality and independent movement of the blood. He considered this the *arché* [origin, first cause] of the organism. He described the reaction and the secondary mechanical transformation of the original movement of the blood brought about by the heart itself; the heart perceiving and able to react, and revitalizing the substance of the blood, as well. Harvey, working as a physician in London, was also a highly educated anatomist and physiologist. Just as Aristotle had done, Harvey pursued the idea of comprehensive views of the organism as a whole. He argued for the primacy of the biological function over the bodily structure, but also for the idea that the heart is an organ of perception for influences upon the soul. Every emotional stirring felt by the soul expresses itself as a movement of the blood, according to Harvey. "Each movement of the blood then influences the pulse and rhythm of the heart, because of the interdependent relationship of the heart and the blood" (Fuchs, loc. cit., p. 102). For more on the deep differences between Harvey and

Aristotle regarding the state of consciousness and physiological self-perception and self-awareness (as a prerequisite of Harvey's external-mathematical context as a rationale for his work and publications), see Steiner's helpful depiction in his Dornach lecture of Dec. 26, 1922 (CW 326 [*Karmic Relationships: Esoteric Studies*, vol. 2. London: Rudolf Steiner Press, 1997]).

278 Ibid., p. 129.

279 CW 326 [*Karmic Relationships*, vol. 2], p. 129.

280 See even the earlier philosophical texts of Steiner, which developed their theses in a logical confrontation with the main spiritual trends of the nineteenth century (CW 2, *Grundlinien einer Erkenntnistheorie der Goetheschen Weltanschauung, mit besonderer Rücksicht auf Schiller* [English trans.: *Goethe's Theory of Knowledge: An Outline of the Epistemology of His Worldview*. Great Barrington, MA: SteinerBooks, 2008], 1892; CW 4, *Die Philosophie der Freiheit* [English trans.: *Intuitive Thinking as a Spiritual Path: A Philosophy of Freedom*. Hudson, NY: Anthroposophic Press, 1995], 1894; CW 5, *Friedrich Nietzsche, ein Kämpfer gegen seine Zeit* [English trans.: *Friedrich Nietzsche: Fighter for Freedom*. Blauvelt, NY: Garber, 1885], 1895; Goethesche Weltanschauung [English trans.: *Goethe's World View*. Spring Valley, NY: Mercury Press, 1987], 1897). See also the philosophical work he finished at the end of the year 1900: *Welt- und Lebensanschauungen im 19. Jahrhundert* [Views on the World and on Life in the Nineteenth Century], and also the numerous writings and lectures of the following two and one-half decades, which expanded the boundaries of the history of consciousness decisively, up to and including depictions of the old mystery teachings, beginning with the two works from 1901 and 1902: CW 7, *Die Mystik im Aufgange des neuzeitlichen Geisteslebens und ihr Verhältnis zur modernen Weltanschauung* [English trans.: *Mystics after Modernism: Discovering the Seeds of a New Science in the Renaissance*. Great Barrington, MA: SteinerBooks, 2000] and CW 8, *Das Christentum als mystische Tatsache* [*Christianity as Mystical Fact: And the Mysteries of Antiquity*. Great Barrington, MA: SteinerBooks, 2006].

281 In 1886, following the same lines of reasoning as Aristotle and Thomas, Steiner characterized psychology as the "first science, in which the spirit must grapple with itself" in his first stand-alone publication (CW 2, *Grundlinien einer Erkenntnistheorie der Goetheschen Weltanschauung* [English trans.: *Goethe's Theory of Knowledge: An Outline of the Epistemology of His Worldview*. Great Barrington, MA: SteinerBooks, 2008]). He wrote: "The spirit stands opposite itself, observing" (p. 121). Aristotle's concept of the soul and the spirit, expanded upon and individualized by Thomas Aquinas, stood at the center of many of Steiner's lectures, both public lectures and those held privately for theosophists just after the turn of the century; as an essential step toward a concrete theory on reincarnation and karma. (On this subject,

see for example the early lecture "Theosophische Seelenlehre I—Körper und Seele" [Theosophical Teachings on the Soul I: Body and Soul], March 16, 1904, in Berlin, CW 52 [not available in English]). Even during his years of university study, he had come into intensive contact with Aristotelian and Thomist teachings, through work done with, among others, the philosophy professor Franz Brentano (see CW 115 [English trans.: *A Psychology of Body, Soul & Spirit: Anthroposophy, Psychosophy, Pneumatosophy*. Great Barrington, MA: Anthroposophic Press, 1999], lecture of Dec. 12, 1911). On the Cistercian clerics working with Maria Eugenia dell Grazie, see among others, CW 240 [English trans.: *Karmic Relationships: Esoteric Studies*, vol. 6. London: Rudolf Steiner Press, 2009], lecture of July 18, 1924. On the deeper fate-connected background behind these events, see the remarkable collection of Steiner's expository remarks put together by Wilhelm Rath: *Rudolf Steiner und Thomas von Aquin* [Rudolf Steiner and Thomas of Aquinas]. Basel, 1991.

282   Ibid., p. 92.

283   CW 239, p. 31.

284   On Rudolf Steiner's evolutionary cosmology, see the written depictions in the publications *Aus der Akasha-Chronik* [English trans.: *Cosmic Memory: The Story of Atlantis, Lemuria, and the Division of the Sexes*. Great Barrington, MA: SteinerBooks, 2006] (1904–1908; CW 11) and *Die Geheimwissenschaft im Umriss* [English trans.: *An Outline of Esoteric Science*] (1910; CW 13), as well as numerous lecture courses intended to deepen our understanding. Among these, see especially the exceptional Berlin presentations *Die Evolution vom Gesichtspunkt des Wahrhaftigen* [English trans.: *Inner Experiences of Evolution*. Great Barrington, MA: SteinerBooks, 2009] (1911; CW 132).

285   Within the framework of his April, 1909 Düsseldorf presentations *Die geistigen Hierarchien und ihre Widerspiegelung in der physischen Welt* [English trans.: *The Spiritual Hierarchies and the Physical World: Zodiac, Planets & Cosmos*. Great Barrington, MA: SteinerBooks, 2008], Steiner portrayed complicated currents and configurations of warmth in connection with the stage in the cosmic development of the earth that Steiner identified with the term "old Saturn." In the lengthy context of this description, he said the following: "On this old Saturn, the first structural foundation of the physical body of the human being was shaped and formed. This very first arrangement was formed out of warmth, but even in this first 'warmth body' the seeds or germs (so to speak) of the organs were placed which would later become all of the organs in the body. At the point where the initial warmth movement had returned to a state of rest, the foundation of a particular organ of the human body arose: the organ that we call the heart. Later, when that organ ceases to move, it sets the entire physical mechanism of the human body into a state of rest [!]. The earliest beginnings of the heart arise in the first impulse of movement, but it can arise in

this initial, structural sense only by means of the fact that the movement is brought to a stop, to a point of quiet, at this place. By means
of this, the heart becomes the organ which brings the entire physical
body and its functions to a standstill when it ceases to beat" (CW 110
[*The Spiritual Hierarchies and the Physical World*], p. 130; see also the
earlier version in CW 102 [not available in English], p. 85). Later in the
Düsseldorf lecture series, Steiner also drew attention to the role played
by the thrones, seraphim, and cherubim (beings active in the zodiacal
region of the constellation of the lion, or Leo) in the quieting of Saturn's warmth activities. Because of this, they were also responsible for
the first extrasensory foundations of the formation of the heart (ibid.,
p. 131 and 133). Fifteen years later he returned to this topic in Prague,
devoting much time to the issue, and emphasizing different aspects of
the questions this time around. In Prague, Steiner characterized the
individual nature of the future heart formation, which will take place
during the post-death existence of the individual, saying: "This outer,
flexible housing, the human heart, is unique to each individual. It is
the result of what was worked out with the gods between death and
a new birth. In working through that intermediate life between death
and a new birth, human beings must work in the direction that leads
from the earth to Leo, the constellation of Leo, which is part of the
zodiac. This direction, this current streaming from the earth toward
the constellation of Leo, is teeming with pure forces. Human beings
must work in this direction, so that they can propel the germ of the
heart onward; inside of it there are nothing but pure cosmic forces.
After they have worked their way through this region, which lies in
the vastness of the cosmos, they must enter regions closer to the earth,
the realm of the sun. Here, too, forces will be developed that bring the
heart closer to completion and perfection. Human beings then enter
the realm where they will be touched by what we can call the warmth
of the earth; out there in cosmic space there is no earth-warmth. It is
entirely different. Here the human heart enters the third stage of preparation. The forces out of which the heart will be prepared are purely
moral and religious forces at first, out in the direction of Leo. Purely
moral and religious forces are secreted in the heart at first. Modern
natural science regards the stars as indifferent, neutral physical masses,
without seeing their moral dimension. To one who truly understands
the formation of the heart, this seems ridiculous. And when the human
being passes through the region of the sun, these moral and religious
forces are usurped by the etheric forces. Not until the human being
gets even closer to the earth, closer to the warmth of the fire realm, can
the last preparative steps be added. At this point the forces become
active, and shape the germ of the physical body for the human being,
who will descend to earth as a soul-spirit being" (CW 239 [*Karmic
Relationships: Esoteric Studies*, vol. 5], pp. 31ff.). In Steiner's Oxford
lecture of Aug. 22, 1922, there is also a reference to the ways in which

the Sun and Leo are related to the formation of the heart (see CW 214 [English trans.: *The Mystery of the Trinity: Human Beings in Relation to the Spiritual World through the Course of Time.* Hudson, NY: Anthroposophic Press, 1991]). For more on the meaning of the sun and warmth qualities for the heart, see below, as well.

286   In Berlin, Steiner discussed this further development of the extrasensory heart on the way to its earthly development, and the equally important integration of these developmental steps inside of the organ itself. He demonstrated the correlation of this development with sickness and health. On October 23, 1909, he said: "Because the heart belongs among the oldest organs of humanity, we actually have a sun portion, a moon portion, a second sun portion, a second moon portion, and also a separate earth portion, following the division of the earth. When all of these portions of one organ, or of the physical body of the human, are acting in harmony, as they fit together in the harmony of the cosmos, then the human being is healthy. As soon as one portion prevails, or outweighs the others, the heart becomes ill; say, for example, the sun portion becomes too large in relation to the moon portion, with respect to the heart" (CW 115 [English trans.: *A Psychology of Body, Soul & Spirit*], pp. 24ff.).

287   CW 55, p. 57.

288   In his *Geheimwissenschaft im Umriss* [*An Outline of Esoteric Science*], Steiner wrote on the early stages of the earth's development, and of the human body, saying that the human beings of that time could feel the "warmth streaming through them" as their Ego, or "I"-being. Further: "In these currents of warmth, woven through with life, we find the first germinal seed of the blood circulation" (pp. 214ff.). In his writing *Aus der Akasha-Chronik* [English trans.: *Cosmic Memory*], he wrote the following on the first stages of the incarnation of the "I": "Essential to the perfection and completion of the physical body is the inclusion of the heart system as the preparer and bringer of the warm blood" (p. 173). Steiner continued to develop Aristotle's idea that the heart cooperates and assists with the preparation of the substance of the blood.

289   "The external organ for the 'I'...is the circulating blood. The 'I' could never work from above to below if it were not able to find its ideal organ in the physical body, one which transverses the human body from above to below in a vertical direction. Where can there be no 'I' of the sort the human beings have? Where the main direction of the blood flow is not from above to below, but rather horizontal. This is the case in the animal world. The collective 'I' of the animals finds no such organ, because their blood flows horizontally. This is the difference. The main blood lines [vessels] of the animals had to stand upright, in order to accommodate the human 'I' into the blood's circulation" (CW 125 [*Wege und Ziele des geistigen Menschen. Lebensfragen im Lichte der Geisteswissenschaft* (Means and Goals of the Spiritual

Human Being: Life Questions in the Light of Spiritual Science); not available in English], pp. 69ff.).

290   Steiner only briefly sketched out this physiological and evolutionary aspect in his writing on the akashic record. "It goes without saying that the sensory system, the glands, and the nervous system must undergo a change in form, so that they can coexist with the newly added warm blood system (following the incorporation of the blood-heart system into the physical body)" (CW 11 [*Cosmic Memory*], p. 173). Shortly thereafter, he held lectures in Prague (CW 128), *Eine Okkulte Physiologie* [English trans.: *An Occult Physiology*. London: Rudolf Steiner Press, 2005], during which he developed these ideas extensively. In the introduction to his presentation there on March 26, 1911, he revisited the subject: "Once the rest of the human organism is built, the human becomes capable of carrying blood, of taking up the task of the circulation of blood. Not until this point can he have the instrument within himself that serves as the tool of our 'I.' For this to happen, the entire human organism must first be constructed. You know that there are other beings upon the earth besides human beings. At the moment, they stand in a certain relationship to the human being, but are not in a state in which they could manifest a human ego. Some portions of their constitution, though they may look similar to those of the human being, are clearly constructed differently. In all of the systems that precede the blood system, the possibility of taking on and accommodating blood must exist as a possibility. That is to say, we must first have the sort of nervous system which can accommodate a blood system of the sort like the human circulatory system. We must have a glandular system of that sort, and a digestive system that are preformed to allow the addition of the human blood system" (p. 114). In connection with this, Steiner depicted the individual details of these prerequisites and necessary processes of transformation.

291   See also the lecture given on April 5, 1919, in CW 180 [English trans.: *Ancient Myths and the New Isis Mystery*. Hudson, NY: Anthroposophic Press, 1994], in which Steiner described the relationships between the physical and etheric corporeality of the heart, which detach themselves from one another. In particular, Steiner emphasized the hazardous moments of this process.

292   See the related statements in the lectures given on September 3, 1906 (Stuttgart; CW 95; English trans.: *Founding a Science of the Spirit*. London: Rudolf Steiner Press, 1999), November 30, 1906 (Cologne; CW 97; English trans.: *The Christian Mystery: Early Lectures*. Hudson, NY: Anthroposophic Press, 1998), April 1, 1907 (Berlin; CW 96; English trans.: *Original Impulses for the Science of the Spirit*. Lower Beechmont, Australia: Completion Press, 2001), and June 29, 1907 (Kassel; CW 100; not available in English). In these lectures, Steiner described future heart processes, which would internalize the process of plant photosynthesis, thus taking the formation of the bodily

substance even further into the forming of the ego. "Certain things
needed in the formation of our bodies must be taken in via nourishment at this stage. Later we will be able to complete these processes
within ourselves, in full consciousness" (CW 97, p. 187). Keeping the
Christological remarks of Thomas Aquinas on the *verbum cordis* in
mind, we should note that Rudolf Steiner closely related two processes
of the larynx and the heart. The continuing formative process of the
larynx, he said, would make it into an organ capable of actual creation
(see also CW 11, pp. 177ff.; English trans.: *Cosmic Memory*), and he
juxtaposed this with the changes in the heart which form substances.
"Just as the nobler side of the human being now produces words, the
human being will someday be able to create and construct by means
of words when his heart becomes the organ of his spirit" (CW 96, p.
294). In addition, Steiner draws our attention to the importance of the
metabolism in several passages. At the present time, this process takes
place physiologically. He also addressed the significant role that the
heart processes play in the formation of human protein (CW 312 [Eng-
lish trans.: *Introducing Anthroposophical Medicine*. Great Barrington,
MA: SteinerBooks, 2010], lecture of Apr. 1, 1920; and CW 313 [not
available in English], lecture of Apr. 16, 1921). He spoke in a general
way of the internalization of nutritive substances, which takes place in
stages (CW 218 [not available in English], lecture of Oct. 22, 1922; and
CW 314 [not available in English], lecture of Oct. 27, 1922).

293   "Tasks performed by plants, external to us, will be completed within
us in the future by the organ into which the heart will transform itself
when it becomes a voluntary muscle" (CW 100, p. 181; not available
in English).

294   See CW 93a (not available in English), p. 45, and the notebook entry
published in the *Beiträge zur Rudolf Steiner Gesamtausgabe* [Contri-
butions to the Complete Edition of Rudolf Steiner] (Nr. 35, 1971), in
which the heart is characterized as a warming oven within the organism (also see below, and see endnote 351; emphasis added).

295   CW 11 (English trans.: *Cosmic Memory*), p. 177.

296   CW 72 (not available in English), p. 131.

297   In light of this, one should take note of the fact that Aristotle and
Thomas Aquinas spoke of modified processes of warmth and movement (compare to the relationship of warmth to the heart processes,
and see below).

298   Only in his presentation on April 22, 1920, did Rudolf Steiner go into
somewhat greater detail on the connections between the feeling processes of the soul and the activities of the blood and heart. At that time,
he said: "What circulates in the blood is the external bodily expression
of our feeling experience. Our emotional-feeling life connects itself, on
the other hand, with our imagination-perception life. Everything we
imprint in our circulatory life vibrates along with the human heart.
Goethe used the expression 'inner living organ' to speak of the eye, and

the heart is just such a living organ. It not only has the task of serving the blood. It is also something that has great importance throughout the human organism. While the eye adapts itself for a short time to the eternal light impressions, to a certain extent, the heart is constantly making small adjustments, which are transferred into the blood under the influence of the emotional-feeling life, and the imaginative-perceptive life with which it is connected. Bit by bit, the heart itself takes into the configuration of its vibration life what, in particular, lives in the emotional-feeling life and the imaginative-perceptive life with which it is connected" (CW 301 [English trans.: *The Renewal of Education.* Great Barrington, MA: Anthroposophic Press, 2001], p. 54). On the effectiveness of the heart processes in the sphere of moral remembering, see below.

299   CW 192 (not available in English), p. 77.

300   CW 204 (English trans.: *Materialism and the Task of Anthroposophy.* Hudson, NY: Anthroposophic Press, 1987), p. 42.

301   CW 324 (not available in English), pp. 89ff.

302   Notebook entry of Rudolf Steiner's (1923). First published in *Beiträge zur Rudolf Steiner Gesamtausgabe* [Contributions to the Complete Edition of Rudolf Steiner], no. 40 (1972), p. 9. According to Steiner it is the task of the breathing to lead the changed life rhythms (alienated from their origin) back into the "general conditions of the cosmos" permanently. Rudolf Steiner designates this process the "original process of healing" (CW 230 [English trans.: *Harmony of the Creative Word: The Human Being & the Elemental, Animal, Plant, and Mineral Kingdoms.* London: Rudolf Steiner Press, 2001], p. 169).

303   See Peter Selg: *Vom* Logos *menschlicher Physis* [On the Logos of Human Physiology], pp. 414ff.

304   For more on this matter, see the summary in Peter Selg, op. cit., pp. 531–540. On Apr. 24, 1920, Steiner spoke very directly on this matter, following many years of depicting the polarity of forces of both substances: "Here you have your blood system in and of itself. By living further between your death and your new birth, these forces, which lie in the blood system, are constantly changing into other forces. And when you next arrive here for a new earthly life, these forces have become the forces of the new nervous system. You can see this yourself in the modern diagrams of the anatomy or physiology, by looking at a picture of the nerve threads and the circulation of the blood. Look at the circulation of the blood: an incarnation. In the next incarnation, this becomes the nervous system" (CW 201 [English trans.: *Mystery of the Universe: The Human Being, Model of Creation.* London: Rudolf Steiner Press, 2001], pp. 125ff.).

305   On the actual formation of the "rhythmic organization" in the middle of the second seven-year period of life, and the profound transformative processes connected with it taking place in the self-life and world-experience of the child, see the related statements from Steiner

in Peter Selg, loc. cit., pp. 613–616. In 1962 the Heidelberg internist Dr. Herbert Plügge published empirical observations on the changing heart-experience of the child during this period of life (*Wohlbefinden und Missbefinden. Beiträge zu einer medizinischen Anthropologie,* Tübingen, 1962, pp. 136–168). Further phenomenologically oriented observations are to be found in the excellent collection and selection of Hans Müller-Wiedemann: *Mitte der Kindheit. Das neunte bis zwölfte Lebensjahr* [The Middle of Childhood. The Ninth to Twelfth Years]. Stuttgart, 1973.

306 CW 314 (not available in English), pp. 45ff.

307 CW 73 (English trans.: *Anthroposophy Has Something to Add to Modern Sciences.* Lower Beechmont, Australia: Completion Press, 2005), p. 271.

308 CW 72 (not available in English), p. 290.

309 "In the head of the human being, the physical organization is a replica of the spiritual individuality. The physical and etheric parts of the head stand as completed pictures of the spiritual. Next to them, with an independent soul-spiritual existence, stand the astral and ego parts. Of the head of a person, we can speak, therefore, of the parallel development of the relatively independent physical and etheric bodies, on the one hand, and the astral and ego organization, on the other. In the metabolic–limb portion of the human being, the four parts of the human being are deeply bound together. The ego and astral parts are not located next to the physical and etheric parts. The ego and astral parts are inside them. They enliven the physical and etheric portions, influencing their growth, their ability to move, and so forth. Because of this, the metabolic–limb system is like a germ or seed that wishes to develop itself further, and is constantly striving to become the head; and it is constantly held back from achieving this, during the entire earthly life of the human being. The rhythmic organization stands in the middle. Here the ego-organization and astral body connect themselves with the physical and etheric part, and then separate themselves from them, over and over, in rotation. Breathing and the circulation of the blood are the physical expression of this uniting and releasing. The events in the arterial blood represent the uniting, and the events in the venous blood depict the releasing" (CW 26 [English trans.: *Anthroposophical Leading Thoughts.* London: Rudolf Steiner Press, 1998], p. 28). For more detailed information on this phenomenon, see: Peter Selg, loc. cit., pp. 418–427.

310 "In the metabolic–limb system, the earth, I would say, is fully in the possession of the human being. That which is earthly predominates over that which is cosmic during the earthly lifespan. In the chest organization, the cosmic balances the earthly. In the head organization, the cosmic outweighs the earthly" (CW 216 [not available in English], p. 38). According to Steiner, this is true in the functional and the morphological sense. "If you acquire...a feeling for this observation of

the chest, you will find the transition point between the form of the organs of the head and the metabolic–limb organs. You will see this in the formation of the skeleton, the organs, and everywhere. Everything that is part of the chest organization is in the middle between the poles of the human organization. Even the shapes of the organs tell you this" (CW 303 [English trans.: *Soul Economy: Body, Soul, and Spirit in Waldorf Education*. Great Barrington, MA: Anthroposophic Press, 2003], p. 106). "You can perceive this easily by looking at a skeleton. If you remove the skull, you have removed the part that is a replica of the cosmos, and what is left over is only half cosmic, in the arrangement of the ribs. This stands under an earthly influence. When you look at the skeleton and see the pipelike bones of the arms and legs, you see purely earthly formations. Look at a skeleton and you will see the vertebra of the spinal cord, the crude vertebra of the spine, on which the ribs sit. You must understand that has developed out of a state of balance between the cosmic and the earthly" (CW 316 [not available in English], p. 47).

311 CW 313 (not available in English), p. 74. Following another thread of thought in his lecture, Rudolf Steiner said: "The breathing function conducts itself in an inverse relationship to the sensory function, in the same way the blood circulation is related to the digestive function. So we could say, if I may express myself rather crudely, that the digestion is, to a certain extent, a compressed version of blood circulation. Or the opposite: what circulates in the blood is a finer version of the digestive process. And the sensory process is a finer version of the breathing process. I could also say the breathing process is a cruder sensory perception process" (CW 319 [English trans.: *The Healing Process: Spirit, Nature & Our Bodies*. Great Barrington, MA: SteinerBooks, 2010], p. 112). For more on this subject see Peter Selg, loc. cit., pp. 505–507.

312 For more details, see CW 312 (*Introducing Anthroposophical Medicine*); particularly the lectures held on Mar. 22, 26–28, and 30, 1920.

313 Ibid., p. 144.

314 "Between the ninth and tenth years of life lies the point in life when what was part of the breathing, and anchored in the upper part of the body, transfers itself, for the most part, into the blood circulation. This is when a marvelous ratio is achieved, of one to four, in what was formerly approximately 18 breaths and 27 pulse beats per minute. This relationship establishes itself at this point in life" (CW 304a [English trans.: *Waldorf Education and Anthroposophy* 2. Hudson, NY: Anthroposophic Press, 1996], p. 46). Steiner described this in greater detail in a lecture course for physicians. In the preceding first seven years of life, this upper organic process and the breathing dominate the human organism. The ego organization of the nerve–sense system works on the human being from the outside. Not until the ninth year (approximately) does the incarnative movement sink itself deeply into the metabolic–limb system. What we could almost call a "coupling of

the ego into the human organism from underneath" is achieved. "The tools of the ego, the polarity of the ego, and also the lower aspect of the ego, which encounters the upper aspect; all of these achieve the proper relationship" (CW 313 [not available in English], pp. 73 and 71). According to Steiner, this process of developmental physiology is connected with profound changes within the warmth organization of the child (and the emergence of an ascendant stream of warmth). (See also Peter Selg, loc. cit., pp. 613–616 and 601–605.)

315 CW 243 (English trans.: *True and False Paths in Spiritual Investigation.* Hudson, NY: Anthroposophic Press, 1985), p. 57.

316 Ibid., p. 38.

317 Even Aristotle was aware of the different qualities of the blood in the upper and lower organism, determined by external sensory processes and the inner activities of the organs, respectively. He found them interesting primarily in terms of the processes taking place inside the human sensory organization. For more on this, see Steiner's remarks within the framework of the Prague course *An Occult Physiology* (CW 128; particularly the lecture held on Mar. 21, 1911, the lectures immediately following). According to Rudolf Steiner, the heart can be spoken of as the organ of "common sense" (Aristotle) to the extent that the sensory processes (mediated by the blood) of the upper and lower organizations come into contact and unite. These would include the classic sense organs of the nerve–sense system, as well as the inner organs of perception located in the metabolic realm (such as the liver, kidneys, and spleen). In addition, Rudolf Steiner spoke about the processes of the blood and rhythmic system occurring in the sense organs. These enable the sensory activities to take place; and, in fact, they virtually constitute these activities (see Peter Selg, loc. cit., pp. 443ff. and pp. 461ff.).

318 CW 301 (English trans.: *The Renewal of Education*), p. 53.

319 CW 145 (English trans.: *The Effects of Esoteric Development.* Great Barrington, MA: SteinerBooks, 2007), p. 39.

320 CW 201 (English trans.: *Mystery of the Universe*), p. 94; emphasis added.

321 Within the context of several lectures given in the fall of 1922, Steiner remarked that the physiological aftereffects of the nightly planetary experiences of the human spirit-soul contribute significantly to the blood circulation (see CW 215 [English trans.: *Philosophy, Cosmology, and Religion.* Hudson, NY: Anthroposophic Press, 1984], lecture of Sept. 10, 1922, and CW 218 [not available in English], lecture of Oct. 9, 1922).

322 CW 319 (English trans.: *The Healing Process*), pp. 58f.; ital. added by Dr. Selg.

323 CW 84 (not available in English), p. 256; ital. added by Dr. Selg.

324 CW 201 (English trans.: *The Mystery of the Universe*), p. 50.

325 For more on the formation of the blood, or "preparation of the blood" as an escalating continuation of the physiological metabolic and substance-transforming events, see the overview of Steiner's corresponding allusions in Peter Selg, loc. cit., pp. 340, 352f., 482, 496ff. (among others). The dematerialization and spiritualization process taking place in the blood reaches its culmination in the heart, in a certain sense, as the substance of the blood becomes "etherized" there.

326 On Steiner's depictions of the incarnative situation of the ego and the soul-body in the sphere of the metabolic–limb system, see Peter Selg, loc. cit., pp. 424ff. Rudolf Steiner spoke of a complete immersion of the spirit–soul in the metabolic realm (CW 314 [not available in English], p. 83). This is a process that serves as the basis of the inner constitution of the human blood and its continual tendency to become spiritualized, as well as its "elementary emotion." In a depiction of the activities of the elements of a being present in the blood, Steiner once said: "First the ego gathers the astral and etheric organizations. It then streams through the physical organism in the blood from the lower part upward. The entire hidden human being thus streams in the blood as a constructive growth process, constantly regenerating the human being through the processing of nourishment. This flowing current streams through the human being from the lower part upward" (CW 221 [not available in English], p. 78). In connection with this, see also Steiner's explanations on the intervention of the higher elements of the being from the end of the third week of embryonic development on (overview in Peter Selg, loc. cit., pp. 582f.). This takes place at the moment when the embryo begins to form its blood, its blood begins to move, and the heart is formed.

327 CW 223 (English trans.: *The Cycle of the Year as Breathing Process of the Earth.* Hudson, NY: Anthroposophic Press, 1988), p. 136.

328 CW 350 (English trans.: *From Mammoths to Mediums…: Answers to Questions*; London: Rudolf Steiner Press, 2000), p. 59.

329 CW 316 (not available in English), pp. 38ff.

330 Notebook entry by Rudolf Steiner (1920). First published in *Beiträge zur Rudolf Steiner Gesamtausgabe* [Contributions to the Complete Edition of Rudolf Steiner], vol. 16 (1966–1967), p. 20.

331 See endnote 295.

332 See CW 205 (not available in English), lecture: July 2, 1921. On the larger anthropologic and physiological context of memory and remembrance in the work of Rudolf Steiner see Peter Selg, loc. cit., pp. 224–226 and 548–558.

333 See CW 128 (not available in English), lecture of Mar. 23, 1911 in reference to the etheric streams depicted there, leading from the heart to the pineal gland [epiphysis] and the counterflow leading from the metabolic–limb system to the pituitary gland.

334 Ibid., p. 105.

335 Steiner elucidated the matter of the boundary structure between the astral and etheric bodies (ibid., p. 118).

336 CW 205 (not available in English), pp. 105ff. and 109ff.

337 In answer to the written question of the physician Ita Wegman, asking to what extent the imminent karma is related to the heart, Rudolf Steiner answered: "The karma constructs itself...in this way: during our life on earth, there is complete unconsciousness in the metabolic–limb organism. In the state of normal consciousness, the human being is in a lasting, dreamless sleep. In this sleeping part of the soul, permeated by archai (archetypal forces), these forces form a judgment on the value (or lack of value) of human actions. The metabolic–limb human being is transformed into the nerve–sense human being of the next earthly life. During this metamorphosis, the judgment of the archai is submitted. The impulse that has undergone metamorphosis (the judgment on the value, or lack of value, of deeds, transformed in the will, which is to be balanced out through other deeds) does not enter the human being consciously. It enters the angel-beings that belong to the person, instead. The karma of the person thus remains in the nescience of that person. The heart is only part of the karma foundation to the extent that it belongs to the metabolic–limb organism. In its role as an organ of the rhythmic system, the heart is not part of the karma formation." (Cited in Peter Selg, loc. cit., pp. 688, 689.

338 CW 74 (English trans.: *The Redemption of Thinking: A Study in the Philosophy of Thomas Aquinas*. Hudson, NY: Anthroposophic Press, 1983), pp. 92ff.

339 CW 317 (not available in English), p. 18.

340 On this topic, see also Thomas Aquinas's corresponding allusions in *De motu cordis*, according to which the formative forces, together with the later life form of the heart, are subject to the *Anima Sensitiva*, living in perceiving, moving, and desiring forces. They also establish a unifying collaboration of the sensing soul with the living body.

341 CW 212 (English trans.: *Introducing Anthroposophical Medicine*), pp. 123ff.

342 Ibid. p. 127.

343 See CW 130 (English trans.: *Esoteric Christianity: and the Mission of Christian Rosenkreutz*. London: Rudolf Steiner Press, 2005), lecture of Dec. 2, 1911. Steiner spoke on the contemporary transfer of the judgeship over human deeds to Christ. He described how the balance of fate, so essential to the individual, could be carried out by the Christ being in the future, strengthened by the general progress made by humankind. "Our karmic bank account will be so balanced in the future, placed in such an ordered world, when we find the way to Christ. The nature of our karmic balance will summon the greatest possible well-being for the rest of the development of the earth. That will be the concern of him who, from this time forward, is the Lord of Karma. It will be the concern of Christ" (ibid., p. 166).

344 CW 107 (English trans.: *The Being of Man and His Future Evolution*. London: Rudolf Steiner Press, 1981), p. 253.

345 CW 143 (not available in English), p. 148.

346 CW 344 (not available in English), p. 146.

347 Ibid., p. 148.

348 CW 342 (English trans.: *First Steps in Christian Religious Renewal: Preparing the Ground for The Christian Community*. Great Barrington, MA: SteinerBooks, 2010), p. 162.

349 In this context we should take note that Steiner declared the Averroeistic interpretation valid and consistent for its time (Aristotle's lifetime and the preceding centuries) in terms of the history of consciousness. That interpretation of Aristotle's concept of the spiritual argued for general, rather than individualized intelligence. Thomas Aquinas took a strong stand against these ideas in the second half of the thirteenth century. Steiner said: "Now you see that what Averroes imagined had been correct until the end of the Alexandrian time. It was simply cosmic-human fact until the end of the Alexandrian time. But Averroes held on to the ideas. The Dominicans took up the evolution of humankind, and said: This is not right! Naturally, they could have said: It was correct once, long ago, but it is no longer correct!" (CW 237 [not available in English], p. 122). Although the individualization of the human spirit and the enabling of an individual course of destiny cannot be conflated into one issue, there are unmistakable connections between these two evolutionary processes.

350 Ibid. p. 115. 347a. "And in everything that lives as freedom within us..., the presence of the sun is at work" (CW 240 [English trans.: *Karmic Relationships*, vol. 6], p. 88). In this larger context, we should take note of Steiner's statement, that an equilibrium between the upper and lower processes of the world takes place in the movements of the heart (CW 312 [English trans.: *Introducing Anthroposophical Medicine*], lecture of Mar. 26, 1920). The "most spiritual" sun is to be seen as the "elevated bearer of the Christ principle," as the "intermediary" of the highest spiritual forces, which "connect the sun-external forces with the sun-internal forces" (CW 266/3 [English trans.: *Esoteric Lessons 1913–1923*], p. 123).

351 With regard to the preparation of the heart during the life between death and a new birth, and the participation of the sun sphere, see the lectures named in endnote 285, and Steiner's exposition of May 25, 1924 (CW 239 [English trans.: *Karmic Relationships*, vol. 5]). These offer additional helpful points of view. In The Hague on Mar. 21, 1913, speaking on the ways the physiological influences of the sun come into force on the blood and heart system of the fully formed human organism, Steiner said: "All of these are connected with the inner forces of the blood circulation, working upon the human heart: the sun forces received by the earth in its solid basic substance; everything the earth receives in its hulls of air and water, and in the changing ratio of

warmth; everything it receives into the light flooding the earth; everything it receives that is not in any way physically perceptible, such as
the earth's portion of the harmony of the spheres; and everything it
receives as life forces that come directly from the sun. Essentially, all
of these forces work on the circulation of the blood and from there,
they work upon the heart. Everything in connection with this that is
external theory, is profoundly wrong. This external theory would have
us consider the heart to be a pump that pumps blood through the body,
so that we would have to see the heart as the organ that regulates
the circulation of the blood. The opposite is true. The circulation of
the blood is the original source, and a resonance of its motion is seen
in the movements of the heart. The blood drives the heart, not the
opposite. However, this entire organism I have described, which is
focused on the activity of the heart, is nothing other than a microcos-
mic human reflection of the macrocosmic effects of the sun upon the
earth. What the earth receives from the sun is reflected in the way the
heart is affected by the blood" (CW 145 [English trans.: *The Effects of
Esoteric Development*], pp. 38ff.).

352 See the overview of Steiner's corresponding descriptions in Peter Selg,
loc. cit., pp. 653–655. In light of the heart theory developed up to this
point, it is particularly interesting that Rudolf Steiner demonstrated
the connection between the gold process working in the heart, and the
enabling of the earthly ego-consciousness or individuality-conscious-
ness. "Everything that offers us stability is compressed at the point
where the heart muscles lie.... Everything that holds us in an earthly
consciousness, in a waking earthly consciousness, everything that
makes this consciousness into a so-called norm,...is the substance,
gold, *Aurum*, which is spread out over the world incredibly finely,
and works on no other organ as directly as it works upon the heart"
(CW 243 [not available in English], pp. 56ff.). At this point Steiner
also pointed out the great closeness between the heart-related gold processes and the individual perceptive and cognitive life of the human
being, as well as the impact of gold on the "thought-world of the ego
organization" (CW 232 [English trans.: *Inner Experiences of Evolution*], p. 209). On the basis of Steiner's observations we can assume that
not only the collective processes of human cardiac function take place
with the help of the active gold sphere. The sun-related heart processes
depend upon it, as well. On the teachings related to the evolution of the
heart in the old mysteries, Rudolf Steiner once said, "We can hardly
understand anything about the ways the old mystery teachers spoke
to their students. Nowadays, if someone wants to explain the human
heart, he takes an embryo and notices how the blood vessels slump,
and how a tube develops, and then how the heart is formed. This is not
the way the old mystery teachers spoke to their students! That would
not have seemed any more important to them than knitting a sock,
because that is what the process would have looked like. Instead, they

emphasized something entirely different, something incredibly important. They said the human heart is the result of the gold, which lives everywhere there is light, streams in from the cosmos, and actually forms the human heart. They were given this as an imaginative picture: Light weaves through the cosmos, and the light carries the gold. Everywhere there is light, there is gold, weaving and living in the light" (CW 291 [not available in English], pp. 212ff).

353   See CW 93a, p. 45.

354   An overview can be found in Peter Selg, loc. cit., p. 548. On March 29, 1920, in his first course for physicians, in Dornach, Steiner said: "It is of the utmost importance that I mention to you, that you should make a rigorous attempt to relate every impairment of the heart that you see, back to a disturbance in human activity. You should undertake investigations on how different the heart activity looks in a person who is, let's say, a farmer who is working his land, and rarely gets away from this activity of working in his fields; how different the heart activity looks in a person who must often drive a car because of his work, or even a train. It would be extraordinarily interesting to instigate a thorough investigation of this. For you would find that the tendency to illnesses of the heart is significantly dependent upon whether a person is driven about by external means such as a train or a car, while the person himself sits still. Passively giving oneself up to movement deforms all of the processes that accumulate in the heart. Now everything is dependent upon what takes place in this person's world, together with the way in which this person warms himself. And there you see the relationship between the heart activity and the impulse of warmth in the world, with which the human being is associated. You see from this that the human being must develop sufficient warmth through his own activity. The fact that he develops sufficient warmth in his life processes through his own activity is at the same time the measure of the health of the human heart" (CW 312 [English trans.: *Introducing Anthroposophical Medicine*], p. 177).

355   CW 343 [not available in English], p. 629. See also the related references from Thomas Aquinas. There is a very special relationship of the will to thought, negotiated or enabled by the heart. This relationship could also be called the intentionality of one's individual, spiritual existence. Its specific physical basis is part of the physiological event which Rudolf Steiner described as the meeting of two etheric streams in the realm of the pineal gland (Oct. 1911 and by implication Mar. and Aug. 1911, as well as Mar. 1920; see the overview discussing the four interpretations in Peter Selg, loc. cit., pp. 226–230). One etheric stream belongs to the actual moral sphere of the will, and the other etheric stream comes out of the heart, or rather, rises up out of the blood which is becoming spiritualized, and is associated with the human capacity for thought and knowledge. (Long ago, Steiner tells us, Aristotle spoke of this etheric stream, which leads from the heart

to the brain. See CW 60 [not available in English], lecture of Jan. 26, 1911.) On Oct. 1, 1911, Steiner reported that in the moments when one is waking up and falling asleep, "a sort of battle" takes place between both streams of forces. This happens during the morning and evening incarnation and excarnation situations, respectively, and in the realm of an organ, and Steiner laid particular emphasis on the evolutionary (see CW 102 [not available in English], p. 85) and reincarnative relationship of that organ with the heart: "Here between birth and death you say, My heart is in my chest, and in my heart the moving fluids of the blood circulation gather together. In a certain state of maturity between death and new birth, you say: Inside of me is the sun, and you mean the actual sun, the one the physicists imagine to be a ball of gas, but which is actually something entirely different. You experience the actual sun. You experience the sun between death and new birth in just that way; the way in which you experience your heart in this life. And just as the sun is visible to the eye, between death and a new birth the heart is on its path of development, on the way to becoming the pineal gland in a wondrous metamorphosis, which is the cause of grand experiences between death and a new birth" (CW 201 [English trans.: *Mystery of the Universe*], p. 127).

356   See the related statements by Steiner in Peter Selg: *Krankheit und Christus-Erkenntnis* [Illness and the Knowledge of Christ], pp. 58–74.

357   Steiner said this in Basel on Oct. 1, 1911, about the blood that becomes etheric in the human heart realm and climbs to the head. Under specific conditions, this blood can unite itself with the etheric blood of Christ, which has been present in the etheric body of the earth since the mystery of Golgotha. Steiner described this as a spiritual and physiological precondition for future Christ-experiences. "The joining of these two streams, however, can take place only when the human being shows the proper understanding of what is contained in the Christ impulse. Otherwise no connection can come about. Instead, the two streams would repel each other, dashing apart just as they had collided together. We can attain understanding only if we adopt this understanding in a manner that is appropriate to this age and stage of the development of the earth. In the time when Jesus Christ was living on the earth, those who had come to Christ's predecessor, John, and allowed themselves to be baptized according to the formula expressed in the Gospel were able to bring the proper understanding to the impending circumstances. They received [the sacrament of] baptism in order to amend for their sins; that is to say, the karma of their previous life, which had come to an end. They also came to be baptized to know that the most important impulse in the development of the earth would now descend to earth in a physical body. But human development continues to make forward strides; and for our time, it is important that the human being realize that he must accept the findings of spiritual science and gradually become so inspired by what is streaming from the heart to the head

that he develops a real understanding for Anthroposophy. The result will be that he can accept what has now begun to intervene in the twentieth century: the etheric Christ, as contrasted with the physical Christ of Palestine" (CW 130 [English trans.: *Esoteric Christianity*], p. 93).

358 See CW 10 (English trans.: *How to Know Higher Worlds*), particularly pp. 125–158.

359 See especially CW 202 (English trans.: *Ancient Myths and the New Isis Mystery*), lecture of Dec. 18, 1920.

360 CW 161 (not available in English), p. 213. On the spiritualizing of thought and desire in the sense of a Christianizing of the heart, see Steiner's remarks in the *Esoterische Betrachtungen karmischer Zusammenhänge* [Esoteric Observations on Karmic Connections] (particularly in CWs 240 [English trans.: *Karmic Relationships*, vol. 6] and 26 [English trans.: *Anthroposophical Leading Thoughts*]), which illuminate these processes in a broad, Christological, and Michaelic context. They work out the future-oriented dimension of the decision: "More than any other battle, this battle will take place in the human heart" (CW 240 [*Karmic Relationships*, vol. 6], p. 183). Steiner's related and profound concept of the heart, forced into use since the Christmas Conference, should receive renewed and strengthened attention from anthroposophists. As is well known, Steiner was not speaking metaphorically when he spoke of the foundation stone being buried "in the bottom of our hearts"(CW 260 [not available in English], p. 64); or when he said that esotericism should be taken up by our "hearts"(CW 240 [*Karmic Relationships*, vol. 6], p. 255). The heart is the organ that will be able to govern the intelligent and will-focused spirituality (CW 26 [*Anthroposophical Leading Thoughts*], p. 240), with the help of the Archangel of the Sun, Michael (ibid., p. 222) working in the rhythmic processes. The heart will be able to unite the cosmic sun forces with the physical and etheric corporeality of the human being "once and for all" (ibid., p. 235), to the extent that the insight into the fate of the individual will be fulfilled in the mystery of Michael; and the individual, karmic connection with Michael will be carried out one day, according to Steiner; "...something, which rests, dreamily sleeping, even if unconsciously, in the deepest corners of the hearts of most anthroposophists" (ibid., p. 188).

361 Rudolf Steiner, CW 268 (not available in English), p. 8.

362 In 1997, Anton Gerretsen published the first outline of the meditations for the sick written by Rudolf Steiner (*Meditationen für Patienten. Meditative Anweiseungen und Texte von Rudolf Steiner, zusammengestellt für Ärzte* [Meditations for Patients. Meditative Instructions and Texts from Rudolf Steiner, Collected for Physicians]. Arlesheim, self-published). His chief resources were the collections of the Arlesheim Clinic, consisting of spiritual exercises that Steiner gave to individual patients during his collaboration with Ita Wegman. After Wegman's death, these were collected by Hilma Walter, Margarethe

Kirchner-Bockholt, and Madeleine van Deventer, and shared privately. During the years 1950 to 1971, Hilma Walter published a series of treatments for illnesses used by Steiner and Wegman. Only a certain percentage of the meditations that were part of individual case reports are included. To the extent that they could be dependably traced back to Steiner, Gerretsen then published these in the volumes named, as well as in the Appendix to the second edition of Hilma Walters' book *Die sieben Hauptmetalle. Ihre Beziehungen zu Welt, Erde, und Mensch* [The Seven Precious Metals. Their Relation to the World, the Earth, and the Human Being](Dornach, 1999), pp. 318ff. Walter was able to gather further materials with help from dependents and relatives, and included meditations formulated by Steiner in the Stuttgart Clinical-Therapeutic Institute, to the extent that these were included in the collection of case histories by Antonij Degenaar (*Krankheitsfälle und andere medizinische Fragen, besprochen mit Dr. Rudolf Steiner* [Case Histories and Other Medical Questions, As Discussed with Dr. Rudolf Steiner], n.d. (recently republished as *Krankengeschichten* [Case Histories]. Verlag am Goetheanum, 2008). Gerretsen's work did not produce a complete set of the meditations for illness, by any means. In the Rudolf Steiner Archive there is further unpublished material. In addition to that, there are various mediations and spiritual exercises that have already been published in the volumes of mantras that are part of the *Gesamtausgabe* [Collected Works], particularly in CW 268. These verses were clearly composed as part of the therapy in cases of illness, rather than for esoteric training in the narrower sense. The questions raised by these meditations are decidedly subtle and complex (see also Gerretsen, loc. cit., p. 1). Nevertheless, some of the central heart mantras were republished in the Epilogue of this volume. The view of the heart made possible by Rudolf Steiner in his work to develop further the ideas of Aristotle and Thomas Aquinas, and their consequences for spiritual Christian medicine, would not be adequately documented without these meditations.

363   CW 266/3 (English trans: *Esoteric Lessons 1913–1923*), p. 126.

Books in English Translation by
Peter Selg

On Rudolf Steiner:

RUDOLF STEINER AND CHRISTIAN ROSENKREUTZ (2012)

RUDOLF STEINER AS A SPIRITUAL TEACHER: From Recollections of Those Who Knew Him (2010)

On Christology:

THE CREATIVE POWER OF ANTHROPOSOPHICAL CHRISTOLOGY: An Outline of Occult Science | The First Goetheanum | The Fifth Gospel | The Christmas Conference (with Sergei O. Prokofieff) (2012)

CHRIST AND THE DISCIPLES: The Destiny of an Inner Community (2012)

THE FIGURE OF CHRIST: Rudolf Steiner and the Spiritual Intention behind the Goetheanum's Central Work of Art (2009)

RUDOLF STEINER AND THE FIFTH GOSPEL: Insights into a New Understanding of the Christ Mystery (2010)

SEEING CHRIST IN SICKNESS AND HEALING (2005)

On General Anthroposophy:

THE AGRICULTURE COURSE, KOBERWITZ, WHITSUN 1924: Rudolf Steiner and the Beginnings of Biodynamics (2010)

THE CULTURE OF SELFLESSNESS: Rudolf Steiner, the Fifth Gospel, and the Time of Extremes (2012)

THE FUNDAMENTAL SOCIAL LAW: Rudolf Steiner on the Work of the Individual and the Spirit of Community (2011)

KARL KÖNIG'S PATH TO ANTHROPOSOPHY (2008)

THE MYSTERY OF THE HEART: The Sacramental Physiology of the Heart in Aristotle, Thomas Aquinas, and Rudolf Steiner (2012)

THE PATH OF THE SOUL AFTER DEATH: The Community of the Living and the Dead as Witnessed by Rudolf Steiner in his Eulogies and Farewell Addresses (2011)

RUDOLF STEINER AND THE SCHOOL FOR SPIRITUAL SCIENCE: The Foundation of the "First Class" (2012)

RUDOLF STEINER'S INTENTIONS FOR THE ANTHROPOSOPHICAL SOCIETY: The Executive Council, the School of Spiritual Science, and the Sections (2011)

On Anthroposophical Medicine and Curative Education:

THE CHILD WITH SPECIAL NEEDS: Letters and Essays on Curative Education (Ed.) (2009)

I AM FOR GOING AHEAD: Ita Wegman's Work for the Social Ideals of Anthroposophy (2012)

ITA WEGMAN AND KARL KÖNIG: Letters and Documents Karl König's Path to Anthroposophy (2009)

KARL KÖNIG: MY TASK: Autobiography and Biographies (Ed.) (2008)

On Child Development and Waldorf Education:

THE ESSENCE OF WALDORF EDUCATION (2010)

A GRAND METAMORPHOSIS: Contributions to the Spiritual-Scientific Anthropology and Education of Adolescents (2008)

I AM DIFFERENT FROM YOU: How Children Experience Themselves and the World in the Middle of Childhood (2011)

THE THERAPEUTIC EYE: How Rudolf Steiner Observed Children (2008)

UNBORNNESS: Human Pre-existence and the Journey toward Birth (2010)

Ita Wegman Institute
for Basic Research into Anthroposophy

PFEFFINGER WEG 1 A CH 4144 ARLESHEIM, SWITZERLAND
www.wegmaninstitute.ch
e-mail: sekretariat@wegmaninstitute.ch

The Ita Wegman Institute for Basic Research into Anthroposophy is a non-profit research and teaching organization. It undertakes basic research into the lifework of Dr. Rudolf Steiner (1861–1925) and the application of Anthroposophy in specific areas of life, especially medicine, education, and curative education. Work carried out by the Institute is supported by a number of foundations and organizations and an international group of friends and supporters. The Director of the Institute is Prof. Dr. Peter Selg.